Homespun
COLLECTIONS

Over 600 Recipes From McBain Amish Community

© Copyright 2014 Edna Mae Schrock

All rights reserved. No part of this publication may be reproduced, stored in a retrieval system or transmitted, in any form, or by any means, electronic, mechanical, photocopying, recording, or otherwise, without the prior permission of the publishers.

For additional copies contact your local bookstore or—
    Pineview Discount
    9200 S Burkett Road
    McBain, MI 49657
    (231) 825-2892

Layout & Design | Maria Yoder

800.927.4196 · carlisleprinting.com
Sugarcreek, Ohio 44681

Introduction

We want to extend a special thank you to Martha, who gave us the idea of this cookbook. The evening she invited us to join her at her quilt was spent in delightful fellowship and lively discussions. We relived our years spent together with all our friends in the McBain Amish Community. Looking ahead and thinking of the changes that could come upon us, we felt urged to have all our contribution bound together as a token of love and memories.

A hearty and sincere thank you to all our friends and church family for the support, recipes, poems, and time contributed to making it possible for organizing this cookbook. We hope it can be more than a collection of recipes, also a treasure of the bond we have shared working together to make our community possible.

To all those who find pleasure in cooking, we hope you find as many pleasant experiences as we have in making memories. Anywhere from cooking to canning for your family, hosting guests to wedding dinners, and learning homespun ways and having your own secret twists to the recipes you try. May you find these pages refreshing and helpful to the glory of God.

The Bunch of Six

Verna Kay Miller   Wilma Fern Schrock
Miriam Miller   Cheryl DeAnn Otto
        Edna Mae Schrock   Esther Miller

Table of Contents

Appetizers, Beverages, Dips................. 1

Breakfast Foods......................... 15

Breads, Rolls........................... 35

Salads, Salad Dressings................... 59

Soups, Vegetables....................... 77

Meats, Main Dishes...................... 87

Cookies, Bars.......................... 129

Cakes, Frostings....................... 167

Desserts.............................. 191

Pies.................................. 231

Candies, Snacks....................... 253

Canning, Freezing..................... 269

Miscellaneous......................... 299

Helpful Hints......................... 313

Canning Guide........................ 323

Index................................ 329

Appetizers Beverages Dips

Appetizers, Beverages, Dips

Apple Fritters............................3	Iced Coffee............................7
Blackberry-Banana Smoothies............3	Iced Coffee............................7
Cappuccino Mocha Mix 5	Ice Tea Concentrate...................11
Caramel Dip for Apples.................11	Icy Holiday Punch......................9
Caramel Fruit Dip....................11	Leanna's Dip 12
Cheese Ball 12	Maple Cream (to spread on bread) 13
Chocolate Syrup 3	Mr. Misty.............................9
Creamy Lemon-Berry Punch............9	Orange Punch 10
Delicious Cappuccino 5	Popsicles 4
Effortless Eggnog......................8	Punch 10
Eggnog...............................8	Rhubarb Juice 10
French Chocolate......................6	Sparkling Grape Juice 8
French Vanilla Cappuccino Mix...........5	Taco Dip 13
Fruit Dip............................11	Tortilla Pinwheels 4
Hot Spiced Cider......................7	Tortilla Roll-Ups 4
Iced Coffee...........................6	

Appetizers, Beverages, Dips

Apple Fritters

1 c. flour
2 Tbsp. sugar
1½ tsp. baking powder
½ tsp. salt
½ c. milk
1 egg
5-6 apples, chopped

Core and peel apples. Combine dry ingredients. Add milk and egg. Add chopped apples. Drop by spoonfuls in hot oil, and fry till golden. Drain on paper towel. May sprinkle with powdered sugar or roll in cinnamon/sugar mixture or eat with maple syrup. Yield: 28 fritters.

Mrs. Ernest Ray Inez Miller

Blackberry-Banana Smoothies

6 oz. blackberries
2 bananas
2 c. yogurt
3 c. ice cream

Mash blackberries and bananas as fine as possible, or use a blender. Add yogurt; when ready to serve, add ice cream. Very refreshing. Serves 6 people.

Mrs. LaVern Linda Miller

Chocolate Syrup

6 c. sugar
2 c. cocoa
2 tsp. salt
4 c. hot water

Mix all ingredients in a 4-6 quart kettle. Heat to boiling; boil for 3 minutes. You can pour it hot into jars when hot and seal. Yield: 2 quarts.

Note: Use this to make your own chocolate milk. You can also add 3-4 tablespoons instant coffee to the hot syrup for cappuccino mix.

Mrs. Wilbur Wilma Miller

Appetizers, Beverages, Dips

Popsicles

1 box Jell-O
1 c. hot water
1 pkg. Kool-Aid
1 c. sugar
3 c. cold water

Stir well and pour in Tupperware popsicle molds or some other small container. Freeze. Yield: 18 popsicles.

Miss Marlys Renae Kauffman
Miss Lyndora Kay Miller

Tortilla Roll-Ups

1 (8 count) pkg. med. tortillas
8 oz. cream cheese
1 pkg. Ranch dressing mix
1 c. chopped broccoli
1 c. chopped cauliflower
1 c. diced ham or any meat
1 c. shredded cheese

Mix cream cheese and ranch. Add vegetables, ham and cheese. Mix together. Spread on tortillas. Roll up and refrigerate. Slice and serve with salsa.

Miss Wilma Fern Schrock

Tortilla Pinwheels

2 c. sour cream
8 oz. cream cheese, softened
1 pkg. Hidden Valley Ranch mix
10 flour tortillas
1 c. broccoli
1 c. cauliflower
1 c. grated cheese
1 c. crumbled bacon or diced ham

Mix sour cream, cream cheese and Ranch mix. Spread on tortillas. Top with remaining ingredients. Roll up and chill overnight or 5-6 hours. Slice ½" thick and serve.

Mrs. Clifford Rhoda Herschberger

Appetizers, Beverages, Dips

Cappuccino Mocha Mix

4 c. non-dairy coffee creamer
2½ c. non-fat dry milk
2 c. sugar (or less)
⅔ c. cocoa
¾ c. instant coffee
½ c. chocolate drink mix
½ c. powdered sugar
⅔ c. instant vanilla pudding
1 lb. French vanilla cappuccino

Mix in a large bowl. To serve: mix 1 tablespoon to a cup of boiling water. Stir well. Yield: 12 cups mix. Delicious!
Note: Deborah adds a small handful of marshmallows and ¼ teaspoon vanilla.

Miss Deborah Ann Miller
Mrs. William Miriam Yoder
Mrs. Delbert Martha Schrock

Delicious Cappuccino

2 c. coffee creamer
2 c. French vanilla creamer
2½ c. non-fat dry milk
2 c. sugar
⅔ c. cocoa
¾ c. instant coffee
1 c. hot chocolate mix
½ c. powdered sugar
dash of salt
⅔ c. instant vanilla pudding
1 lb. French vanilla cappuccino mix

Mix in a large bowl. To serve: mix 3 heaping teaspoons to a cup of boiling water and stir well. Store in air-tight container. The best!

Mrs. Leon Cristina Wagler

French Vanilla Cappuccino Mix

4 c. French vanilla creamer
2 c. dry milk
¼ c. chocolate Nesquik
¾ c. instant coffee
1 c. sugar

Mix all together and store in an air-tight container. Use 3 tablespoons mix with 1 cup hot or boiling water.

Miss SueEllen Miller

Appetizers, Beverages, Dips

French Chocolate

¾ c. chocolate chips
½ c. light corn syrup
⅓ c. water
1 tsp. vanilla

1 pt. whipping cream
  or Rich's topping
2 qt. milk

Blend chocolate chips with syrup and water over low heat till chocolate is melted. Add vanilla; cool. Beat cream till thick, then slowly beat in chocolate mixture. It should mound slightly when dropped from a spoon. Chill. Just before serving, scald milk. Fill cups half full of chocolate mixture, then pour in hot milk. Adjust to taste. Serves 6-8 people.

Miss Cheryl DeAnn Otto

Iced Coffee

10 c. strongly brewed coffee
⅓ c. instant coffee
¾ c. sugar

1 Tbsp. vanilla
1 can sweetened condensed
  milk

Dissolve instant coffee in brewed coffee. Add sugar and vanilla. Stir until dissolved, then add condensed milk. Cool. When ready to serve, combine half mix and half milk. Add ice. Mix may be stored in refrigerator up to 2 weeks.

Miss Dorcas Miller

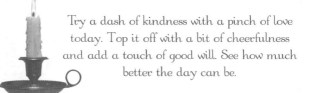

Try a dash of kindness with a pinch of love today. Top it off with a bit of cheerfulness and add a touch of good will. See how much better the day can be.

Appetizers, Beverages, Dips

Iced Coffee

½ c. instant coffee
½ c. instant vanilla pudding
2 c. sugar
2 c. regular creamer
1 c. hazelnut creamer
2 qt. water
3 qt. milk
dash of salt
vanilla to taste

Mix first 3 ingredients well. Add the rest of the ingredients. If you are using powdered creamer use hot water to dissolve creamer. Serve slushy. Enjoy with your friends and family. Serves 30 people.

Miss Rosetta Kay Wagler
Miss Susanna Schrock

Iced Coffee

1 c. sugar
3 Tbsp. instant coffee
3 c. strongly brewed coffee
1 tsp. vanilla
milk
ice

Mix sugar, instant coffee, brewed coffee and vanilla in a gallon pitcher. Stir until sugar is dissolved. Add milk until half full. Fill with ice. Stir.

Mrs. Clifford Rhoda Herschberger

Hot Spiced Cider

2 qt. cider
¼ c. brown sugar
12 whole cloves
10 whole allspice
4 (3") cinnamon sticks

Bring cider to a boil. Add rest of ingredients and steep 3-5 minutes. Enjoy!

Mrs. Perry Delores Herschberger

Appetizers, Beverages, Dips

Effortless Eggnog

½ gal. cold milk, divided
1 pkg. instant vanilla pudding
¼ c. sugar
2 tsp. vanilla
½ tsp. cinnamon
½ tsp. nutmeg

In a large bowl, whisk ¾ cup milk and pudding mix until smooth. Whisk in sugar, vanilla, cinnamon and nutmeg. Stir in remaining milk. Refrigerate.

Mrs. Isaac Daisy Troyer

Eggnog

5 eggs
1 qt. creamy milk
½ c. maple syrup
½ tsp. salt

Beat eggs; add remaining ingredients and beat again. Chill and serve.
Note: Be sure to use only eggs that have no broken lining prior to using.

Mrs. Wilbur Wilma Miller

Sparkling Grape Juice

2 (12 oz.) cans grape juice concentrate
4 c. water
⅔ c. lemon juice
1 (12 oz.) can orange juice concentrate
1½ c. sugar
1 (2 liter) Sprite

Mix all ingredients except Sprite in a gallon container. Add Sprite and serve immediately. Yield: 1½ gallon.

Miss Dorcas Miller

Appetizers, Beverages, Dips

Creamy Lemon–Berry Punch

chopped strawberries, as many as desired
2 c. vanilla ice cream
2 qt. pink lemonade
Sprite
chopped ice cubes

Mix strawberries and ice cream and freeze till hard. Mix lemonade and ice cream/strawberry mixture. Stir vigorously. Last add Sprite and ice cubes. Sip and enjoy on a hot summer day! Serves approximately 12 people.
Note: This is an original recipe from my sister Rebekah.

Mrs. Ernest Ray Inez Miller

Mr. Misty

6 oz. Jell-O
1½ c. sugar
1 qt. boiling water
1 (46 oz.) can pineapple juice
2 qt. cold water
7-Up to taste

Mix Jell-O, sugar and boiling water. Mix well. Add pineapple juice and freeze. When ready to drink, add 7-Up to make slushy. Serves: 15 people.

Miss Lyndora Kay Miller

Icy Holiday Punch

6 oz. cherry Jell-O
¾ c. sugar
2 c. boiling water
1 (46 oz.) can pineapple juice
6 c. cold water
2 (2 liter) ginger ale, chilled

In a 4 quart freezer-proof container, dissolve Jell-O and sugar in boiling water. Stir in pineapple juice and cold water. Cover and freeze overnight. Remove from freezer 2 hours before serving. Place in a punch bowl; stir in ginger ale just before serving. Serves 32 people.

Mrs. Delbert Martha Schrock

Appetizers, Beverages, Dips

Orange Punch

16 oz. frozen orange juice concentrate
16 oz. frozen lemon juice concentrate
1 qt. orange sherbet
2 lg. bottles ginger ale

Mix frozen juice and sherbet together till slightly thawed. Beat till foamy. Last add ginger ale. Yield: approximately 1½ gallon.

Mrs. Joseph Lucinda Miller

Punch

16 oz. can frozen orange juice, concentrate
16 oz. can frozen lemonade, concentrate
2 pkg. cherry Kool-Aid
2 c. sugar
3 qt. water
1 qt. ginger ale

Mix and chill. Add ginger ale just before serving. A refreshing drink.

Miss Wilma Fern Schrock

Rhubarb Juice

2 qt. rhubarb juice
2½ c. sugar
2 Tbsp. strawberry Jell-O
2 c. hot water
2 c. pineapple juice
½ c. ReaLemon

Cut up rhubarb; cover with water and boil for 10 minutes. Drain. Use 2 quarts of the juice. Add all the other ingredients. You can cold pack for 15 minutes or put in containers to freeze. To serve: mix with one can of 7-Up or Sprite. Sunday afternoon specialty.

The Bunch of Six

Appetizers, Beverages, Dips

Ice Tea Concentrate

4 c. boiling water
2 c. loose tea or 2 tea bags
2 c. sugar

Put tea in boiling water. Let steep for 15 minutes. Strain. Add sugar. Boil for 15 minutes. This will make a quart of concentrate. Put 2 tablespoons concentrate in a glass full of water. This recipe makes 1 gallon of tea depending on strength desired. Very refreshing on a warm summer day!

Mrs. Clifford Rhoda Herschberger

Caramel Dip for Apples

½ c. butter
½ c. Karo
1 c. brown sugar
1 c. sweetened condensed milk

Mix all. Bring to a boil on low heat, stir constantly as it will burn easily.

Mrs. Reuben Marilyn Schrock

Caramel Fruit Dip

8 oz. cream cheese
1 c. sour cream
1 c. brown sugar
vanilla
caramel flavoring

Beat well and serve with your favorite fruit. Serves 10 people.

Miss Rachel Fern Kauffman

Fruit Dip

1 (13 oz.) jar marshmallow creme
12 oz. cream cheese, softened

Mix until well blended. Use as a dip with your favorite fruit. Very good with apples. Yield: 3½ cups.

Miss Gloria Faith Schrock

Appetizers, Beverages, Dips

Cheese Ball

16 oz. cream cheese
4 oz. Velveeta cheese
1 Tbsp. liquid smoke
2 tsp. Worcestershire sauce
1 pkg. dried beef or bologna
1 tsp. Lawry's salt
pinch of garlic powder
2 tsp. chopped onions

Mix all together and refrigerate.

Mrs. Reuben Marilyn Schrock

Leanna's Dip

1 lb. Velveeta cheese
8 oz. cream cheese
½ c. milk
1 pkg. Hidden Valley Ranch, dip mix
1½ c. sour cream
diced ham

Put Velveeta cheese, cream cheese and milk in oven on low heat to melt; stir occasionally. When melted, add Hidden Valley Ranch, sour cream and diced ham. Serve with raw vegetables or a variety of crackers.

Miss Cheryl DeAnn Otto

Appetizers, Beverages, Dips

Maple Cream
(to spread on bread)

Fill a kettle one third full with maple syrup, then spread butter around top of kettle so it doesn't boil over, (repeat from time to time if syrup rises too high while boiling.) Bring to boil and put in a candy thermometer. Keep boiling until 242°-245°, then set on a cooling rack undisturbed until it's just a little warm, not cold. Then have 2 people ready with a wooden spoon, a table knife, a potato masher and some cream or milk. Stir, scraping sides from time to time till syrup becomes waxy and tawny colored. Never let it set long without stirring; things can happen fast with hard-boiled syrup. Now add a little cream and more as needed to make it manageable. If it starts getting unmanageable, use knife to scrape sides and masher to make it smooth. Experience is the best teacher, and if it doesn't go quite like you think it should, adjust temperature a little next time. I got these detailed instructions from my friend, David Esther, and it worked good. You may want to time your maple cream making with fresh bread out of the oven, then spread it on with butter. So-o-o good!

Mrs. Ernest Ray Inez Miller

Taco Dip

15 oz. can refried beans
8 oz. cream cheese
16 oz. sour cream
1 pkg. taco seasoning
shredded lettuce
shredded cheese
diced tomatoes
diced green peppers
nacho chips

Spread can of beans on tray. Mix cream cheese, sour cream and taco seasoning until smooth; spread on top of beans. Top with lettuce, cheese, tomatoes and peppers to cover. Serve with cheesy nacho chips.

Miss Edna Mae Schrock

My Kitchen

God bless my little kitchen,
I love its every nook;
And bless me as I do my work,
Wash pots and pans and cook.

And the meals that I prepare,
Be seasoned from above,
With Thy blessing and Thy grace,
But most of all Thy love.

As we partake of earthly food,
The table for us spread,
We'll not forget to thank Thee, Lord,
Who gives us daily bread.

So bless my little kitchen, God,
And those who enter in,
May they find naught but joy and peace,
And happiness therein.

Breakfast Foods

Breakfast Foods

Baked Oatmeal 29	Good Morning Brain Pancakes 25
Baked Omelet Roll 19	Granola 29
Blueberry French Toast 18	Granola 30
Bran Muffins 17	Granola Breakfast Cereal 30
Breakfast Bake 20	Granola Cereal 31
Breakfast Burritos 21	Granola Cereal 31
Breakfast Favorite 20	Grape Nuts 32
Breakfast Pizza 24	Grape Nuts 33
Breakfast Pizza Delight 24	No-Cook Mush 28
Breakfast Tortilla 21	Not Too Sweet Pancake Syrup 27
Brunch Enchiladas 22	Pancake Pizza 27
Cinnamon French Toast 18	Pancakes 25
Cornmeal Mush 27	Quick Fried Mush 28
Corn Mush 28	Ron's Pancakes 25
Egg and Gravy Bake 22	Skier's French Toast 17
French Breakfast Puffs 19	Sour Cream Waffles 26
Gold Rush Brunch 23	Tasty Granola 32
Gold Rush Brunch Casserole 23	Tasty Waffles 26

Breakfast Foods

Bran Muffins

2 c. whole wheat flour
½ c. brown sugar
2 tsp. baking powder
½ tsp. soda

1 tsp. salt
¾ c. sour milk
½ c. vegetable oil
1 egg

Mix all together, beat well. Bake at 350° for 15-20 minutes. Serve warm with milk and fresh strawberries. Yield: 12 muffins.

Mrs. Nelson Ruth Miller

Skier's French Toast

¼ c. Karo
¾ c. butter
1 c. brown sugar, heaping
¼ c. water
12 slices bread

1 lb. sausage, fried
8 eggs, beaten
1½ c. milk
1 tsp. vanilla
1 tsp. salt

Bring first four ingredients to a boil in medium saucepan. Pour in a 9"x13" pan and place 6 slices bread on top of syrup. Add sausage, then remaining 6 slices bread Mix beaten eggs, milk, vanilla and salt; pour over all. Bake at 375° for 45-60 minutes. When top is done, flip over so syrup side is up. Serves 8-10 people.

Note: We like putting maple syrup on top before eating it.

Mrs. Clifford Rhoda Herschberger
Miss Deborah Ann Miller

Breakfast Foods

Cinnamon French Toast

½ c. brown sugar
1½ c. maple syrup
½ c. butter
8 slices homemade bread
4 tsp. sugar

1 tsp. cinnamon, heaping
10 eggs
1 tsp. salt
4 c. milk

Heat first 3 ingredients in a saucepan till butter is melted. Pour into a 10"x15" pan. Lay bread slices on top. Try to have the whole pan covered with bread. Mix sugar and cinnamon and sprinkle on top. Beat eggs, add salt and milk, pour over bread. Bake at 350° for 30-40 minutes, uncovered. If using store-bought bread, put 2 layers of bread. This can be made the evening before and kept refrigerated. Serves 8 people.

Mrs. Wilbur Wilma Miller

Blueberry French Toast

12 slices bread
16 oz. cream cheese
1 c. blueberries

12 eggs, beaten
2 c. milk
½ c. maple syrup

In the bottom of a greased 9"x13" pan, put 6 slices bread, cut into 1" cubes. Next cut cream cheese in little cubes and drop on bread. Spread fresh or frozen blueberries on top. Cut 6 more slices of bread in 1" cubes and spread over top evenly. Beat eggs well and add milk and maple syrup. Pour mixture over all. Bake at 350° for 1 hour. Serve with blueberry sauce or syrup. For the blueberry lover! Serves 12 people.

Miss Miriam Miller

Breakfast Foods

French Breakfast Puffs

⅓ c. shortening
½ c. sugar
1 egg
1½ c. flour
½ tsp. baking powder
½ tsp. salt

¼ tsp. nutmeg, opt.
½ c. milk
½ c. butter
½ c. sugar
1 tsp. cinnamon

Mix shortening, sugar and egg. Sift flour, baking powder, salt and nutmeg. Stir in alternating with milk. Fill small greased muffin tins and bake for 20-25 minutes at 350°. Immediately roll muffin in melted butter, then roll in mixture of sugar and cinnamon. Yield: 2 dozen.

Miss Cheryl DeAnn Otto

Baked Omelet Roll

6 eggs, beaten
1 c. milk
½ c. flour
½ tsp. salt

¼ tsp. pepper
¾ c. diced ham
1½ c. shredded cheese

Beat first 5 ingredients together. Pour into a greased 9"x13" pan. Bake at 450° for 18-20 minutes or until eggs are set. Sprinkle ham and cheese over the top. Roll up omelet in pan. Place the seam-side down on a serving platter. Cut into 6 slices. Some like it served with Ranch dressing. Serves 6 people.

Miss Edna Mae Schrock

Breakfast Foods

Breakfast Bake

1 lb. sausage
1 (4 oz.) can mushrooms
2 c. shredded cheddar cheese
6 eggs
3 c. milk

1 c. Bisquick
½ c. butter, melted
½ tsp. salt
pepper and other
   seasonings to taste

Brown sausage and mushrooms in a skillet. Drain. Put mixture in a 9"x13" pan that has been sprayed with nonstick cooking spray. Add cheese. Mix eggs, milk, Bisquick, butter, salt and other seasonings. Pour mixture over the sausage/cheese blend. Bake at 350° for 45 minutes. Can be mixed the night before and baked in the morning. Serves 8 people.
Note: We like to add some crumbled bacon.

Miss Cheryl DeAnn Otto

Breakfast Favorite

1 can buttermilk biscuits
Velveeta cheese
12 eggs

1 lb. sausage
½ c. flour
3½ c. milk

Press biscuits in bottom of buttered 9"x13" baking pan. Bake at 350° till lightly browned. Cover with cheese slices. Scramble and fry eggs and put on top of cheese. Fry sausage and add flour, then add milk. Season your gravy to taste and pour over eggs. Enjoy!

Mrs. Ernest Sara Schrock

The richest person is one who finds pleasure in everyday duties.

Breakfast Burritos

2 cans cream of mushroom soup
16 oz. sour cream
4 tortillas
4 med. potatoes, fried
1 lb. sausage, browned
10 eggs
½ c. milk
onions and peppers, chopped
salt
pepper
Velveeta cheese slices
shredded mozzarella
    and cheddar cheese

Mix together soup and sour cream. Spread half into bottom of 9"x13" pan. Cover with 2 tortillas. Layer potatoes and sausage next. Beat eggs and milk. Add salt, pepper, onions and peppers to taste. Scramble together. When almost done, put on top of sausage and cover with Velveeta. Add the 2 remaining tortillas and the soup/sour cream mixture. Bake at 350° for 30-45 minutes. Top with shredded cheese.

Mrs. Kenneth Leanna Kauffman
Miss Esther Miller
Miss SueEllen Miller

Breakfast Tortilla

8 tortillas
10 eggs, scrambled
2 c. meat, (ham, hot dogs, etc.)
shredded cheese
sour cream

Spread sour cream on tortillas. Put eggs, meat, and cheese in layers down the middle of the tortillas. Fold sides of tortillas in and place seam-side down on cookie sheet. Bake at 350° for 10 minutes. Serves 8 people.

Note: Onions and peppers can be added to eggs while scrambling. Shredded, fried potatoes can also be added.

Miss Denise Ann Kauffman

Breakfast Foods

Egg and Gravy Bake

12 eggs
3 Tbsp. butter
½ c. flour
1½ c. milk
½ tsp. dry mustard

¾ tsp. salt
⅛ tsp. black pepper
3 slices bread
softened butter

Break eggs into a greased 10"x15" pan, leaving yolks whole. Sprinkle with salt and pepper. Melt butter in saucepan, add flour and stir well. Add milk slowly, stirring constantly until it boils. Add dry mustard, season to taste. Pour gravy over eggs. Spread bread with softened butter and crumble over gravy. Bake at 325° for 20-30 minutes. Serves 8-10 people.

Note: Cheese or meat may also be added.

Mrs. Wilbur Wilma Miller

Brunch Enchiladas

16 (8") flour tortillas
¾ c. chopped onions
¾ c. chopped green peppers
¼ c. butter
2 c. chopped ham
2 c. sausage crumbs
sour cream

shredded cheddar cheese
16 eggs
1½ c. milk
2 Tbsp. flour
salt and pepper to taste
sour cream
salsa

In a saucepan, sauté onions and peppers in butter till soft; add meat and cook till hot. Spread a strip of sour cream down the center of each tortilla. Add ⅓ cup of meat mixture, top with ¼ cup cheddar cheese. Roll up and place seam-side down in two 9"x13" pans. Beat eggs, milk, flour, salt and pepper together and pour over tortillas. Refrigerate overnight. Remove from refrigerator 30 minutes before baking. Bake uncovered at 350° for 45-60 minutes. They're done once a knife inserted in the center comes out clean. Add a thin layer of shredded cheddar cheese. Let set 5 minutes. Serve with sour cream and salsa.

Note: If you only need one 9"x13" for your family, just freeze the other pan for later. Thaw before baking.

Mrs. Kenneth Marilyn Otto

Breakfast Foods

Gold Rush Brunch

8 med. potatoes, shredded
½ c. chopped onions
2 Tbsp. parsley flakes
8 eggs

1 lb. sausage, bacon or ham
1½ lb. shredded cheese, divided
1 can mushrooms, opt.

White Sauce:
¼ c. butter
2 c. milk
¼ c. flour

¼ tsp. salt
1 c. sour cream

Lightly fry potatoes, onions and parsley. Put in a 9"x13" pan. Fry eggs just until set; put on top of potatoes. Fry meat and put on top of eggs. Then cover with half of cheese and mushrooms. Pour white sauce over casserole, then top with remaining cheese. Bake at 350° for 40 minutes. Can be made the day before. Serves 8-10 people.

Mrs. Wilbur Wilma Miller

Gold Rush Brunch Casserole

4 lg. potatoes, cooked and shredded
2 Tbsp. chopped onions
2 Tbsp. parsley flakes

8 eggs
1 lb. ham or bacon, fried
1½ lb. shredded cheese, divided

White Sauce:
¼ c. butter
¼ c. flour
¼ tsp. salt

1¾ c. milk
1 c. sour cream

Lightly fry potatoes, onions and parsley. Put in a greased 9"x13" pan. Fry eggs. Spread 1 pound cheese over potatoes, then layer meat and eggs. Pour white sauce over casserole and top with remaining cheese. Bake at 350° for 30-40 minutes. For white sauce: Combine melted butter and flour; add salt and milk. When thickened add sour cream.

Miss Mary Edna Miller

Breakfast Pizza

biscuit dough
1 can cream of mushroom soup
fried potatoes
scrambled eggs
fried and crumbled bacon
onions

green peppers
fresh mushrooms
ham
ripe olives
shredded cheddar cheese

Sausage Gravy:
1 lb. sausage, crumbled
4½ c. milk, divided

½ c. flour
salt and pepper to taste

Mix enough biscuit dough to press on bottom of 9"x13" pan. Bake to light golden—do not over bake. Spread mushroom soup over crust. Spread the rest of the ingredients on the biscuits using whatever you wish. Bake until heated then top with cheese. Serve with sausage gravy. For sausage gravy: Brown sausage and add 3½ cups milk. Bring to a boil. Mix 1 cup milk with flour and add to sausage and milk mixture. Cook 1 minute. Serves 12 people.

Mrs. Monroe Elsie Miller

Breakfast Pizza Delight

1½ lb. fried sausage
1½-2 c. pizza sauce
bread, thinly sliced
melting cheese

3 c. milk
1 tsp. salt
5 eggs

Cover the bottom of a 9"x13" pan with slices of bread. Top with cheese slices. Add sausage mixed with pizza sauce, then add another layer of bread. Beat the last 3 ingredients together and pour over everything. Bake at 350° for 35-40 minutes or until done and golden brown. Serves 10-12 people.

Note: This can be made ahead of time and refrigerated overnight. You may wish to add more milk if it looks too dry. When prepared ahead, this is a simple but complete hot dish for company or a busy morning.

Mrs. Samuel Rachel Chupp

Breakfast Foods

Good Morning Brain Pancakes

1½ c. flour
¾ c. ground flax seed
¼ c. raw sugar
4 tsp. baking powder
½ tsp. salt

1 egg
2 egg whites
2 Tbsp. vegetable oil
2 c. milk

Mix dry ingredients, add the rest. Beat till smooth. Fry. Serve with blueberries and your schoolchildren will have a good start to their day! Yield: 16 (4") pancakes.

Mrs. Ernest Ray Inez Miller

Pancakes

1¾ c. flour
3¾ tsp. baking powder
3 Tbsp. sugar

3 eggs
1½ c. milk
3 Tbsp. vegetable oil

Mix together and fry. Serves 6 people.

Mrs. Isaac Daisy Troyer

Ron's Pancakes

2 c. flour
1½ tsp. salt
4 tsp. baking powder
¼ c. sugar

2 eggs
¼ c. vegetable oil
2 tsp. vanilla
1½ c. milk

Mix dry ingredients in a bowl. In another bowl mix wet ingredients. Mix wet ingredients slowly into dry ingredients. If you prefer thinner pancakes add more milk. Fry in hot oiled griddle. Eat with maple syrup and enjoy! Serves 6 people.

Note: Good to serve with butter, peanut butter, whipped topping, ice cream or your choice of fruit pie filling.

Mrs. Monroe Elsie Miller

Breakfast Foods

Sour Cream Waffles

1½ c. flour
2 tsp. baking powder
½ tsp. soda
1 Tbsp. sugar
3 eggs, separated

¾ c. sour cream
¾ c. milk
¼ c. vegetable oil
¼ c. butter, melted

Sift dry ingredients together. Beat egg yolks, sour cream and milk. Add dry ingredients, alternating with oil and butter cooled down to room temperature. Stir until batter is smooth and free of lumps. In separate bowl, beat egg whites until stiff; fold into batter. Slightly more than a cup will make the waffle pan nicely filled. Enjoy! Serves 5 people.

Miss Susanna Schrock

Tasty Waffles

3 eggs
2 c. milk
2¼ c. flour
1 Tbsp. baking powder

1 tsp. salt
6 Tbsp. butter, melted
1 Tbsp. vanilla, opt.

Beat eggs till light. Add milk, then dry ingredients. Beat in butter and vanilla till smooth. Have your sprayed or greased waffle iron medium-hot, with both sides having a turn on burner. Pour waffle batter on least hot side first. Fry 2½ minutes then flip iron and fry 2½ minutes on that side. Only grease iron the first time. Yield: 5 large waffles.

Mrs. Ernest Ray Inez Miller

Breakfast Foods

Pancake Pizza

pancake batter
scrambled eggs
meat of your choice
cheese
gravy

Put a thin layer of pancake dough into a cake pan and bake. Prepare scrambled eggs; fry in a pan along with meat and cheese. Then make your gravy (to put on top). Once everything is done, put in layers, and it's ready to serve.

Note: Be sure to use only a small amount of dough. We like hamburger gravy best. Good luck and happy eating!

Mrs. Howard Ellen Schrock

Not Too Sweet Pancake Syrup

½ c. sugar
3 Tbsp. Perma Flo
⅛ tsp. salt
2 c. hot water
3 Tbsp. brown sugar
2 Tbsp. butter
1 tsp vanilla
1 tsp. maple flavoring

Combine first 3 ingredients. Stir in water. Cook 4-5 minutes, or until clear. Remove from heat and add rest of ingredients.

Mrs. William Miriam Yoder

Cornmeal Mush

6 c. water
3 c. cornmeal
¾ c. flour
1 Tbsp. salt
3 c. cold water

Heat 6 cups water to boiling in a stew pan. Put cornmeal, flour and salt in a bowl, stir in 3 cups cold water, then add to boiling water. Keep stirring until it boils and simmer for 15 minutes. Pour in a 9"x13" pan which has been rinsed in cold water. Cover with wax paper and let stand overnight. Slice and fry in shortening.

Mrs. Kenneth Leanna Kauffman

Breakfast Foods

Corn Mush

4½ c. cornmeal
¾ c. flour
1½ tsp. salt
3 qt. boiling water

Mix cornmeal, flour and salt and pour into boiling water. Heat to a boil. Pour into a 9"x13" pan and cool overnight. Next morning slice the mush thinly, fry and serve with apple butter.

Mrs. Steven Katie Jantzi

No-Cook Mush

1 c. cornmeal
2 Tbsp. flour
1 tsp. salt
2 c. boiling water

Add the boiling water all at once and stir well with a wire whip. Drop by tablespoonfuls in hot pan greased with lard or oil. When frying turn patties, then flatten to desired thickness. This fries quicker. Eat with liverwurst and ketchup. It is also good with maple syrup. Serves 4 people.

Mrs. Ernest Mary Ellen Miller

Quick Fried Mush

1 c. cornmeal
½ tsp. salt
1 Tbsp. flour, slightly rounded
1 c. boiling water, approx.

Mix cornmeal, salt and flour in a medium bowl. Add hot water and stir till mixed. Add more hot water if too thick. Drop by tablespoonfuls into hot skillet with grease. When turning patties, flatten to desired thickness. Fry to a golden brown on each side. Serves 6 people.

Mrs. Joe Lorene Miller

Baked Oatmeal

½ c. butter, melted
or vegetable oil
1 c. brown sugar
2 eggs, beaten
3 c. oatmeal

2 tsp. baking powder
1 tsp. salt
1 c. milk
½ tsp. vanilla or maple flavoring
½ c. coconut

Mix and bake in a 9"x13" pan at 350° for 30 minutes. Serve warm. Serves 6-12 people.

Miss Lovina Eicher

Granola

24 c. quick oats
3-4 c. coconut
3-4 c. sunflower seeds
3-4 c. brown sugar (honey may be used)

2 boxes graham crackers, crushed
1 box Cheerios
2 lb. butter, melted (may use part oil)

Mix dry ingredients-then mix in butter. Bake at 250°-300°, stirring occasionally-until toasted to your liking. We like ours just dried.

Note: Raw sunflower seeds, (versus roasted) makes a better flavor. Roasted have a tendency to make granola taste old.

Mrs. Howard Ellen Schrock

If one lives to be 70 years old and is an average person, he spent 6 years eating.

The best place to put your troubles in, is your pocket... the one with a hole in it.

Breakfast Foods

Granola

10 c. oatmeal
2 pkg. graham crackers, crushed
1 c. brown sugar
2 c. coconut
1½ c. butter
½ c. water
2 tsp. maple flavoring

Pour butter mixture over dry ingredients and mix well. Bake at 250° for 1 hour, stirring every 15 minutes. Yield: 1 gallon.
Note: Sometimes we like to add butterscotch chips when partially cooled.

Miss Edna Mae Schrock

Granola Breakfast Cereal

21 c. quick oats
1 (14 oz.) box graham crackers, crushed
7 c. wheat germ
1 Tbsp. salt
2 Tbsp. cinnamon
1½ c. coconut oil
1½ c. honey
2 Tbsp. vanilla
1 c. flax seeds, opt.

Mix together all the dry ingredients. Melt the oil, honey and vanilla, then pour over the dry ingredients and mix well. Pour into 2 large casserole dishes and toast in 250° oven. Stir the granola every 25-30 minutes until lightly browned and not wet-feeling to the touch. Store in air-tight containers. Yield: approximately 2-2½ gallon.

Mrs. Dennis Marilyn Hershberger

Breakfast Foods

Granola Cereal

10 c. oatmeal
2 c. wheat germ
1½ c. brown sugar
4 c. Rice Krispies
1 c. coconut

½ c. butter, melted
1 c. peanut butter
½ c. corn syrup
2 tsp. vanilla
pinch of salt

Mix together oatmeal, wheat germ, brown sugar, Rice Krispies and coconut in a large bowl. Mix together the rest of ingredients and heat in small saucepan till peanut butter is dissolved and mixture is smooth. Pour over oatmeal mixture and mix till crumbly. Put in 2 cake pans and toast in oven at 275° for 1 hour. Stir every 20 minutes.

Mrs. Joe Lorene Miller

Granola Cereal

22 c. oatmeal
3 pkg. graham crackers, crushed
4 c. coconut
1 c. pecans

4 tsp. soda, scant
2 tsp. salt
2 c. wheat germ
2 c. butter
2¾ c. honey

Combine dry ingredients. Melt butter and add honey, then mix into granola. Toast at 275° until coconut is golden brown, stirring occasionally.

Miss Marietta W. Miller

Breakfast Foods

Tasty Granola

14 c. quick oats
4 c. coconut
2 tsp. salt
2 c. brown sugar
6 c. Honey Nut Cheerios
2 pkg. graham crackers, crushed
1¾ c. butter
1 c. peanut butter
2 c. chocolate chips

Mix dry ingredients. Melt butter and peanut butter together. Add to dry ingredients and mix well. Spread on sheet pans and toast at 250° until golden brown. Let cool awhile then add chocolate chips. Let set until chips are warm and soft. Mix with your hands until evenly coated. Cool completely.

Mrs. Nelson Ruth Miller

Grape Nuts

12½ c. whole wheat flour
5 c. sugar
2 tsp. salt
5½ c. buttermilk or sour milk
2 Tbsp. soda
½ c. butter, melted
¾ tsp. maple flavoring
1 Tbsp. vanilla

Mix flour, sugar and salt. Add soda to buttermilk; stir, then add to dry ingredients. Last, add butter and flavorings, mix well. Put in 2 pans (9"x13" and 10"x15" work well) and spread evenly. Bake in 350° oven until done, approximately 1 hour and 15 minutes. Grind or put through salad master to make crumbs. Spread in pans and dry at 225°, stirring every 15 minutes.

Mrs. Wilbur Wilma Miller

Breakfast Foods

Grape Nuts

3 c. brown sugar
9 c. whole wheat flour
1½ tsp. salt
½ c. butter, melted

1 qt. milk
2¼ tsp. soda
2 tsp. vanilla
1 tsp. maple flavoring

Bake in two 9"x13" pans for 30-35 minutes at 350°. Cool. Grind with salad master or screen, then toast.

Mrs. Isaac Daisy Troyer

What Words Do

A careless word may cause strife;
A cruel word may wreck a life.
A bitter word, hate instill;
A brutal word, smite and kill.
A joyous word, light the day;
A gracious word, smooth the way.
A timely word, lessen stress;
A loving word, heal and bless.

God's Flowers

My two small daughters, in a childish hour,
Thrilled by the beauty of our grounds in flower.
Gathered the heads of all my choicest bloom,
With skirts like baskets full, they sought my room.

Aghast, I chided, and the joyous light
Left their sweet faces, while in hurried flight,
They dropped their blossoms in a jeweled heap.
Lip quivering, the baby turned to weep.

"Come, sister," said the elder one, "let's go
To the big field where all the daisies grow."
She whispered as they went out hand in hand.
"We'll pick God's flowers. He will understand."

Breads Rolls

Breads, Rolls

100% Whole Wheat Bread 40	Golden Cornbread 50
100% Whole Wheat Bread 40	Homemade Tortillas 58
Amish Friendship Bread or Cake 41	Italian Cheese Bread 43
Angel Biscuits 49	Jiffy Pizza Dough 45
Biscuit Mix 49	Maple Twists 55
Blueberry Sour Cream Streusel Muffins . . . 53	Melt in your Mouth Biscuits 50
Bread Sticks 47	Melt in your Mouth Dinner Rolls 51
Bread Sticks 47	Pecan Roll Syrup 58
Bread Sticks 48	Pizza Crust 45
Cinnamon Rolls 56	Pizza Crust 46
Cinnamon Rolls 56	Pizza Crusts 46
Cinnamon Rolls 57	Pizza Hut Pizza Crust 46
Cinnamuffins 54	Pumpkin Bread 44
Cloud Biscuits 49	Pumpkin Cinnamon Rolls 57
Cornbread 50	Refrigerator French Bread 42
Corn Pone 51	Rhubarb Nut Bread 44
Danish Braids 54	Rich Dinner Rolls 52
Der Dutchman Bread 37	Soft Pretzels 48
Donuts 52	Starter for 10 Day Friendship Bread 41
Donuts 53	Wheat Bread 38
Favorite Bread Recipe 37	White Bread 38
Flour Tortillas 58	Whole Wheat Bread 39
Garlic Bread 42	Whole Wheat Bread 39
Garlic Bubble Loaf 43	Zucchini Nut Bread 45

Der Dutchman Bread

2½ qt. warm water
2½ c. sugar
½ c. salt, scant
1 c. yeast

flour
2 c. vegetable oil
2 eggs
flour

Mix first 5 ingredients, adding just a little flour. Add rest of ingredients adding flour till it is the right consistency. Let rise till almost double and punch down, let rise again, then put in bread pans. Bake at 350° for 30 minutes. Yield: 10-12 loaves.

Note: I usually use half wheat flour.

Mrs. Samuel Dorothy Miller

Favorite Bread Recipe

4 c. warm water
2 Tbsp. yeast
½ c. sugar
4 tsp. salt

⅓ c. lard
1 egg
8 c. flour, (4 c. white
  and 4 c. Prairie Gold)

Dissolve yeast in warm water and let set for 5 minutes. Then add rest of ingredients except flour and mix well. Next add 4 cups flour and mix well with wire whip. Slowly keep adding flour and kneading until smooth and not sticky anymore. Let rise till double, punch down and let rise till double again. Put in pans and let rise approximately 30 minutes. Bake 10 minutes at 325° then 20 minutes at 350°. Yield: 5 loaves.

Miss Cathy Wagler

Always remember to forget the troubles that passed away. But never forget to remember the blessings that come each day.

Breads, Rolls

Wheat Bread

6½ c. warm water
2 Tbsp. salt
⅓ c. sugar
1 c. vegetable oil or lard
¼ c. yeast
5 c. whole wheat flour
9-10 c. seal of Minnesota flour

Whip together first 6 ingredients with a wire whisk. Stir in remaining flour to desired consistency. Let rise 30 minutes, punch down and allow to rise again 30 minutes. Shape into loaves and put into bread pans and let rise another 15-20 minutes. Bake at 350° for 25 minutes. Yield: 6 large or 7 small loaves.

Mrs. Vernon Rachel Herschberger

White Bread

4¾ c. water
¾ c. vegetable oil
½ c. sugar
3 Tbsp. salt
2 Tbsp. do-cel, rounded
2 Tbsp. yeast
15 c. flour, divided

Mix water, oil, sugar and salt. Mix in 3 cups flour. Add 3 more cups flour, yeast and do-cel. Mix. Slowly add and mix in the rest of the flour. Knead until well mixed, using oil. Let rise until double in size. Put in 5 pans. Let rise again. Bake at 350° for 30 minutes.

Miss Ruth Miller

Don't be afraid to try new recipes. The worst that can happen is that you will have to eat them yourself.

Whole Wheat Bread

3 eggs, beaten
¾ c. lard
¾ c. honey
1 Tbsp. liquid lecithin
1 Tbsp. apple cider vinegar
3 Tbsp. sorghum
5 Tbsp. yeast
2 Tbsp. salt
18-19 c. whole wheat
   Prairie Gold flour, approx.

Beat eggs, adding hot water to measure 6½ cups. Add next 4 ingredients and stir till dissolved. Your liquid should be about lukewarm before adding yeast. Stir well, add salt. Mix in 6 cups flour and beat well with wire whip. Add remaining flour and mix with hands. Let rise, then shape in 6 loaves. You should have enough for 6 loaves and a small amount of dough left over for your small child to shape and bake in their own small dish. (A small stainless steel bowl works well and they love it!) You may also use potato water, mashed potatoes, milk or buttermilk for part of the liquid. Yield: 6 loaves.

Mrs. Wilbur Wilma Miller

Whole Wheat Bread

4½ c. warm water
¾ c. lard
½ c. honey
1 Tbsp. salt
1 Tbsp. guar gum
3 Tbsp. yeast
12-14 c. whole wheat flour

Dissolve lard in warm water and add honey and salt. Next mix 1 cup flour into the water. Then mix the guar gum and yeast with a cup of flour and add it to the water mixture, stirring well till all the lumps disappear. Continue adding whole wheat flour until dough is the consistency you like. Let rise. Put in 5 pans and bake at 350° for 28 minutes. Yield: 5 loaves.

Note: For softer crusts, put a small bowl of hot water in oven while the bread is baking.

Mrs. Dennis Marilyn Hershberger

Breads, Rolls

100% Whole Wheat Bread

3 eggs
6½ c. water
1½ c. vegetable oil, divided
3 Tbsp. salt
1 c. honey

3 Tbsp. wheat gluten
¼ c. yeast
1½ Tbsp. lecithin
16½ c. 100% Prairie Gold flour
2 Tbsp. guar gum, opt.

Beat eggs; add warm water and 1 cup oil, add the rest of ingredients except guar gum. Beat flour into mixture with egg beater 2 cups at a time. When it's too hard to beat, stir with large spoon, 2 cups at a time. Now add the guar gum. When it's too hard to stir, knead in the last portion of flour with your hands. When all is kneaded in good, add ½ cup oil and knead till that is all worked in. Let rise to twice the size. Knead and let rise again. Divide into 6 portions and roll out with rolling pin. Roll up dough and place into bread pans. Let rise to twice the size and bake at 350° for 30 minutes or until golden brown. Yield: 6 loaves.

Mrs. Monroe Elsie Miller

100% Whole Wheat Bread

2 eggs
4¼ c. warm water
1 c. vegetable oil
¾ c. honey
2 Tbsp. salt

1 Tbsp. liquid lecithin
2 Tbsp. wheat gluten
2 Tbsp. do-cel
2 Tbsp. yeast
12 c. Prairie Gold flour

Mix the first 6 ingredients well with a wire whip. Add 3 cups flour and mix well. Sprinkle 2 more cups flour over the mixture in your large bowl, then add gluten, do-cel, and yeast over that flour, mix it all in together. Mix well. Remove wire whip. Use a spoon or scraper to add the rest of flour until read to use hands. Add oil to finish mixing it. Mix well! Let rise 1½ hours. Punch down a few times. Bake at 350° for 30 minutes. Yield: 5 loaves.

Note: Some white flour can be used instead of all whole wheat.

Mrs. Ernest Mary Ellen Miller

Breads, Rolls

Starter for 10 Day Friendship Bread

1½ tsp. yeast
1 c. warm water

1 c. flour
2 Tbsp. sugar

Mix yeast and warm water together, then add flour and sugar. Pour into a 1 gallon ziploc bag. Keep in cool place. Do not refrigerate.

The Bunch of Six

Amish Friendship Bread or Cake

flour
sugar
milk
vegetable oil
eggs
vanilla

baking powder
salt
cinnamon
instant pudding
nuts

Day 1: Do nothing. Day 2-5: Squeeze the bag 2 times a day. Day 6: Add 1 cup flour, 1 cup sugar and 1 cup milk to the mixture in the bag. Squeeze, mixing well. Day 7-9: Squeeze and let air out of bag 2 times a day. Day 10: Pour and squeeze contents into a large bowl. Add 1 cup flour, 1 cup sugar and 1 cup milk, stir and pour 4 (1 cup) starters into 4 one-gallon ziploc bags. Give one bag to each of your friends along with a copy of this recipe. Keep one for yourself. You should have 1 cup starter left; if not use one more cup from a reserved bag. Add 1 cup oil, ½ cup milk 3 eggs and 1 teaspoon vanilla. Mix well. Then add 2 cup flour, 1 cup sugar, 1½ teaspoon baking powder, 1 teaspoon salt, 2 teaspoon cinnamon, 1 (3.4 oz.) box vanilla instant pudding mix and 1 cup chopped nuts. Mix well Mix a little sugar and cinnamon to sprinkle on the bottom of pans and to sprinkle on top of batter. If making bread, pour batter into 2 bread pans. Bake at 325° for 1 hour. If making a cake pour batter into a 9"x13" pan and bake at 325° for approximately 45 minutes or until toothpick inserted near center comes out clean.

The Bunch of Six

Breads, Rolls

Refrigerator French Bread

2¼ c. water
2 Tbsp. butter
2 pkg. yeast
1 Tbsp. sugar
1 Tbsp. salt

6½ c. flour, divided
vegetable oil
1 egg white
1 Tbsp. water

Heat water and butter to 120°. In a large bowl, combine 3 cups flour, yeast, sugar, salt and warm water mixture. Gradually add enough remaining flour to form a stiff dough. Knead till smooth and satiny. Place dough in a greased bowl, turning once to grease top. Cover and let rise in a warm place for 30 minutes. Punch down and divide into 2 equal parts. Roll each into a rectangle on lightly floured board. Roll up tightly, jelly-roll style, beginning with long side. Seal edges and ends well by rolling with hands. Place seam-side down, on greased baking sheet. Brush with vegetable oil. Cover. Refrigerate 2-24 hours. When ready to bake, remove from refrigerator. Let stand 10 minutes. Brush with slightly beaten egg white and water. Slash tops of loaf diagonally at 2" intervals with sharp knife. Bake in preheated oven at 400° for 35-40 minutes.

Miss Cheryl DeAnn Otto

Garlic Bread

1 loaf Italian bread
10 Tbsp. butter, softened
1 egg, beaten
1 tsp. garlic powder

¼ c. Parmesan cheese
2 c. shredded cheese
2 Tbsp. parsley

Slice bread in half, lengthwise. Beat egg, then mix with softened butter. Add remaining ingredients and spread on bread slices. Regular homemade bread is fine or you can bake your own loaf, shaped like Italian bread. Sprinkle oregano on top, then put in broiler until cheese is melted. Serves 12 people.

Mrs. Kenneth Marilyn Otto
Miss Marietta W. Miller

Breads, Rolls

Garlic Bubble Loaf

1 Tbsp. yeast
¼ c. warm water
2 c. milk
2 Tbsp. sugar
1 Tbsp. shortening
2 tsp. salt
2 c. flour
½ c. butter
1 Tbsp. parsley flakes
2 tsp. garlic powder

Dissolve yeast in warm water. Let set for 5 minutes. Add milk, sugar, shortening, salt and flour. Beat until smooth, then stir in enough flour to form a soft dough. Turn out onto a floured surface. Knead until smooth and elastic about 6-8 minutes. Place in a greased bowl, turning once to grease top. Cover. Let rise until double in bulk. Melt butter. Add parsley flakes and garlic powder. When punched down divide dough into 4 parts, then divide each part in 12 pieces. Roll into balls, dip into butter mixture, then place balls into 2 bread pans. Pour remaining butter mixture over dough. Let rise until double in bulk. Bake at 375° for 35-40 minutes. Cool and remove from pans. Serve warm. Very good.

Mrs. David Verda Miller

Italian Cheese Bread

1½ c. warm water
2 Tbsp. yeast
1½ tsp. salt
1½ tsp. sugar
1½ Tbsp. vegetable oil
3 c. flour
½ tsp. garlic salt
Italian dressing
¼ tsp. oregano
¼ tsp. Italian seasoning
dash of pepper
¼ c. grated Parmesan cheese
shredded mozzarella cheese

Mix the first six ingredients, knead 2 minutes. Let rise 15 minutes. Spread on an 11"x16" pan. Brush with Italian dressing. Combine seasonings; sprinkle over top. Sprinkle with Parmesan cheese and shredded mozzarella cheese. Bake at 450° until golden brown. Serve with barbecue sauce or salsa.

Note: Bread dough can be used instead of the above mixture. Use enough for about 2 loaves.

Mrs. Steven Katie Jantzi

Breads, Rolls

Pumpkin Bread

2/3 c. shortening
2 2/3 c. sugar
1 tsp. vanilla
4 eggs
2 c. pumpkin
1 tsp. cinnamon
1/2 tsp. baking powder

2 tsp. soda
1 1/2 tsp. salt
1 tsp. nutmeg
3 c. flour
1 c. walnuts or raisins
2/3 c. water

Cream shortening, sugar and vanilla add beaten eggs and pumpkin. Stir in dry ingredients alternately with water, just until smooth. Pour into bread pans and bake at 350° for 45-55 minutes. Fills approximately 4 bread pans.

Miss Lovina Eicher

Rhubarb Nut Bread

1/2 c. brown sugar
1/3 c. vegetable oil
1 egg
1 c. sour milk
1 tsp. vanilla

1 tsp. soda
1/2 tsp. salt
2 1/2 c. flour
1/2 c. rhubarb, cut fine
1/2 c. chopped nuts

Sugar Mixture:
1/2 c. sugar

1 tsp. cinnamon

Mix brown sugar, oil, and egg. Add sour milk and vanilla. Add dry ingredients and mix well. Stir in rhubarb and nuts. Put in 2 bread pans. Sprinkle the sugar mixture on top. Bake at 325° for 40 minutes.

Mrs. Wilbur Wilma Miller

Breads, Rolls

Zucchini Nut Bread

2½ c. sugar
2 tsp. soda
¼ tsp. baking powder
2 tsp. cinnamon
1 tsp. salt
3 c. flour

1 c. vegetable oil
4 eggs
1 Tbsp. vanilla
3 c. raw zucchini, shredded
1 c. chopped nuts

Mix dry ingredients, add oil, then beaten eggs and vanilla, Stir in zucchini and nuts. Put in 2 bread pans and bake approximately 1 hour.
Note: You can also bake in a 9"x13" pan as a cake.

Mrs. Wilbur Wilma Miller

Jiffy Pizza Dough

2 c. flour
1 Tbsp. baking powder
1 tsp. salt

⅔ c. milk
⅓ c. vegetable oil

Mix together and press into a 10"x15" pan. Sprinkle top with chopped herbs or Italian seasoning. Bake at 350° for 10 minutes.

Mrs. Vernon Rachel Herschberger

Pizza Crust

1½ c. warm water
1½ Tbsp. dry yeast
3 Tbsp. sugar
2¼ tsp. salt
½ c. vegetable oil, scant

4½ c. flour
½ tsp. oregano
½ tsp. basil
½ tsp. garlic powder

Add yeast, sugar, salt and oil to warm water, then add the rest of ingredients. Put in cookie sheet, let rise 20 minutes. Prebake crust at 325° for 20 minutes. Put on toppings and bake at 350° for 30-35 minutes.

Mrs. Perry Delores Herschberger

Breads, Rolls

Pizza Crust

1 c. warm water
1 Tbsp. yeast
2 Tbsp. sugar

2 Tbsp. vegetable oil
2½ c. flour
1 tsp. salt

Mix together and let stand 5 minutes. Pat in large cookie sheet. If too sticky, sprinkle with flour. Do not add more flour to dough. Bake at 350°-375° for 25 minutes.
Note: I don't prebake crust, but most people do.

Mrs. Howard Ellen Schrock

Pizza Crusts

1½ Tbsp. yeast
2 c. warm water
2 Tbsp. sugar
¾ tsp. salt

½ tsp. oregano
2 tsp. Italian seasoning
5¼ c. flour
2¼ Tbsp. vegetable oil

Mix together yeast and warm water. In a mixing bowl combine yeast mixture, sugar, salt and seasonings, oil and flour. Let rise. Spread out on 2 11"x16" greased cookie sheets. Bake at 375° for 15-20 minutes.

Mrs. Joe Lorene Miller

Pizza Hut Pizza Crust

2 Tbsp. yeast
2 Tbsp. sugar
⅔ c. warm water
3 Tbsp. vegetable oil
2 tsp. salt

¼ tsp. garlic powder
½ tsp. oregano
2 c. cold water
6½-7 c. flour

Dissolve yeast and sugar in warm water. Combine other ingredients in a bowl, except flour. Add yeast mixture and slowly knead in flour until dough is smooth. Grease 2 cookie sheets and roll out crusts. Let rise a little. Bake at 450° until lightly browned. Yield: 2 crusts.

Miss Cathy Wagler

Bread Sticks

1 c. warm water
1 Tbsp. yeast
2 Tbsp. sugar

1 tsp. salt
2 Tbsp. vegetable oil
2½ c. flour

Mix first five ingredients and let stand for a few minutes. Add flour, then let dough rise for 25 minutes. Roll out on a large cookie sheet. Use pizza cutter and cut into strips. Let rise for a few more minutes. Bake at 350° for 15 minutes or until golden. Brush with butter and sprinkle with garlic powder, Parmesan cheese and parsley flakes. Soft and delicious. Yield: 18 sticks.

Miss Cathy Wagler

Bread Sticks

1½ c. warm water
1 Tbsp. yeast
1 Tbsp. sugar

1¼ tsp. salt
3 Tbsp. vegetable oil
4 c. flour

Butter Mixture:
¾ c. butter, melted
3 Tbsp. Parmesan cheese
1 Tbsp. garlic powder

1 Tbsp. parsley flakes
1 Tbsp. Italian seasoning

Mix dough. Let rise until double in size. Roll out in large squares and cut in strips. Dip in butter mixture, twist, and place on cookie sheets. Let rise a little, then bake at 350° until golden brown. Eat with cheese dip. Delicious! Serves 10 people.

Mrs. LaVern Linda Miller

Breads, Rolls

Bread Sticks

2½ c. flour
2 Tbsp. sugar
1 tsp. salt
1 c. warm water

1 Tbsp. vegetable oil
1½ tsp. garlic powder
1½ tsp. oregano
1 Tbsp. yeast

Topping:
¾ c. Parmesan cheese
1½ tsp. garlic powder
1½ tsp. Ranch seasoning
2 Tbsp. chives

1 Tbsp. Italian seasoning
1 Tbsp. oregano
1½ tsp. minced onion

Mix and press dough into cookie sheet and let rise 30 minutes. Add toppings and cut into 1" strips. Bake at 375° until golden. Dip into pizza sauce, cheese sauce or Ranch dressing. Serves 10 people.

Miss Deborah Ann Miller

Soft Pretzels

1½ Tbsp. yeast
1¾ c. warm water
¼ tsp. salt
½ c. brown sugar

4-5 c. flour
1 c. hot water
4 tsp. soda
pretzel salt

Mix first 5 ingredients together. Let rise ½-1 hour. Mix and knead. Do not punch down. Cut into strips and roll or twist them. Mix the hot water and soda. Dip pretzels in soda mixture. Sprinkle with pretzel salt. Bake at 500° till brown, about 10-15 minutes. Spread butter on top. Yield: approximately 15 pretzels.

Mrs. Joseph Lucinda Miller

Angel Biscuits

5 c. flour
1 Tbsp. baking powder
1 tsp. soda
1 tsp. salt
3 Tbsp. sugar
1 Tbsp. instant yeast
¾ c. shortening
2½ c. buttermilk

Sift first 5 ingredients together. Cut in shortening thoroughly. Add buttermilk and yeast. Mix with spoon until flour is moistened. Cover bowl and put into refrigerator until ready to use. When ready to use, take out as much as needed, roll out on floured board to ½-¾" thickness and cut. Put on a cookie sheet. Bake at 400° for about 12 minutes. The dough will keep for several weeks in the refrigerator. Yield: approximately 24 biscuits.

Mrs. Kenneth Leanna Kauffman

Cloud Biscuits

1 egg
⅔ c. milk
½ c. shortening or butter
1 Tbsp. sugar
4 tsp. baking powder
½ tsp. salt
2 c. flour

Mix egg and milk, add the rest of the ingredients and beat as little as possible. Bake at 450° for 10-15 minutes. Yield: 12 biscuits.
Note: You can use 1 cup applesauce instead of shortening, egg, and milk.

Miss Lovina Eicher

Biscuit Mix

8 c. flour
3 Tbsp. sugar
⅓ c. baking powder
2 tsp. cream of tartar
2 tsp. salt
1¾ c. shortening

Sift together dry ingredients and cut in shortening. Pack loosely in airtight container. When ready to use: Mix 1 cup mix to ⅓ cup milk, blend lightly with fork only until flour is moistened and dough pulls away from sides of bowl. Place on lightly greased pan. Bake at 450° for 10-12 minutes.

Miss Cheryl DeAnn Otto

Breads, Rolls

Melt in your Mouth Biscuits

3 c. flour
1 Tbsp. baking powder
¾ tsp. cream of tartar
¾ tsp. salt
3 Tbsp. sugar
¾ c. butter
2 eggs
1 c. milk

In a large bowl add ingredients in order given. Yield: 15 biscuits.

Mrs. Isaac Daisy Troyer

Cornbread

2 c. cornmeal
2 c. whole wheat flour
½ c. sugar
8 tsp. baking powder
1 tsp. salt
3 eggs
2 c. milk
½ c. lard

Mix together dry ingredients, add milk, eggs and lard. Bake in greased pans for 30 minutes or till done. Enough for 2 pans. Cornbread and chili is a family favorite.

Mrs. Leroy Barbara Weaver

Golden Cornbread

1 c. cornmeal
1 c. flour
3 Tbsp. sugar
4 tsp. baking powder
½ tsp. salt
1 c. milk
1 egg
¼ c. vegetable oil

Preheat oven to 450°. In large bowl, combine cornmeal, flour, sugar, baking powder and salt. Add milk, egg, and oil. Beat until fairly smooth. Bake in a greased 8" square pan 20-30 minutes, or until toothpick comes out clean. This is very good with chicken gravy.

Mrs. Jerry Esther Schrock

Corn Pone

½ c. sugar
½ c. cornmeal
1 c. flour
pinch of salt

2 tsp. baking powder
1 egg
½ c. milk
½ c. butter, melted

Mix dry ingredients together then add egg and milk, last add melted butter. Put in 9" pan. Bake at 350° for 30 minutes.

Note: We like to eat corn pone with hamburger gravy or chicken broth gravy.

Mrs. Ervin Ella Miller

Melt in your Mouth Dinner Rolls

1 Tbsp. yeast
½ c. warm water
1 Tbsp. sugar
1 tsp. baking powder
⅓ c. butter, melted

1 c. milk, scalded
⅓ c. sugar
⅛ tsp. salt
2 eggs, beaten
4½ c. flour

Dissolve yeast in warm water. Add sugar and baking powder. Let stand for 20 minutes. Meanwhile, mix butter, milk, sugar and salt; cool. Add eggs. Mix all ingredients together, adding flour last. Stir with a spoon, as it is very sticky. Cover and refrigerate overnight. Shape into balls and place in greased muffin pans or a 9"x13" pan. Let rise for 2 hours. Bake at 425° until golden.

Mrs. LaVern Linda Miller

Rich Dinner Rolls

1½ c. milk
⅓ c. butter
¾ c. sugar
1½ tsp. salt
3 Tbsp. yeast

¾ c. warm water
¾ tsp. sugar
3 eggs
7¼ c. flour

Scald milk with butter. Add sugar and salt cool to lukewarm. Stir yeast, sugar, and warm water together. Add beaten eggs to milk mixture along with yeast. Add some flour and mix well. Add rest of flour and mix by hand. Dough will be soft. Let rise till double. Shape in small balls or buns and place on two greased cookie sheets. Bake at 350° for 15 minutes.

Mrs. Kenneth Marilyn Otto

Donuts

3 c. milk
4½ c. water
¾ c. sugar
6 Tbsp. butter

¼ tsp. salt
½ c. yeast
9 c. donut mix
9 c. bread flour

Heat milk and butter until melted. Add water, sugar and salt. Add donut mix and blend very well. Add yeast and 1 cup flour. Mix thoroughly. Add rest of flour. Let rise until double in bulk. Roll out and cut with donut cutter. Let rise to right size and fry in oil at 367°. Dip in glaze. Yield: approximately 80 donuts.

Mrs. Joe Laura Hershberger

Breads, Rolls

Donuts

5 c. warm water
⅓ c. brown sugar
⅓ c. vegetable oil
2 eggs

11 c. donut mix, divided
4 Tbsp. yeast
6 c. flour

Glaze:
1-2 lb powdered sugar
1 c. water

vanilla

Mix first 4 ingredients till egg yolks are broken, then add 6 cups donut mix with yeast on top of donut mix. Mix. Add 5 more cups donut mix and the flour. Mix well then let rise in bowl until double. Roll out ½" thick on a greased surface. Cut donuts and place on a greased cookie sheet. Let rise again until double. Then fry in 350°-375° oil. Frost with glaze. Yield: approximately 5 dozen donuts.

Miss Verna Kay Miller

Blueberry Sour Cream Streusel Muffins

1 c. flour
1 tsp. baking powder
¼ tsp. soda
¼ tsp. salt
1½ tsp. sugar

1 egg, beaten
½ c. sour cream
2 Tbsp. milk
2 Tbsp. vegetable oil
¾ c. blueberries

Streusel Topping:
¼ c. brown sugar
2 Tbsp. flour

½ tsp. cinnamon
1½ Tbsp. butter, softened

Sift flour with baking powder, soda, salt and sugar. Beat egg with sour cream, milk and oil. Stir only until blended. Carefully fold in blueberries. Spoon into greased muffin tins. Mix brown sugar with flour and cinnamon. Cut in butter until crumbly. Sprinkle over muffins. Bake at 425° for 15-20 minutes or until topping is golden brown and toothpick comes out clean. Yield: 6 muffins.

Miss Melissa Joy Otto

Breads, Rolls

Cinnamuffins

¼ c. vegetable oil
¼ c. honey
¼ c. molasses or sorghum
1 c. applesauce
½ c. raisins

1½ tsp. baking powder
1½ tsp. cinnamon
½ tsp. soda
dash of salt
1½ c. wheat flour

Mix all ingredients well. Bake in muffin tins at 400° for 20 minutes. Very simple, healthy and delicious! We like to eat these with butter and honey, or fruit and milk. Yield: approximately 10 muffins.

Mrs. Leroy Barbara Weaver

Danish Braids

1 c. water
2 Tbsp. yeast
5 c. flour
1 c. butter

½ tsp. salt
3 eggs, beaten
½ c. sugar

Filling:
8 oz. cream cheese, softened
½ c. sugar

4½ Tbsp. flour
3 Tbsp. lemon juice

Glaze:
2 Tbsp. hot milk
6 Tbsp. butter, melted

1 tsp. vanilla
3 c. powdered sugar

Dissolve yeast in warm water. Cut butter into flour and salt. Add yeast mixture, eggs and sugar. Mix all together. Let stand in cool place for several hours or overnight. Divide dough into 3 parts. Roll out and put on greased 10"x15" pans. Divide and put the filling down the center third of the dough. Top with fruit pie filling of your choice. Cut the sections of dough on either side of filling in to strips 1" wide by 3" long from the edge in to where the filling is. Crisscross strips over fruit filling. Let rise 20-30 minutes and bake at 350° for 20-25 minutes. Glaze when cooled.

Mrs. Joe Lorene Miller

Maple Twists

1 c. warm water
1⅓ Tbsp. yeast
½ c. butter, softened
¼ c. brown sugar
¼ c. dry milk

1 tsp. salt
2 eggs, beaten
4 c. flour, approx.
a few drops maple flavoring

Maple Nut Filling:
6 oz. cream cheese
¼ c. butter, melted
½ c. sugar
½ c. brown sugar

2 tsp. cinnamon
½ tsp. maple flavoring
1 c. chopped nuts, opt.

Dissolve yeast in warm water. Add the rest of the ingredients except for the flour; add flour gradually and knead till smooth. Put in a large bowl and let rise till double in size. Next divide into 3 pieces. Roll one piece in to a 14" circle and put on a large greased pizza pan. Mix filling ingredients except nuts and spread half of it on the circle and sprinkle with ½ cup nuts. Repeat with second circle, putting the second circle on top of the first one. Put rest of filling on top, then roll out the third one and place on top. Beginning at edge of pan, cut dough into wedges like a pie but leaving a circle in the middle uncut. Twist each wedge 3 times and then let rise again. Bake at 325° for 20-23 minutes. Ice with your favorite maple or brown sugar icing while still warm.

Mrs. Leon Christina Wagler

Breads, Rolls

Cinnamon Rolls

2 eggs
2 c. warm water
¼ c. brown sugar
2 Tbsp. vegetable oil

2 tsp. yeast
½ tsp. salt
6 c. flour

Frosting:
½ c. water
½ c. brown sugar

½ c. butter

Beat eggs; until fluffy, then add warm water, sugar, oil yeast, salt and half of flour; mix well. Add rest of flour a little at a time mixing well. Let rise till double then roll out on a greased counter. Sprinkle with a little brown sugar and cinnamon, then roll up and cut in 1" slices. Let rise 10 minutes. Bake at 350° till light brown. Yield: 1 large cookie sheet.

Mrs. Samuel Dorothy Miller

Cinnamon Rolls

2 Tbsp. yeast, rounded
1 c. warm water
2 c. milk
1 c. butter
2 c. sugar
2 tsp. salt

2 c. mashed potatoes
1½ tsp. vanilla
1½ tsp. lemon juice
4 eggs
10 c. flour

Dissolve yeast in warm water. Heat milk to scalding. Add butter, sugar, salt, potatoes and flavorings. Beat eggs and add to mixture. Cool to lukewarm then add yeast and part of flour. Beat well. Add remaining flour while mixing. Let rise 1 hour. Roll out and spread with melted butter and cinnamon mixed with sugar. Roll up and cut pieces 1" thick and put in buttered pans. Let rise again, then bake at 350° for 20 minutes or until lightly browned. Frost and serve. Yield: 2 cookie sheets.

Mrs. Ernest Sara Schrock

Breads, Rolls

Cinnamon Rolls

8 eggs
1 c. water
2 c. brown sugar
2½ Tbsp. salt

2 c. butter, melted
1 qt. milk, scalded
½ c. yeast
15 c. flour

Beat water and eggs in a large bowl. Add brown sugar, salt, melted butter and scalded milk. Mix in yeast with the flour. Let rise 1 hour. Roll out; spread with melted butter, brown sugar and cinnamon. Roll up and cut; let rise again. Bake at 350° for 20 minutes. Rotate after 10 minutes. Yield: 3 cookie sheets plus a cake pan. Serves 85 people.

Mrs. Ernest Mary Ellen Miller

Pumpkin Cinnamon Rolls

1½ c. milk, scalded
1 c. cooked and mashed pumpkin
½ c. white sugar
2 tsp. salt

½ c. shortening
2 eggs, beaten
2 Tbsp. yeast
½ c. warm water
7 c. flour

Pour scalded milk over pumpkin, sugar, salt, and shortening. Cool to lukewarm. Add eggs, yeast, water and half of flour. Beat well, add rest of flour. Let rise once, then roll out. Spread with butter and sprinkle with brown sugar and cinnamon. Roll up and cut like cinnamon rolls. Place in pans and let rise again. Bake at 350° for 20 minutes. When cool; frost with your favorite frosting.

Mrs. Eldon Ray Denise Miller

Breads, Rolls

Pecan Roll Syrup

1 c. butter
4 c. brown sugar
1 c. water
¾ c. corn syrup

Heat mixture to melt sugar. Pour a thin layer in pie pan and sprinkle with nuts. Put your favorite cinnamon rolls on top and bake like usual. When cooled slightly put them upside down on a plate and remove pan. No frosting needed. Yield: approximately 6 pans.

Miss Susanna Schrock

Flour Tortillas

2 c. flour
1 tsp. baking powder
1 tsp. salt
¼ c. vegetable oil
¾ c. hot water

Mix and roll out into 10" rounds (or size you prefer). Fry on dry griddle until a light golden brown on each side.

Miss Esther Miller

Homemade Tortillas

1 c. whole wheat flour
1 c. flour
½ tsp. salt
¼ c. lard
⅔ c. warm water

Mix salt, flour and lard together with your fingers until fine crumbs form. Pour water into dry ingredients and mix with a fork. Sprinkle with flour and knead for two minutes. Cover dough and let set for 20-30 minutes. Pinch off walnut-sized balls of dough. Roll out really thin. Bake each tortilla 45-60 seconds on each side on a hot ungreased skillet until lightly browned. Stack tortillas in a tightly covered container to keep them soft. Yield: 12-14 tortillas.

Mrs. Dennis Marilyn Hershberger

Salads Salad Dressings

Salads, Salad Dressings

Applesauce Jell-O and Cottage Cheese 71
Bacon/Chicken Salad. 61
BLT Chicken Salad 61
Broccoli and Cauliflower Salad 62
Cabbage Salad 63
Cherry Salad 72
Coleslaw 63
Cornbread Salad 64
Corn Chip Salad 65
Cottage Cheese Salad. 72
Cranberry Salad. 72
Deluxe Cheeseburger Salad 62
French Dressing. 74
French Dressing. 74
French Dressing. 74
Hot Taco Salad 69
Pasta Salad. 65
Pineapple Cheese Salad 73
Potato Salad. 66
Potato Salad. 66
Ribbon Salad 73
Springtime Potato Salad 67
Sweet and Sour Dressing 75
Taco Salad 67
Taco Salad 68
Taco Salad Dressing. 75
Tomato/Cucumber Salad. 69
Vegetable Pizza 70
Vegetable Pizza 71
Western Dressing. 75

BLT Chicken Salad

1 head lettuce, chopped
2 lg. tomatoes, diced
3 hard-boiled eggs, sliced
1 lb. bacon, fried and crumbled

3 c. cooked and sliced
　chicken breast
shredded cheese

Dressing:
1 c. Miracle Whip
½ c. barbecue sauce
2 Tbsp. chopped onions, opt.

2 Tbsp. lemon juice
¼ tsp. salt
¼ tsp. pepper

Put lettuce on a large serving plate. Sprinkle with tomatoes, eggs, chicken and cheese. Garnish with bacon. Drizzle with dressing just before serving. For dressing: Mix all together in a bowl and refrigerate until ready to pour over salad.

Miss Wilma Fern Schrock

Bacon/Chicken Salad

½ c. mayonnaise
5 Tbsp. barbecue sauce
3 Tbsp. chopped onions
½ tsp. salt
1 Tbsp. lemon juice
3 Tbsp. sugar
¼ tsp. pepper
¼ tsp. liquid smoke, opt.
4 c. torn lettuce

4 c. torn spinach
2 lg. tomatoes, cut up
1½ lb. boneless, skinless, cubed
　and cooked chicken breasts
10 bacon strips, cooked
　and cubed
2 hard-boiled eggs, sliced
shredded cheese, opt.

Combine the first 8 ingredients; mix well, then chill until ready to serve. Place greens on a large platter; spread tomatoes, chicken, bacon and eggs over greens. Drizzle dressing over all.

Mrs. Kenneth Marilyn Otto

Salads, Salad Dressings

Broccoli and Cauliflower Salad

1 head broccoli
1 head cauliflower

Dressing:
1 c. Miracle Whip
1 c. sour cream
¼ c. sugar

1 c. shredded cheese
1 lb. bacon, fried and crumbled

1 tsp. salt
1 Tbsp. Hidden Valley Ranch powder

Serves 20 people.

Miss Rosanna Jantzi

Deluxe Cheeseburger Salad

1 lb. ground beef
½ c. finely chopped dill pickles
⅔ c. ketchup

2 tsp. mustard
⅓ c. onion powder
⅔ c. cheese

Salad Layers:
6 c. chopped lettuce
warm meat mixture
3 c. shredded cheese

1 c. diced tomatoes
½ c. bacon

Fry hamburger and add rest of ingredients. Serve warm on top of lettuce. Layer in order given in a 9"x13" pan. Serve while meat mixture is still warm.

Mrs. LaVern Linda Miller

Cabbage Salad

4 c. shredded cabbage
1 c. chopped broccoli
1 c. chopped cauliflower
½ lb. bacon
1 c. Miracle Whip

½ c. sour cream
1 tsp. salt
2 Tbsp. sugar
1 red pepper, opt.
1 c. shredded cheese

Mix the shredded cabbage, broccoli and cauliflower. Fry the bacon and crumble, set aside. Mix Miracle Whip, sour cream, salt and sugar with the cabbage mixture. Add chopped peppers if desired. Top with crumbled bacon and shredded cheese. A favorite! Serves 12 people.

Mrs. Monroe Elsie Miller

Coleslaw

6 med. head cabbage

2 c. carrots

Dressing:
3 c. sour cream
3 c. mayonnaise or salad dressing
2 c. sugar

½ c. vinegar
1 Tbsp. celery seed
2 Tbsp. salt

Shred cabbage and carrots into a 13-quart bowl. Mix together the dressing ingredients in a smaller bowl, then pour on top of cabbage and mix thoroughly. Yield: 2½ gallons. Serves 70-75 people.

Mrs. Ernie Freeda Yoder

Salads, Salad Dressings

Cornbread Salad

1 (8 oz.) Jiffy cornbread mix
1 (4 oz.) can green chilies
⅛ tsp. cumin
⅛ tsp. oregano
⅛ tsp. sage
3 med. tomatoes, chunked
2 c. shredded cheese
1 (15 oz.) can whole kernel corn
1 c. green peppers
1 (15 oz.) can kidney beans
1 c. green onions
10 slices bacon, fried and crumbled
1 c. mayonnaise
1 c. sour cream
1 env. Ranch dressing mix

Mix cornbread according to directions on package, adding green chilies, cumin, oregano, and sage yet before baking. Bake at 400° for 20-25 minutes. Cool. In a small pan mix mayonnaise, sour cream and Ranch dressing mix. Set aside. Crumble ½ of cornbread in a 9"x13" pan. Layer with half of rest of ingredients in this order: beans, dressing mix, corn, tomatoes, peppers, onion, cheese, bacon. Then repeat for second layer. Refrigerate at least 2 hours. Serves 15 people.

Note: SueEllen uses ½ cup corn and 1 cup kidney beans.

Miss SueEllen Miller,
Miss Sarah Mae Jantzi

Always remember you are absolutely unique. Just like everyone else.

Salads, Salad Dressings

Corn Chip Salad

1 head lettuce, chopped
1 lb. bacon, fried and crumbled
6 hard-boiled eggs
2 c. shredded cheese
4 c. crushed corn chips

Dressing:
1 c. mayonnaise
¼ c. brown sugar
¼ c. sugar
¼ c. milk
2 Tbsp. vinegar

In a bowl mix lettuce, bacon, eggs, cheese and chips. Mix dressing ingredients. Just before serving, mix all together. Mix only enough for one meal. It's not good leftover as the chips will get soggy. Serves: 12-14 people.
Note: Lyndora adds onions and tomatoes to taste; also one more cup chips.

Miss Edna Mae Schrock
Miss Lyndora Kay Miller

Pasta Salad

1½ lb. spiral macaroni
8 oz. cubed ham
½ c. celery
2 med. tomatoes
1 med. onion
1 green pepper
2 c. shredded cheddar cheese

Dressing:
3 c. Miracle Whip
¼ c. brown and spicy mustard
¾ c. vegetable oil
½ tsp. salt
¼ c. vinegar
1½ c. sugar
1 Tbsp. salt
½ Tbsp. celery salt

Mix and pour over pasta. Refrigerate and serve.

Mrs. Eldon Ray Denise Miller

Salads, Salad Dressings

Potato Salad

12 c. cooked potatoes
12 hard-boiled eggs

1½ c. celery, chopped
1 c. cooked macaroni

Dressing:
3 c. salad dressing
2 Tbsp. mustard
¼ c. vinegar

2½ c. sugar
4 tsp. salt
½ c. milk

Cook potatoes till soft. Put through salad master. Add other ingredients. Mix dressing ingredients and combine with cooled potato mixture.

Mrs. Joseph Lucinda Miller

Potato Salad

12 c. shredded potatoes
12 hard-boiled eggs

1½ c. chopped onions
1½ c. chopped celery

Dressing:
3 c. mayonnaise
3 Tbsp. vinegar
3 Tbsp. mustard

4 tsp. salt
2 c. sugar
½ c. milk

Cook and shred potatoes. Cool and mix with the other ingredients. Add dressing and mix well. Let sit in refrigerator overnight for best results. Fills an ice cream pail. Serves approximately 20 people.

Mrs. Leon Christine Wagler

Springtime Potato Salad

6 c. cooked and diced potatoes
4 hard-boiled eggs, chopped
½ c. chopped celery
½ c. chopped sweet pickles
⅓ c. chopped onions
⅓ c. chopped radishes
½ c. mayonnaise

3 Tbsp. sugar
1 Tbsp. vinegar
1 Tbsp. milk
1½ tsp. mustard
½ tsp. salt
paprika, opt.

Combine potatoes, eggs, celery, pickles, onions and radishes. In another bowl, combine mayonnaise, sugar, vinegar, milk, mustard and salt. Mix well. Pour over potato mixture, stirring to coat. Chill. Sprinkle with paprika if desired.

Mrs. Delbert Martha Schrock

Taco Salad

2 lb. hamburger
2 med. onions
1 Tbsp. taco seasoning
2 lg. head lettuce
1 lb. shredded cheese

4 med. tomatoes, chunked
1 (15 oz.) can kidney or chili
   beans, drained
1 bag taco chips, crushed

Dressing:
16 oz. Thousand Island dressing
¼ c. sugar

½ Tbsp. taco seasoning

Brown hamburger with chopped onions and taco seasoning. Cool. Chop lettuce in a large bowl. Add cheese, beans, tomatoes and hamburger. Mix well. Just before serving add dressing and taco chips. Fills a fix and mix bowl. For dressing: Mix all ingredients well. Pour desired amount of dressing over lettuce mixture. Serve immediately.

Mrs. Monroe Elsie Miller

Salads, Salad Dressings

Taco Salad

2 lb. hamburger
2 med. onions
1 Tbsp. taco seasoning
2-3 head lettuce
4 med. tomatoes, chunked

1 (15 oz.) can kidney or chili beans, drained
1 lb. shredded cheese
1 bag taco chips, crushed

Dressing:
2 c. salad dressing
1 c. sugar
¼ c. vinegar
½ c. ketchup
1 Tbsp. vegetable oil

¾ tsp. salt
½ tsp. paprika
½ tsp. pepper
½ tsp. garlic powder
2 Tbsp. taco seasoning

Brown hamburger with chopped onions and taco seasoning. Cool. Chop lettuce in large bowl; add beans, shredded cheese, tomatoes, hamburger. Mix well. Just before serving add dressing and taco chips. For dressing: Mix all ingredients well. Toss desired amount of dressing with lettuce and chip mixture. Serve immediately.

Mrs. Perry Delores Herschberger

Happiness is like potato salad when you share it with others, it's a picnic.

Salads, Salad Dressings

Hot Taco Salad

2 lb. hamburger
1 onion, chopped
¼ tsp. salt
4 c. cheddar cheese
1 c. Thousand Island dressing
2 Tbsp. hot sauce

1 can kidney beans or pork
   and beans
1 head lettuce, chopped
4 tomatoes, diced
1 pkg. nacho chips
sour cream

Thousand Island Dressing:
2 c. salad dressing
¼ c. relish

2 Tbsp. ketchup
onion, chopped

Cook hamburger, onion and salt; then drain. Add cheese, dressing, hot sauce and kidney beans. Simmer a little, Serve with the lettuce, tomatoes, chips and sour cream like a haystack.

Note: Thousand Island dressing can also be used for dressing in taco salad.

Miss Ruth Miller

Tomato/Cucumber Salad

cucumber
tomato
green or red onion
cheese, cubed

Italian dressing
salad supreme seasoning
pepper
onion powder

Use whatever amounts you like. Drain cucumber and tomato after you cut them up and before mixing with other ingredients. Pepper and onion powder are opt. Leftovers are as good as fresh.

Note: Salad supreme seasoning can be found in Pineviews salvage section.

Mrs. Ernest Ray Inez Miller

Salads, Salad Dressings

Vegetable Pizza

Crust:
¼ c. margarine
2 Tbsp. sugar
¼ c. boiling water
1 Tbsp. active dry yeast
¼ c. warm water
1 egg, beaten
1½ c. all-purpose flour
1 tsp. salt

Dressing:
8 oz cream cheese
1 c. sour cream
1 env. Hidden Valley Ranch
1 Tbsp. sugar

Toppings:
chopped broccoli
chopped cauliflower
chopped lettuce
chopped peppers
chopped tomatoes
shredded cheese

For Crust: Combine margarine, sugar and boiling water in a mixing bowl. Stir until the margarine is melted. Dissolve yeast in warm water, then add yeast and egg to butter mixture. Add flour and salt, mix well. Spread on greased 10"x15" pan. Bake at 325° just until golden brown. Combine dressing ingredients. Spread on cooled crust. Put on toppings.

Mrs. Eldon Ray Denise Miller

Love Faith Hope

Love, makes our friends a little dearer.
Joy, makes our hearts a little lighter.
Faith, makes our path a little clearer.
Hope, makes our lives a little brighter.
Peace, brings us a little nearer.

Vegetable Pizza

Crust:
3 c. whole wheat flour
1½ Tbsp. sugar
1½ Tbsp. baking powder
1½ tsp. salt
¾ c. butter
1 c. water

Dressing:
8 oz. cream cheese
2¼ c. sour cream
1 Tbsp. Ranch dressing powder

Toppings:
½ head broccoli
½ head cauliflower
3 lg. tomatoes
3 c. grated cheese
¾ lb. bacon, fried and crumbled

For Crust: Combine dry ingredients. Cut in butter. Add water and mix. Roll out dough on cookie sheet and bake at 350° for 10-15 minutes. For Dressing: Combine cream cheese, sour cream and Ranch dressing powder. Spread on cooled crust. Top with chopped vegetables, cheese and bacon. Serves 15 people.

Miss Rosanna Jantzi

Applesauce Jell-O and Cottage Cheese

3 (3 oz.) boxes strawberry Jell-O
3 (3 oz.) boxes cherry Jell-O
1 Tbsp. cinnamon hearts
2 c. boiling water
1 c. cold water
4 c. applesauce

Melt cinnamon hearts in 2 cups boiling water. Pour over Jell-O. Let set till it starts to thicken, then add applesauce. Pour into Jell-O mold. When hard, place upside down on flat plate and fill center with cottage cheese. Serves 12 people.

Miss Julia Jantzi

Salads, Salad Dressings

Cottage Cheese Salad

24 oz. cottage cheese
6 oz. dry Jell-O (no water)
20 oz. crushed pineapple, drained
12-16 oz. Cool Whip

Mix cottage cheese and Jell-O, then add pineapple. Fold in Cool Whip.
Note: This recipe times 3 fills a fix and mix bowl.

Mrs. Jerry Esther Schrock
Miss SueEllen Miller

Cherry Salad

5 c. milk
½ c. sugar
½ c. Perma Flo, scant
¼ tsp. almond flavoring
1 qt. cherries, drained
5 sliced bananas
1 c. pecans
¾ c. coconut

Cook together milk, sugar and Perma Flo until thickened. Add flavoring. When cold, add to fruit and nuts. Serves 10 people.

Mrs. Kenneth Leanna Kauffman

Cranberry Salad

3 oranges
4 apples
1 pkg. cranberries
3 c. sugar
1 c. cherry Jell-O
1 c. orange Jell-O
4 c. boiling water
2 c. cold water

Grind together oranges, apples and cranberries. Leave peelings on 1 orange. Add sugar. Combine Jell-O with sugars. Chill Jell-O until partially set, add fruit mixture and put into bowls you wish to serve it in. Sprinkle with nut meats. A Thanksgiving special served with pumpkin pie. Serves 20 people.
Note: May add Cool Whip before serving.

Miss Susanna Schrock

Salads, Salad Dressings

Pineapple Cheese Salad

1 (46 oz.) can pineapple juice
1¼ c. sugar
1 c. water
½ c. Perma Flo, rounded
1 lb. Velveeta cheese, cubed
3 c. marshmallows
1½ c. nuts, chopped
1 (20 oz.) can crushed pineapple

Mix sugar and pineapple juice in a 6-quart saucepan and bring to a boil. Mix the water and Perma Flo and slowly pour into pineapple juice and heat till it boils. Cool, then add crushed pineapple, cheese, marshmallows and nuts. Serves 15 people.

Mrs. Ernest Sara Schrock

Ribbon Salad

Layer 1:
6 oz. lime Jell-O
2 c. boiling water
2 c. cold water

Layer 2:
1 (20 oz.) can crushed pineapple
3 oz. lemon Jell-O
1 c. boiling water
½ c. miniature marshmallows
8 oz. cream cheese
1 c. Rich's topping, whipped
1 c. salad dressing

Layer 3:
6 oz. cherry Jell-O
2 c. boiling water
2 c. cold water

Layer One: Dissolve lime Jell-O in boiling water. Stir in the cold water. Pour into a 9"x13" pan. Chill until partially set. Layer Two: Drain pineapple, reserving 1 cup juice. Set aside. Dissolve lemon Jell-O in boiling water in a double boiler. Add marshmallows and stir until melted. Remove from heat. Add 1 cup reserved juice and cream cheese. Beat with egg beater until well blended. Stir in pineapple. Cool. Fold in whipped Rich's topping and salad dressing. Chill until thickened. Pour over first layer. Chill until almost set. Layer Three: Stir in cold water. Chill until thick and syrupy. Pour over pineapple layer. Chill completely before serving.

Miss Margaret Jantzi

French Dressing

1 c. sugar
2 Tbsp. vinegar
1 Tbsp. Worcestershire sauce
1 c. vegetable oil
¾ c. ketchup
pinch of salt

Combine all ingredients in a mixing bowl and beat with egg beater for several minutes. Delicious on any salad.

Mrs. Samuel Rachel Chupp

French Dressing

2 c. salad dressing
2 c. sugar
¼ c. vinegar
½ c. ketchup
2 tsp. mustard
1 tsp. paprika
½ c. vegetable oil
½ tsp. salt
4 tsp. water

Mix all ingredients together and serve with tossed salad.

Mrs. Perry Delores Herschberger

French Dressing

2 c. sugar
2 c. Wesson oil
¾ c. ketchup
⅓ c. vinegar
2 Tbsp. Worcestershire sauce
1 c. salad dressing
pinch of salt
½ c. chopped onions, opt.

Mix together and refrigerate. Use for tossed salads.

Mrs. William Miriam Yoder

Sweet and Sour Dressing

1 c. sugar
¼ tsp. pepper
1 tsp. celery seed
1 Tbsp. mustard

1 med. onion, chopped
3 Tbsp. Miracle Whip
1 c. vegetable oil
⅓ c. vinegar

Mix all together and store in refrigerator. Use on tossed salads. This is also good on haystacks.

Mrs. Joe Laura Hershberger

Taco Salad Dressing

2 c. mayonnaise
1 c. sugar
¼ c. vegetable oil
½ c. ketchup
dash of vinegar

1 tsp. salt
½ tsp. onion salt
dash of paprika
dash of garlic powder

Beat all together with a wire whip and store in refrigerator till ready to use. Double this recipe for a fix and mix bowl.

Mrs. Leon Christine Wagler

Western Dressing

2 c. Miracle Whip
1 c. sugar
¼ c. vinegar
½ c. ketchup
2 tsp. mustard

1 tsp. paprika
4 tsp. water
½ c. vegetable oil
½ tsp. salt

Blend all together. Awesome! Yield: 1 quart.
Note: Marietta uses mayonnaise and ½ cup more sugar. She says it's good on lettuce salad or taco salad.

Mrs. Ray Marjorie Wagler
Miss Marietta W. Miller

A Talk With God

Sometimes we talk with God in tears—
We do not say a word;
We only kneel and softly weep
And believe our prayer is heard.

Sometimes we talk with God in song
Throughout the busy day.
How it refreshes mind and soul,
To talk with Him that way!

Sometimes we talk with God in church
While his servant leads in prayer
And deepest longings fill the soul—
We feel His presence there.

And in devotion's quiet time,
To talk with Him is sweet.
Christ comforts, warns, forgives and guides
While we sit at His feet.

Soups Vegetables

Soups, Vegetables

Asparagus Delight 79
Baked Beans 85
Cheddar Chowder 79
Cheeseburger Soup 80
Cheese Soup 81
Cheesy Ham Chowder. 80
Elephant Stew 81
Hamburger Stew 82
Pepper Poppers 85
Stuffed Green Pepper Soup 82
Taco Soup 83
Vegetable Soup 83
Venison Stew 84
Zippy Corn Chowder 84

Soups, Vegetables

Asparagus Delight

1 lb. asparagus
¾ c. butter
¾ c. flour
4 c. milk
1 qt. chicken broth
1 lb. cubed ham

1 c. shredded cheese
8 hard-boiled eggs, sliced
½ tsp. salt
⅛ tsp. pepper
10-12 biscuits

Dice asparagus, cook in small amount of water for nearly 5 minutes; drain. Melt butter in 6-quart kettle, then stir in flour until smooth. Add milk and broth. Bring to a boil. Cook and stir for 2 minutes. Add rest of ingredients. Heat. Serve over biscuits. Serves 12 people.

Miss Susanna Schrock

Cheddar Chowder

2 c. water
2 c. diced potatoes
½ c. diced carrots
½ c. chopped celery

White Sauce:
¼ c. butter
¼ c. flour
2 c. milk

¼ c. chopped onions
1 tsp. salt
¼ tsp. pepper

2 c. grated cheddar cheese
1 c. cubed ham

Combine water, potatoes, carrots, celery, onions, salt and pepper in a 3-quart kettle. Boil 10-12 minutes. Meanwhile in a smaller saucepan, make the white sauce. Melt butter and add flour. Stir until smooth (about 1 minute). Slowly add milk; cook until thickened. Add grated cheese to white sauce; stir until melted. Add white sauce and ham to vegetables that have not been drained. Heat through. Serves 6 people.

Mrs. Ernie Freeda Yoder

Soups, Vegetables

Cheesy Ham Chowder

1½ c. diced ham
3 c. potatoes
1½ c. carrots
2 Tbsp. chopped onions
2 qt. milk

1⅝ c. flour
¼ c. chicken soup base
6 Tbsp. butter
8 oz. Velveeta

Cook potatoes, carrots and onions in a kettle. Whip together cold milk and flour, then cook till it thickens. Add ham, vegetables, chicken base, butter, and cheese. Simmer till cheese is melted. Serves 8 people.
Note: You can substitute cheddar cheese powder for some of the Velveeta.

Mrs. Vernon Rachel Herschberger

Cheeseburger Soup

½ lb. ground beef
½ c. chopped onions
¾ c. carrots
¾ c. celery
2 Tbsp. parsley
6 Tbsp. butter, divided
3 c. chicken broth

4 c. diced potatoes
¼ c. flour
1 tsp. salt
½ tsp. pepper
milk
Velveeta cheese

Brown beef. Sauté onions, carrots, celery and parsley with 3 tablespoons butter for 10 minutes. Add broth, potatoes and beef. Simmer for 10 minutes. Melt the rest of the butter and add flour, salt and pepper. Add this to the other mixture. When ready to serve add milk and cheese to your liking. Heat but do not boil, especially when reheating leftovers as the milk and cheese will separate and become curdly. Serves 16-20 people.

Miss Cathy Wagler

Soups, Vegetables

Cheese Soup

3 c. diced potatoes
2 c. diced carrots
1 c. diced celery
¾ c. diced onions

3 c. broccoli and cauliflower
1 qt. chicken broth
1 c. flour
1 lb. Velveeta cheese

Put vegetables in kettle and add water till almost covered. In separate saucepan, heat chicken broth. Thicken with flour and water. When vegetables are soft, mix all together. Add salt and chicken seasoning to taste. Add cheese and stir well. Yield: approximately 1 gallon of soup.

Mrs. Wilbur Wilma Miller

Elephant Stew

1 med. elephant
1 ton peppers
2000 bushels carrots
2 small rabbits, opt.

1 ton salt
500 bushels potatoes
4000 sprigs parsley

Cut elephant into bite-size pieces. (This will take about 2 months.) Place meat in pan and cover with 1000 gallons of gravy. Simmer for 4 weeks. Shovel salt and pepper to taste. When meat is tender, add vegetables. (Steam shovel is useful here.) Simmer slowly for 4 weeks. Garnish with parsley. Serves 3800 people.

Note: If more are expected, add the 2 rabbits. (This is not recommended, as very few people like hare in their stew.)

Soups, Vegetables

Stuffed Green Pepper Soup

1 lb. ground beef
1 env. dry onion soup mix
1 (14.5 oz.) can diced tomatoes
1 (15 oz.) can tomato sauce
1 c. cooked white rice
1 beef bouillon cube

2 large green bell peppers, chopped
2 Tbsp. brown sugar, packed
2 Tbsp. apple cider vinegar
1¼ c. water
mozzarella cheese, opt.

In a large pot, brown beef thoroughly. Drain off grease and return to pot. Stir in dry soup mix and heat thoroughly. Add remaining ingredients (except rice) and bring to a boil. Reduce heat and simmer for 30-40 minutes or until peppers are soft. Add rice and heat through. Scoop into bowls and sprinkle with mozzarella cheese. Serves 5 people.

Mrs. Kenneth Marilyn Otto

Hamburger Stew

2 Tbsp. lard
1 lb. hamburger
½ c. chopped onions
2 c. canned tomatoes
½ c. diced celery
2 c. cubed, raw potatoes

2 med. diced carrots
2 tsp. salt
½ tsp. pepper
¼ c. rice
1½ qt. water

In a large kettle, brown meat and onions. Add other ingredients. Simmer slowly until vegetables are down. Serves 4-6 people.

Miss Lovina Eicher

Soups, Vegetables

Taco Soup

2 lb. hamburger
1 med. onion
1 med. pepper
salt and pepper to taste
1 pkg. taco seasoning
1 qt. water

1 qt. pizza sauce
1 can hot chili beans
chopped lettuce
sour cream
shredded cheddar cheese
taco chips

Brown hamburger with chopped onions and peppers, season with salt and pepper to taste. Add taco seasoning. Mix browned hamburger, water, pizza sauce and chili beans. Simmer. Serve with chopped lettuce, sour cream, grated cheddar cheese and crumbled taco chips.

Miss Ruth Miller

Vegetable Soup

1 qt. cooked and chopped roast beef
1 quart rich broth from roast
1 c. chopped celery
1 c. chopped onions
1 qt. cubed potatoes
1 qt. cubed carrots
1 qt. green beans

1-2 bags frozen mixed vegetables
1 qt. chopped cabbage
2 cloves garlic, chopped
1 Tbsp. Italian seasoning
2-3 bay leaves
2 anise stars
1-2 qt. tomato juice

Sauté onion, celery and garlic. Add all the raw vegetables and cover with water; cook until tender. Add the roast beef, broth, green beans and frozen vegetables. Add 1-2 quarts tomato juice and seasonings with salt and pepper. Simmer at least 30 minutes to mingle flavors.

Note: Sometimes I use leftover roast. Our family prefers it with no cabbage.

Mrs. Kenneth Marilyn Otto

Soups, Vegetables

Venison Stew

2 lb. stew meat
3 Tbsp. vegetable oil
½ c. chopped onions
2 tsp. Mrs. Dash
¼ tsp. pepper
1 Tbsp. salt
3 c. water
2 c. beef broth
3 c. sliced red potatoes
2 c. sliced carrots
2 c. diced celery
2 c. corn
2 c. tomatoes
1 c. ketchup
¼ c. barbecue sauce
½ tsp. dill weed, scant
2 c. chopped cabbage
½ c. flour

Brown meat with oil. Add onion and Mrs. Dash to the meat. Add liquids, vegetables and seasonings and cook until tender; then add cabbage last. The flour can be added to the browned meat or thicken with the flour after vegetables are tender. Serves 40-50 people.

Mrs. Ernest Mary Ellen Miller

Zippy Corn Chowder

1 med. onion, chopped
1 med. green pepper, chopped
2 Tbsp. butter
2 c. chicken broth
2 lg. potatoes, cubed
2 tsp. mustard
1 tsp. salt
½ tsp. paprika
3 c. corn
3 c. milk
¼ c. flour
Lawry's seasoning salt, opt.
chicken seasoning, opt.

Melt butter; add onion and pepper. Sauté till brown. Add chicken broth and potatoes, simmer 15-20 minutes. Add rest of ingredients except flour. When hot, add paste made of ½ cup milk and ¼ cup flour. Do not boil.
Note: Rachel serves with Cajun seasoning.

Miss Rachel Fern Kauffman
Mrs. Perry Delores Herschberger

Soups, Vegetables

Pepper Poppers

peppers
cream cheese
2 eggs, beaten
½ c. milk
1 c. flour

1 tsp. baking powder
1½ tsp. salt
1 tsp. vegetable oil
½ tsp. paprika
½ tsp. garlic powder

Take small peppers (Jalepenos or Yum-yums). Cut off the top and take out seeds. Fill with cream cheese. Cover with dough and deep fat fry at 350°-375°. Eat with dip. Yield: Approximately 12 peppers.

Note: This recipe can also be used for fish or chicken.

Miss Susanna Schrock

Baked Beans

1 lb. dry beans
½ c. mustard
2 tsp. salt
3 c. tomato juice

1½ c. brown sugar
½ lb. home-cured bacon
1 med. onion
½ c. ketchup

Soak and cook beans. Fry bacon. Add bacon and drippings to rest of ingredients. Simmer or bake 2 hours. Improves flavor to let stand overnight. Recipe can also be multiplied and canned.

Mrs. Isaac Daisy Troyer

Good character, like good soup, is usually homemade.

"Slow Me Down, Lord"

Ease the pounding of my heart
By the quieting of my mind!
Steady my hurried pace
With a vision of the eternal reach of time!
Give me, amidst the confusion of my day,
the calmness of the everlasting hills.
Break the tension of my nerves and muscles
With the soothing music of the singing stream.
Help me to know the magical,
Restorative power of Thy touch.
Teach me the art of taking minute vacations,
Slowing down to look at a flower,
To chat with a friend, to pet a dog.
Remind me each day of the hare
And the tortoise,
So that I may know
That the race is not always to the swift,
There is more in life than increasing its speed.
Let me look upward
into the branches of the towering oak,
And know that it grew great,
Because it grew slowly and well.
Slow me down, Lord! Inspire me to send,
My roots deep into the soil
of Life's enduring values. Amen."

—Selected

Meats Main Dishes

Meats, Main Dishes

Bacon Cheeseburger Casserole 106
Baked Beans 104
Baked Beans (large recipe) 103
Baked Chicken Breast 91
Baked Macaroni and Cheese 113
Baked Red Potatoes 109
Barbecue Chicken Pizza 124
Barbecued Hamburgers 99
Barbecued Meatballs 95
Barbecue Sauce for Chicken 93
BLT Pizza 124
Brine for Turkey 95
Brown Gravy 116
Cheesy Enchiladas 117
Chicken and Rice Bake 91
Chicken Breading 93
Chicken Breast Casserole 89
Chicken Dressing 89
Chicken Pot Pie 90
Chicken Stockpot Noodles 114
Corn Dogs 102
Deep Dish Taco Squares 123
Delicious Homemade Sub-Sandwiches . . 102
Enchiladas 117
Favorite Meatballs 96
Favorite Meat Loaf 98
Frankfurter Bake 112
Hamburger Casserole 104
Hamburger Rice Casserole 105
Hamburgers to Grill 100
Ham Loaf 97
Haystack Casserole 119
Homemade Tater Tots 112
Horseshoe Special 119
Hungarian Chicken Casserole 90
Hush Puppies 116
Lasagna 113
Long John Silver's Fish Batter 95
Marinade for Chicken 94
Marinade for Chicken 94
Marinade for Chicken, Turkey or Pork . . . 94
Meatballs 96
Meatballs 97
Meat Loaf 99
Mexican Casserole 120
Mexican Pizza 125
Mock Ham Loaf 98
Mock Turkey 106
Mom's Baked Chicken Breast 91
Mom's Fried Chicken 92
One Dish Meal 107
Oven Barbecue 100
Oven Fried Potatoes 109
Parmesan Potatoes 110
Pepperoni Rolls 127
Poppy Seed Chicken 92
Potato Haystack Casserole 108
Potato Ranch Casserole 108
Potluck Eggs Benedict 114
Quick and Easy Potatoes 110
Quick Potato and Bean Casserole 109
Rice Casserole 105
Skillet Casserole 107
Sloppy Joes 100
Sloppy Joes 101
Stromboli 121
Stuffed Pizza 125
Taco Casserole 121
Taco Pie 122
Taco Pie Casserole 122
Taco Pizza 126
Taco Shells and Dressing 128
Taco Squares 123
Tater Tot Casserole 111
Tater Tot Casserole 111
Tender Chicken Nuggets 92
Tostado (Mexican Haystack) 120
Tuna Patties 103
Upside Down Pizza 126
Wet Burrito Casserole 118
Wet Burrito Casserole 118
You Ain't Nothin' but a Hound Dog 101
Yummy Chicken Nuggets 93
Zucchini Casserole 115
Zucchini Casserole 115
Zucchini Patties 103
Zucchini Pizza 127

Chicken Breast Casserole

2½ lb. chicken breast, cooked and cut up
2 cans cream of chicken soup
2 c. chicken broth
2 boxes prepared Stove Top Dressing, or your own mix
4 qt. mashed potatoes
3 c. sour cream

Put chicken breast in bottom of large roaster. Mix cream of chicken soup and chicken broth and pour over chicken pieces. Put dressing on top. Mash potatoes and add sour cream and put on top. Put cheese on potatoes and bake at 350° till hot. Gravy will come to the top.

Miss Wilma Fern Schrock

Chicken Dressing

1 (9"x13") pan toasted bread
1 qt. chicken broth (with chicken bits)
1 pt. canned mixed vegetables
½ c. chicken seasoning
1 tsp. salt
2 Tbsp. celery flakes
⅛ tsp. pepper
4 eggs
1½ c. milk
½ c. butter, melted

In large bowl beat eggs; combine all the rest of the ingredients except bread. Mix well. Add bread; pour into greased 9"x13" pan. Bake at 350° for 1 hour.

Mrs. Jerry Esther Schrock

Forgiveness is an opportunity to shower back our gratitude to the one who forgave us everything.

Meats, Main Dishes

Hungarian Chicken Casserole

4 c. chicken broth
4 c. water and extra broth
½ c. flour
2 c. macaroni
salt to taste
½ lb. cheese, diced
1 c. bread crumbs
4 Tbsp. butter

Cook macaroni in water and drain. Thicken broth/water with flour and mix with chicken and macaroni. Mix in salt and cheese. Brown bread crumbs in butter and spread on top. Bake in a casserole dish or 9"x13" pan for 30 minutes at 325°.

Note: Sometimes I also add cooked, cubed carrots and potatoes for a more complete meal.

Mrs. Samuel Rachel Chupp

Chicken Pot Pie

3 c. Bisquick
1 c. diced potatoes
1 c. diced carrots
1 c. peas
½ c. chopped onions
2 c. chicken broth
1 c. chicken pieces
½ tsp. black pepper
1 tsp. salt
2 tsp. chicken seasoning
1 c. milk
¼ c. flour

Mix Bisquick according to directions on box. Use rolling pin and roll out like pie dough, reserve some dough for top of pies. Cook vegetables and broth together until vegetables are tender. Add chicken pieces and seasonings. Mix together milk and flour; add to vegetables. Fill pies with filling and use remaining dough to make tops for the pies. Bake uncovered at 350° for 20 minutes. Yield: 2 (9") pies.

Mrs. LaVern Linda Miller

Chicken and Rice Bake

1 qt. chicken broth with meat
2 c. water
½ tsp. chicken base
2 c. uncooked rice
½ c. diced potatoes
½ c. diced carrots
¼ c. diced onions
salt and pepper to taste
1 can cream of chicken soup

Mix all together and bake. Vegetables may be raw or cooked. This casserole can be put into a cold oven at 8:00 am. Turn oven to 200°-220° and you can leave the house. When you return at 12:00, dinner is ready as quickly as you can add shredded cheese and cornflake crumbs on top. Serves 12-15 people.

Mrs. Nelson Ruth Miller

Baked Chicken Breast

3 lb. chicken breasts
1 c. sour cream
1 can cream of chicken soup
3 pkg. Ritz crackers
½ c. butter, melted

Soak chicken breast with ¼ cup salt and enough water to cover breast. Let stand overnight or 24 hours. Drain. Mix sour cream and cream of chicken soup and layer with chicken breast (2-3 layers.) Mix Ritz crackers and melted butter and put on top. Bake at 350° for 1 hour or until meat is done.

Mrs. Monroe Elsie Miller

Mom's Baked Chicken Breast

Chicken breasts
Lawry's or regular salt
Ranch dressing
saltine crackers

Slice chicken breast lengthwise, approximately ⅜" thick. Sprinkle with Lawry's or regular salt. Dip in Ranch dressing and roll in crushed saltine crumbs. Place on cookie sheet and bake in a preheated oven at 400° for 7 minutes.

Mrs. Vernon Rachel Herschberger

Meats, Main Dishes

Mom's Fried Chicken

2 c. whole wheat flour
4 tsp. celery salt
4 tsp. Season All

Put a thin layer of vegetable oil on baking pan. Put flour mixture in a plastic bag and put chicken pieces in and shake to coat well. Put in greased pans and bake at 350° for 45 minutes, turning chicken after 15-20 minutes. This is delicious!

Mrs. Delbert Martha Schrock

Poppy Seed Chicken

2 lb. cooked chicken breasts
1 can cream of chicken soup
1 c. sour cream
½ c. butter
1½ c. crushed Ritz crackers

Put chicken in buttered 8"x8" dish. Mix chicken soup and sour cream. Pour over chicken. Melt butter and mix with crackers. Put on top. Sprinkle with poppy seeds. Bake at 350° for 40 minutes.

Miss Ruth Miller

Tender Chicken Nuggets

1 c. crushed cornflakes
½ c. Parmesan cheese
½ tsp. salt
¼ tsp. pepper
⅛ tsp. garlic powder
¼ c. Ranch salad dressing
1 lb. boneless, skinless chicken breasts

Combine first 5 ingredients. Place dressing in another bowl. Cut chicken in small cubes. Toss chicken cubes in dressing, then roll in cornflake mixture. Place in greased 9"x13" baking pan. Bake uncovered at 400° for 12-15 minutes.

Miss Cheryl DeAnn Otto

Meats, Main Dishes

Yummy Chicken Nuggets

2 cubed chicken breasts
2 c. saltine cracker crumbs
vegetable oil

Preheat vegetable oil to 375°. While vegetable oil is heating, cube chicken breasts in bite-sized pieces and roll in crushed saltines. Deep fat fry at 375° until golden brown. Sprinkle with salt to taste. Serves 12 people.

Mrs. Vernon Rachel Herschberger

Chicken Breading

3 boxes saltine crackers
3 (18 oz.) boxes cornflakes
2¾ c. whole wheat flour
¼ c. pepper
1¼ c. Lawry's seasoned salt
⅜ c. paprika
2 Tbsp. Accent
⅜ c. lemon pepper
⅝ Tbsp. salt

Crush crackers and cornflakes finely. Mix in rest of ingredients. To use: roll chicken pieces in melted butter, then in breading. Lay on foil-lined pans. Bake boneless breasts 30 minutes at 350°, then bake 30 minutes longer. (I put drumsticks in first, then lower temperature and put breasts in to finish together.) Next put all into a roaster, cover and keep in 250°-300° for another 1½-2 hours. Yield: approximately 2 ice cream pails full of crumbs.

Mrs. Ernest Ray Inez Miller

Barbecue Sauce for Chicken

¾ c. vinegar
1 Tbsp. garlic powder
¼ c. sugar
¼ c. salt
1 tsp. pepper
3 c. water
1 Tbsp. Worcestershire sauce

Boil all together. Cool. Soak chicken for a day then use to dip chicken in while grilling.

Mrs. Reuben Marilyn Schrock

Meats, Main Dishes

Marinade for Chicken

2 c. water
2 c. vinegar
½ c. butter
¼ c. salt

2 Tbsp. pepper
5 Tbsp. Worcestershire sauce
1 Tbsp. garlic powder

Mix all ingredients together and soak chicken for 6-8 hours prior to grilling. Grill chicken till basically done, then bake it in the remaining marinade at 350° for 1½ hours. This is enough marinade for two chickens.

Miss Cathy Wagler

Marinade for Chicken

1 gallon water
½ c. Tender Quick
1 c. brown sugar

2 Tbsp. Worcestershire sauce
1 bottle Italian dressing

Mix together. Let chicken soak in marinade 24 hours in a cool place. Grill and enjoy!
Note: This is a large recipe. Enough brine to soak 6-8 chickens.

Mrs. Perry Delores Herschberger

Marinade for Chicken, Turkey or Pork

2 Tbsp. sugar
2 Tbsp. vegetable salt
2 Tbsp. salt
4 c. water divided

1 tsp. garlic salt
1 Tbsp. Worcestershire sauce
¼ c. butter
1 Tbsp. vinegar

Heat 2 cups water; add salts and sugar. Stir to dissolve, then add butter, vinegar and Worcestershire sauce. Add 2 cups cold water and chicken or turkey steaks. I soak a fryer or steaks and pork chops etc. in brine overnight. Makes tender meat. Fry or grill meat as desired. Yield: Enough for 2 fryers.

Miss Verna Kay Miller

Meats, Main Dishes

Brine for Turkey

1½ gal. water
1 c. Tender Quick
¼ c. liquid smoke
¾ c. salt

3 Tbsp. brown sugar
1 tsp. pepper
¼ tsp. red pepper

Mix all ingredients together and completely cover a 10-12 pound turkey with brine. Soak 2 days. Bake in a turkey-size oven bag and follow baking instructions on chart.

Miss Wilma Fern Schrock

Long John Silver's Fish Batter

1 egg white
1 Tbsp. baking powder
1 Tbsp. vegetable oil

1 Tbsp. salt
1 c. flour
3½ lb. fish

Beat egg white until stiff. Mix remaining ingredients with ¾ cup water, then add to egg white. Dip fish into mixture and deep-fat fry.

Mrs. Ernest Sara Schrock

Barbecued Meatballs

3 lb. hamburger
1½ c. oatmeal
1 c. chopped onions
½ tsp. garlic powder

2 tsp. salt
½ tsp. pepper
2 tsp. chili powder

Sauce:
3 c. ketchup
1¼ c. brown sugar
1½ tsp. liquid smoke

¾ tsp. garlic powder
½ c. chopped onions, opt.

Mix meatball ingredients and form into balls. Place in flat pan, one layer at a time. Bake at 350° for 1 hour. Heat sauce and pour over baked meatballs.

Mrs. Joe Laura Hershberger

Meats, Main Dishes

Favorite Meatballs

1 can evaporated milk
 or regular milk
1½ lb. ground beef
1½ lb. sausage
2 c. quick oats
2 eggs

1 c. chopped onions
½ tsp. garlic powder
2 tsp. salt
½ tsp. pepper
2 tsp. chili powder

Sauce:
2 c. ketchup
1-2 Tbsp. liquid smoke
1½ c. brown sugar

1 tsp. garlic powder
½ c. chopped onions

Mix and shape into balls. Place in cake pan and pour sauce over them. Bake covered at 350° for 1 hour. Serves 20 people.

Mrs. Leon Christina Wagler

Meatballs

2 qt. hamburger
3 c. oatmeal
1½ c. milk
2 eggs
2 sm. onions

¼ c. Worcestershire sauce
2 tsp. salt
1 tsp. dry mustard
½ tsp. pepper

Sauce:
2 c. ketchup
1 c. brown sugar
⅔ c. sugar
½ c. maple syrup

2 tsp. mustard
½ tsp. salt
1 Tbsp. Worcestershire sauce
½ tsp. liquid smoke

Mix well and shape into meatballs. Bake until almost done, then drain off some of the juice or as much as possible. Top with sauce and bake a little longer till done. Serves 20 people.

Note: I sometimes use half hamburger and half sausage.

Mrs. Samuel Dorothy Miller

Meats, Main Dishes

Meatballs

2 lb. ground beef
1 lb. ground pork
1 (5 oz.) can evaporated milk
2 c. quick oats
½ tsp. pepper

Sauce:
2 c. ketchup
¾ c. brown sugar

1 tsp. chili powder
¼ tsp. garlic powder
1 Tbsp. salt
2 eggs
¼ c. chopped onions

1 tsp. liquid smoke

Mix all ingredients together. Shape into balls. (A cookie scoop works good to measure and shape). Place in 9"x13" baking pan, in single layer. Combine sauce ingredients and pour over meatballs. Bake at 350° for 1 hour. Yield: approximately 30 meatballs.

Mrs. Joe Lorene Miller

Ham Loaf

1¼ lb. ground ham
⅔ lb. sausage
⅔ lb. hamburger

Sauce:
1 c. brown sugar, packed
½ c. vinegar

2 eggs
1 c. cracker crumbs
salt and pepper to taste

2 tsp. mustard
½ c. water

Shape meat in a loaf or balls. Pour sauce over top and bake for 1 hour at 350°. Use a 9"x13" pan for a loaf.

Miss Cheryl DeAnn Otto

Meats, Main Dishes

Mock Ham Loaf

1 lb. hamburger
½ lb. ground hot dogs
1 c. crushed saltine crackers

1 egg, beaten
1 tsp. salt
½ tsp. pepper

Glaze:
¾ c. brown sugar
½ c. water

1 Tbsp. vinegar
½ tsp. dry mustard

Mix glaze, add half of glaze to the meat, and add all the other ingredients. Put meat into a 9"x 9" pan. Pour rest of glaze on top and bake at 350° for 30-40 minutes.
Note: Marilyn uses 1 teaspoon vinegar instead of 1 tablespoon.

Mrs. Reuben Marilyn Schrock
Mrs. LaVern Linda Miller

Favorite Meat Loaf

1½ lb. ground beef
1½ lb. sausage
1½ c. milk
1 c. rolled oats
1 c. cracker crumbs
2 eggs

½ c. chopped onions
1 tsp. garlic powder
1 tsp. salt
1 tsp. pepper
1 tsp. chili powder

Sauce:
¾ c. brown sugar
¼ c. chopped onions
½ c. ketchup

1 tsp. garlic powder
½ tsp. liquid smoke

Mix meat loaf ingredients well and press into a large pan. Bake at 350° for 45 minutes. Mix sauce and put on meat and bake another 20 minutes. Serves 25 people.

Mrs. Leon Christina Wagler

Meats, Main Dishes

Meat Loaf

3 lb. ground beef
2 c. milk
1½ c. quick oats
2 eggs
½ c. chopped onions
1 Tbsp. salt
½ tsp. pepper

Combine all ingredients. Mix well and press in 9"x13" pan. Bake at 350° about 1 hour. Serves 8 people.

Mrs. Isaac Daisy Troyer

Barbecued Hamburgers

3 lb. hamburger
½ c. sauce
2 eggs
⅔ c. oatmeal
½ tsp. onion salt
½ tsp. garlic salt
½ tsp. pepper
½ tsp. salt

Sauce: (for 12 lb. hamburger)
4 c. ketchup
2 c. brown sugar
1⅓ c. sugar
1 c. pancake syrup
8 tsp. mustard
1 tsp. Worcestershire sauce
1 tsp. liquid smoke
1⅓ c. honey

Mix ingredients in order given. Extra sauce can be stored in refrigerator for weeks.

Miss Ruth Miller

If we fill our hours with regrets of yesterday and with worries of tomorrow, we have no today in which to be thankful.

Meats, Main Dishes

Hamburgers to Grill

2 lb. hamburger
1½ tsp. salt
1 tsp. pepper
½ tsp. Worcestershire sauce
½ c. crushed crackers
¼ c. milk
1 tsp. Lawry's salt
½ c. oatmeal
1 egg, beaten

Mix all ingredients. Use a ⅓ cup measure to make hamburgers. Top with barbecue sauce while grilling. Very delicious!

Mrs. Jerry Esther Schrock

Oven Barbecue

10 lb. hamburger
1 qt. ketchup
½ c. chopped onions
3 Tbsp. salt
⅓ c. Worcestershire sauce
1½ tsp. pepper
2 c. quick oats
⅓ c. mustard
2 c. barbecue sauce

Mix all together well. Put in roaster and bake 2 hours, stirring occasionally.

Mrs. Nelson Ruth Miller

Sloppy Joes

10 lb. hamburger
1½ qt. ketchup
2-3 onions
2 c. quick oats
pepper to taste
¼ c. salt
⅓ c. Worcestershire sauce
1 c. brown sugar
⅓ c. mustard

Mix all together. Bake 2 hours. Stirring occasionally. Yield: 3½ gallons. Serves 100 people.

Mrs. David Verda Miller

Meats, Main Dishes

Sloppy Joes

5 lb. hamburger
4 tsp. salt
2 c. oatmeal
2 c. milk
4 c. barbecue sauce
½ tsp. pepper

Mix all ingredients thoroughly. Put in a large roaster. Bake at 350° for 1 hour, stirring every 20 minutes. Yield: Fills 40-45 regular size buns.

Mrs. Steven Katie Jantzi

You Ain't Nothin' but a Hound Dog

½ lb. ground beef
2 Tbsp. chopped onions
¾ c. ketchup
¼ c. water
1½ tsp. Worcestershire sauce
¾ tsp. chili powder
¼ tsp. pepper
⅛ tsp. cayenne pepper
8 cooked hot dogs

In saucepan, cook beef and onions till meat is no longer pink; drain. Stir in ketchup, water, Worcestershire sauce, chili powder, pepper and cayenne. Bring to a boil. Reduce heat; simmer uncovered for 5 minutes or until mixture is desired thickness. Place hot dogs in buns. Top each with about 2 Tbsp. beef mixture.

Miss Lyndora Kay Miller

Meats, Main Dishes

Corn Dogs

2 Tbsp. vegetable oil
2 Tbsp. sugar
1 c. flour
1 tsp. salt
1½ tsp. baking powder
¾ c. cornmeal
¾ c. milk
1 egg
16 hot dogs

Mix all ingredients except the hot dogs. Wipe hot dogs dry; dip in batter and deep fry until brown. Drain on paper towel. Serve with ketchup. Serves 8 people.
Note: These can be individually wrapped and frozen for quick school lunches.

Mrs. Dennis Marilyn Hershberger

Delicious Homemade Sub-Sandwiches

1 bottle Ranch dressing
2 different meats
chopped peppers
chopped onions
bacon, fried and crumbled
shredded cheese

Use the Melt-In-Your-Mouth Dinner Roll recipe (page 51). Make 1 recipe and flatten onto 2 cookie sheets, then prick with a fork like you would for pie crusts. Cut both sheets into 6 pieces. (I cut lengthwise then in half and 4 cuts crosswise. Buns are approximately 4½"x 9"). Bake at 425° until lightly golden. Fold each piece in half while still warm. After cool, fill each sandwich with the above toppings in order given. Wrap each sandwich individually and warm in oven at 350° for 15-20 minutes. A family favorite. Serves 12 people.

Mrs. LaVern Linda Miller
Mrs. Perry Delores Herschberger

Tuna Patties

2 cans tuna
¼ c. mayonnaise
2 c. bread crumbs, divided

Add mayonnaise and 1 cup bread crumbs to meat. Roll patties in other cup of bread crumbs. Fry in oil. Serve with tartar sauce.

Miss Bethany Kay Otto

Zucchini Patties

⅔ c. Bisquick baking mix
¼ c. Parmesan cheese
2 eggs
2 c. grated zucchini
½ tsp. salt
¼ tsp. black pepper
½ tsp. Lawry's salt

Combine ingredients and drop by spoonfuls onto heavy skillet with a thin layer of oil or lard. Spread out batter, flatten slightly as you turn them with spatula. Fry until golden brown on both sides. This makes a favorite summer sandwich with tomatoes and onions. Serves 5 people.

Note: To make your own Bisquick mix: 12 cups flour, 2 tablespoons salt, ¼ cup baking powder, 2½ teaspoons cream of tartar, 2 cups lard. Store in airtight container.

Mrs. Wilbur Wilma Miller

Baked Beans (large recipe)

5-6 qt. cooked, drained, and salted beans
5 c. brown sugar
2½ c. ketchup
2 Tbsp. mustard
2 tsp. liquid smoke
1 onion
2 lb. hamburger, fried

Mix well. Bake 1½ hours at 350°. This can be canned in pressure cooker at 10 pounds for 45 minutes. Serves 40-45 people.

Mrs. Monroe Elsie Miller

Meats, Main Dishes

Baked Beans

3 c. precooked beans
½ c. brown sugar
½ c. ketchup
2 tsp. mustard
3 Tbsp. butter

1 c. cream
½ c. chopped onions
bologna or other meat, opt.
cheese, opt.

Mix all together and pour into 5 quart roaster. Bake at 350° for 45 minutes or till onions are soft. Add cheese just a little before done.
Note: This is good with cornbread.

Mrs. Jacob Elsie Mishler

Hamburger Casserole

1 lb. hamburger
1 c. uncooked rice
1 c. diced carrots
1 c. chopped onions
1 can mushroom soup

2 c. boiling water
1 qt. tomato juice
1 tsp. salt
pepper to taste

Cover and bake for 2 hours at 325°. May be sprinkled with grated cheese 10 minutes before removing from oven. Serves 4-6 people.

Miss Lovina Eicher

Deal with the faults of others
as gently as your own.

Hamburger Rice Casserole

1½ lb. hamburger
½ c. chopped onions
1 c. rice
3 c. water
seasoning salt

salt and pepper
1 can cream of mushroom soup
1 can cream of chicken soup
1½ c. frozen peas, thawed

Topping:
12 oz. sour cream
2 c. cornflakes, crushed

¼ c. butter, melted

Brown hamburger and onion together. Season with seasonings. Boil rice in water until tender. Mix with the rest of ingredients and put in a 9"x13" pan. Topping: Cover with sour cream, then the cornflakes mixed with melted butter. Bake at 350° until hot. Do not overbake. Serves 10-12 people.

Mrs. William Miriam Yoder

Rice Casserole

1 lb. ground beef
1 c. diced celery
1 lg. onion, minced
1 c. minute rice
3 Tbsp. soy sauce

pinch of salt
1 can cream of mushroom soup
1 can cream of chicken soup
1 soup can water

Brown meat with celery and onion, then add the rest of the ingredients. Pour into a 2-quart casserole dish and bake for 30 minutes (more if using regular rice) at 350°. Serves 8-10 people.

Mrs. Ernest Mary Ellen Miller

Meats, Main Dishes

Mock Turkey

2 lb. hamburger
1 onion
2 tsp. salt
½ tsp. pepper
2 cans cream of chicken soup
1 can cream of celery soup
4 c. milk
1 lg. pkg. bread stuffing
    or 1 loaf bread, cut up

Brown hamburger and onion in butter. Add salt and pepper. Mix soups and milk with wire whip, add meat and stuffing. Pour in buttered 9"x13" pan and bake at 350° for 45 minutes. Serves 12 people.

Mrs. Monroe Elsie Miller

Bacon Cheeseburger Casserole

hash browns
1 lb. hamburger
8 slices bacon, fried
    and crumbled
¼ c. chopped onions
1 can cream of celery soup
1 tsp. Worcestershire sauce
salt and pepper to taste
½ tsp. garlic, opt.
Velveeta cheese slices or
    cheese of your choice

Brown hamburger, bacon and onions. Add celery soup, Worcestershire sauce and seasonings. Put a layer of hash browns in greased casserole, top with half of meat and slices of cheese. Repeat layers. Cover and bake at 350° for 45 minutes or until heated through. Serves 6-8 people.

Mrs. Gerald Betty Kauffman

Meats, Main Dishes

One Dish Meal

1½ lb. hamburger
2 med. onions, chopped
salt and pepper to taste
1c. water or tomato juice
3 lg. potatoes, shredded
3 lg. carrots, shredded
1 can cream of mushroom soup
Velveeta cheese

Brown hamburger and onions in a 10" skillet. Season with salt and pepper. Pour water or tomato juice over hamburger, then layer potatoes and carrots, sprinkling with salt between each layer. Cover and simmer for 20 minutes. Spread soup over all and cover with cheese. Ready to serve when cheese is melted.

Mrs. Kenneth Leanna Kauffman

Skillet Casserole

1½ lb. hamburger or sausage
5 med. potatoes, shredded
salt and pepper to taste
3 med. carrots, shredded
1¼ c. water
cheese
1 sm. onion

Fry hamburger with onion in 10" skillet. Add potatoes, salt and pepper. Top with carrots. Pour 1¼ cup water in pan and cover. When it's cooking, turn heat lower. Simmer for 20 minutes. Cover with cheese. May use beans instead of carrots. Use the leftovers to make soup for supper. Just add chicken broth, milk and some thickener, season with chicken seasoning, celery salt or whatever your family likes. I like to make this for a quick meal.

Mrs. Ernest Sara Schrock

The Lord wants our precious time, not our spare time.

Meats, Main Dishes

Potato Haystack Casserole

8-10 boiled, peeled and shredded potatoes
2 pkg. Ranch dressing mix
2 c. sour cream
2 c. milk

4 lb. hamburger
salt and pepper to taste
1-2 pkg. taco seasoning
cheese
nacho chips

Layer these in casserole in order given, then put cheese on top. Cover and bake until hot at 350°. Just before serving, put crushed nacho chips on top.

Note: Can also wait to put cheese on until the last 10 minutes that way you can bake it faster, uncovered.

Mrs. Delbert Martha Schrock

Potato Ranch Casserole

3 lb. hamburger
1 med. onion
salt and pepper to taste
2 cans cream of mushroom soup
4 qt. cooked and shredded potatoes

16 oz. sour cream
2 c. Ranch dressing
16 oz. mozzarella or marble cheese
1 lb. bacon, fried and crumbled

Brown hamburger and onion. Add salt and pepper. Mix soups and hamburger and put in large roaster. Place potatoes on top of hamburger. Mix sour cream and Ranch dressing and spread over potatoes. Bake until heated through. Top with cheese and bacon and return to oven till cheese melts.

Mrs. Gerald Betty Kauffman
Miss SueEllen Miller

Quick Potato and Bean Casserole

4 sm. potatoes, cooked and sliced
1 qt. green beans
1 (16 oz.) pkg. hot dogs, sliced
1 med. onion, chopped
1 can cream of mushroom soup
salt and pepper to taste
a little milk

Put in oven at 350° until good and hot. Put Velveeta cheese slices on top and return to oven until melted.
Note: This is a casserole I like to make when I have leftover potatoes and I am in a hurry. This will make a small roaster full.

Mrs. Ray Marjorie Wagler

Baked Red Potatoes

1 c. butter, melted
1 tsp. salt
1 tsp. Lawry's salt
2 Tbsp. parsley
½ tsp. pepper
½ tsp. paprika
4 qt. quartered potatoes

Mix seasonings with melted butter, then toss with potatoes. Put in casserole dish and cover tightly. Bake at 350° for 1 hour. Serves 32 people.

Mrs. Eldon Ray Denise Miller

Oven Fried Potatoes

8 lb. potatoes
¼ c. flour
¼ c. Parmesan cheese
½ tsp. salt
½ tsp. seasoning salt
½ tsp. paprika
½ tsp. garlic powder
¼ c. butter

Peel and chunk potatoes. Combine flour, cheese and seasonings in a plastic bag. Shake and coat well. Put on greased pan. Dot potatoes with butter and bake at 375° for about one hour turning once during baking. They are ready when they are golden brown.

Mrs. Eldon Ray Denise Miller
Mrs. Kenneth Marilyn Otto

Meats, Main Dishes

Parmesan Potatoes

1 gal. potatoes, peeled and cut up
¾ c. butter, melted
2 c. Parmesan cheese
1 c. flour
2 Tbsp. seasoned salt
1 Tbsp. salt
1 Tbsp. garlic powder
1 Tbsp. Italian seasoning

Put potatoes in a bowl. Pour butter over potatoes. Cover and shake well, then add rest of ingredients. Shake well again, then put on a buttered cookie sheet. Bake at 350° till potatoes are soft, approximately 1 hour. Stir once or twice while baking. Serves 12 people.

Mrs. Samuel Dorothy Miller

Quick and Easy Potatoes

8 med. potatoes
1-2 c. chopped ham or meat of your choice
¼ c. chopped onions
minced garlic, opt.
salt and pepper to taste
6 Tbsp. butter, melted
cheese slices

Thinly slice peeled potatoes into casserole dish. Mix in ham, onions, garlic, salt and pepper. Pour butter over all. Bake in 400° oven for 45 minutes. Cover with cheese slices and allow to melt before serving.

Note: This is enough for our family of 8. You can add ingredients to suit your taste, such as different seasonings, no cheese, or Parmesan cheese, etc. Quick meal!

Mrs. Ernest Ray Inez Miller

Meats, Main Dishes

Tater Tot Casserole

2 lb. tater tots
1 pt. sour cream
2 cans cream of chicken soup
2½ c. milk
½ c. chopped onions
1 lb. Velveeta cheese
1 tsp. salt
½ tsp. pepper
2 lb. hamburger, fried
2 c. crushed cornflakes
½ c. butter, melted

Mix sour cream, soup, milk, onions, cheese, salt and pepper. Layer tater tots on the bottom, then hamburger and soup mixture. Mix cornflakes and melted butter. Pour this on top of casserole. Bake at 350° for 45-60 minutes. Use large size roaster.

Note: You can add peas or mixed vegetables.

Mrs. Joe Laura Hershberger

Tater Tot Casserole

1 lb. hamburger, browned and seasoned
1½ c. mixed vegetables, cooked
1 can cream of chicken soup
1 soup can milk
cheese
1 lb. tater tots

Put the browned hamburger and mixed vegetables in a 2-quart casserole dish. Dilute the soup with the milk and pour over the layers of meat and vegetables. Cover with cheese slices and top with frozen tater tots. Bake covered at 350° for 1¼ hour. Serves 6 people.

Miss Edna Mae Schrock

Meats, Main Dishes

Homemade Tater Tots

8 potatoes, peeled and cooked
4 Tbsp. flour, rounded
1 tsp. salt
dash of pepper
oil to fry

Cook potatoes till tender then peel and shred finely or use ricer while still warm. Stir in flour salt and pepper. Heat oil in a heavy pan so the tater tots can float while frying. Now form potatoes in small balls to fry. Fry until golden. Drain on a paper towel then freeze. To serve bake single layer on a cookie sheet at 400° until desired crispness. Serves 10 people.

Mrs. LaVern Linda Miller

Frankfurter Bake

1 lb. pkg. noodles
2½ c. grated cheese
2½ c. milk
½ c. margarine
¼ c. flour
1 tsp. salt
2 lb. hot dogs, sliced
½ c. brown sugar
½ c. salad dressing
2 Tbsp. mustard

In a large kettle cook noodles, drain. Return to kettle. Stir in margarine, flour, milk, cheese and salt. Pour into a well greased 9"x13" pan. Mix hot dogs, brown sugar, salad dressing and mustard. Spoon hot dog mixture evenly over noodles. Bake at 375° for 25 minutes. Serves 12 people.

Note: An excellent dish to take to school for hot lunch. A children's favorite!

Miss Denise Ann Kauffman

Lasagna

8 lasagna noodles
1 lg. onion
3 lb. hamburger
1 pt. pizza sauce
3 Tbsp. mustard

2 Tbsp. chili powder
1/3 c. ketchup
1/3 c. Open Pit barbecue sauce
salt and pepper
1 pkg. mozzarella cheese

Cook noodles. Fry hamburger and onion. Drain. Add pizza sauce, mustard, chili powder, ketchup, barbecue sauce, salt and pepper. Start with noodles and put in layers with meat and cheese. Spread cheese on top. Bake at 350°.

Mrs. Reuben Marilyn Schrock

Baked Macaroni and Cheese

4 c. dry macaroni
1/2 c. butter
1/4 c. chopped onions
1/2 c. flour

1 tsp. salt
4 c. milk
1-1½ lb. or 4-6 c. Colby
    cheese, grated

Bring 4-5 quarts water to a boil. Add a tablespoon of salt. Add macaroni; cook uncovered 10 minutes, or until tender. Stir occasionally; drain. Melt butter; add chopped onions and cook several minutes. Blend in flour and salt. Gradually stir in milk. Boil one minute. Add most of cheese (if using Velveeta, delete flour); stir until melted. Add macaroni. Bake uncovered at 350° for 30 minutes, or until hot. Sprinkle with remaining cheese the last 15 minutes of baking. Serves 15 people.

Miss Miriam Miller

Meats, Main Dishes

Chicken Stockpot Noodles

2 qt. chicken pieces
1½ qt. chicken broth
2½ gal. water
1¾ c. chicken soup base
5 lb. homemade noodles
4 cans cream of chicken soup
1 c. water
1½ c. butter, browned

Bring first 4 ingredients to a boil. Add noodles, then cook for 5 minutes. Mix cream of chicken soup with 1 cup water, pour over top. Pour browned butter on top of that. Do not stir. Put lid on and let set for 1 hour before serving. Yield: 1 (20-quart) stockpot full. Serves 80 people.

Mrs. Perry Delores Herschberger

Potluck Eggs Benedict

1 lb. fresh asparagus, trimmed
¾ c. butter
4 c. milk
1 (14.5 oz.) can chicken broth
1 lb. fully cooked ham, cubed
1 c. shredded cheddar cheese
8 hard-boiled eggs, quartered
1½ tsp. salt
⅛ tsp. cayenne pepper
10-12 biscuits, warmed
¾ c. all-purpose flour

Cut asparagus into ½" pieces, using only tender parts of spears. Cook in a small amount of boiling water until tender, about 5 minutes; drain. Set aside to cool. Melt butter in a saucepan; stir in flour until smooth. Add milk and broth; bring to a boil. Cook and stir for 2 minutes. Add ham and cheese; stir until the cheese melts. Add eggs, salt, cayenne and asparagus; heat through. Serve over biscuits. Put in casserole dish and bake at 350° until hot. Serves 10-12 people.

Mrs. Delbert Martha Schrock

Meats, Main Dishes

Zucchini Casserole

2-3 sm. zucchini, shredded
2 lb. sausage or hamburger, fried
1 onion, chopped

1 pkg. saltines, crumbled
½ c. flour
2½ c. milk

Put a layer of shredded zucchini in a medium casserole dish. Fry meat and onion. Put a layer of meat, then half of the saltines; then repeat layers. Reserve some meat crumbles, stir in flour and milk gradually, stirring constantly till it boils. Season to taste. (We like to use sausage seasoning.) Pour gravy over top and bake uncovered approximately 1 hour. Serves 10 people.

Mrs. Wilbur Wilma Miller

Zucchini Casserole

3 eggs
¼ c. vegetable oil
½ c. flour
1½ tsp. baking powder
1 tsp. salt

dash of pepper
½ c. grated cheese
2 c. grated zucchini
½ c. chopped onions
¼ c. chopped parsley

Beat eggs and vegetable oil. Stir together flour, baking powder, salt, pepper and cheese. Add to egg mixture. Add rest of ingredients and stir. Pour in greased casserole dish. Bake at 350° for 45 minutes.

Note: Some hamburger or bologna can be used instead of the cheese.

Mrs. Jacob Elsie Mishler

Meats, Main Dishes

Hush Puppies

1 c. Bisquick
1 c. cornmeal
1 tsp. salt

1 egg
¾ c. milk
½ c. chopped onions

Drop by spoonfuls into hot oil to deep fat fry. Eat with chicken or sausage gravy. Serves 5 people.

Miss Susanna Schrock

Brown Gravy

1 c. butter
1 c. flour
4 c. water

1 can cream of mushroom soup
1 tsp. salt
½ tsp. pepper

Melt butter. Stir in flour and brown. Stir in water, then the rest of ingredients. It will seem lumpy at first but will smooth when cooking if stirred with wire whip.

Note: This recipe is for a large 10" skillet.

Mrs. Howard Ellen Schrock

Giving up doesn't always mean you are weak. Sometimes it means you are strong enough to let go.

Cheesy Enchiladas

Cheese sauce:
¼ c. flour
3 c. milk
8 oz. Velveeta

½ c. butter
8 oz. sour cream

Meat Mixture:
2 lb. hamburger, browned
1 onion, chopped
2 Tbsp. taco seasoning

1 can kidney beans or refried beans
10 flour tortillas

Place meat mixture in tortillas. Roll up and place in buttered baking dish. For Cheese Sauce: Heat milk, drop in cheese and butter. Mix flour with a little milk then stir into hot milk. Add salt to taste. Pour cheese sauce over top. Bake at 350° until cheese starts to bubble. Serve with lettuce, chopped tomatoes and salsa.

Mrs. Eldon Ray Denise Miller

Enchiladas

3 lb. ground beef
¼ c. taco seasoning
16 flour tortillas

1¾ c. pizza sauce
1 can cream of mushroom soup
2 lb. grated cheese

Cook ground beef and taco seasoning together. Put meat in tortillas, roll up and place tightly together in 9"x13" pan. Mix sauce and mushroom soup together. Pour over tortillas. Top with cheese. Bake at 350° for 20-30 minutes. Delicious! Serves 10 people.

Mrs. Steven Katie Jantzi

Meats, Main Dishes

Wet Burrito Casserole

1 c. hamburger, browned
chopped onions
chopped peppers
salt to taste
¼ c. baked beans

1 Tbsp. taco seasoning
4 flour tortillas
1 can cream of mushroom soup
¼ c. milk
shredded or American cheese

Brown hamburger with onions and peppers, salt and seasonings of your choice. Mix beans and taco seasoning with browned hamburger. Spoon into tortillas, roll up and put into baking dish. In a small bowl, whip together mushroom soup and milk; pour over tortillas. Top with cheese. Bake at 350° for 30 minutes. Serves 4 people.

Mrs. Vernon Rachel Herschberger

Wet Burrito Casserole

1½ c. sour cream
1 can cream of mushroom soup
1 lb. hamburger
1 med. onion, chopped
1 med. green pepper, diced

1 tsp. taco seasoning
1 (10 oz.) can mushrooms
1 (16 oz.) can refried beans
10 flour tortilla
4 c. shredded cheese

Mix sour cream and cream of mushroom soup. Put half in bottom of 9"x13" pan, fry hamburger, onions and peppers. Add mushrooms, taco seasoning and beans. Divide meat mixture onto tortilla shells. Roll up shells and place on top of sour cream and soup in pan. Top with rest of soup mixture. Sprinkle cheese on top. Bake at 350° for 30 minutes. Serves 12-15 people.

Note: Marilyn uses 1 package taco seasoning.

Miss SueEllen Miller
Mrs. Reuben Marilyn Schrock

Meats, Main Dishes

Haystack Casserole

2 lb. hamburger or sausage
2 Tbsp. taco seasoning
1 tsp. salt

1 qt. pizza sauce
2 c. uncooked rice

Topping:
chopped lettuce
green peppers
onions

tomatoes
shredded cheese
crushed tortilla chips

Cook rice, add salt to taste. Put into casserole dish. Brown meat, add taco seasoning, salt and pizza sauce. Spread on top of rice. Bake at 375° for 15 minutes. Add toppings of your choice just before serving. May be served with or without cheese sauce of your choice. Serves 15 people.

Mrs. Nelson Ruth Miller

Horseshoe Special

toast
sloppy joe or barbecue sauce

hash browns
cheese sauce

Cheese Sauce:
½ gal. milk
1 lb. cheese
¾ c. butter

¾ c. flour
1 Tbsp. salt
2 tsp. pepper

Put toast in plate. On top of toast, put sloppy joe, then your hash browns. Top with cheese sauce. For cheese sauce: Heat milk, drop in cheese and butter. Mix flour with a little milk then stir into hot milk. Add salt and pepper. Bring to a boil. Enjoy!

Miss Verna Kay Miller

Meats, Main Dishes

Mexican Casserole

3½ lb. hamburger, fried
2 cans kidney beans
3 Tbsp. taco seasoning
6 c. pizza sauce
2 c. uncooked rice
cheese sauce

2 c. sour cream
lettuce
tortilla chips
tomatoes
shredded cheese

Cheese Sauce:
2 c. hot milk

1 lb. Velveeta cheese

Brown hamburger, add beans, taco seasoning and pizza sauce. Cook the rice then add cheese sauce. Layer the rice, then hamburger in a large roaster. Bake at 350° for 30 minutes. Do not cover. Put sour cream on top while still hot. Top with lettuce, crushed tortilla chips, tomatoes and shredded cheese.

Miss Marietta W. Miller

Tostado (Mexican Haystack)

Meat Mixture:
2 lb. hamburger, browned
1 can refried beans

1 pkg. taco seasoning
¾ c. water

Toppings:
1 pkg. tortilla chips, crushed
hot meat mixture
1 head lettuce, shredded
4 chopped tomatoes

1 lb. shredded Colby cheese
2 qt. hot cheese sauce
sour cream
salsa

Mix meat mixture ingredients and bring to a boil, simmer for 10 minutes. Layer all the food in a stack on your plate.

Mrs. David Verda Miller

Meats, Main Dishes

Stromboli

1 c. warm water
1 Tbsp. yeast
1 Tbsp. sugar

1 tsp. salt
2½-3 c. flour

Filling:
ham
bacon
pepperoni

onions
peppers
cheese

Dissolve yeast in warm water. Add rest of ingredients. Knead a few times and let set a few minutes. Divide dough in half for 2 smaller pans. Roll on floured pan and fill with your choice of fillings. Put filling in middle and fold 2 sides of dough up over the top, sealing edges or ends of roll. Bake at 400° for 15-20 minutes. Brush with butter when done and you can sprinkle top with garlic salt or seasoning of your choice.
Note: One batch serves 8-10 people with one piece each.

Mrs. Leon Christine Wagler

Taco Casserole

2 lb. ground beef
2 c. chopped onions
1 c. chopped green or red peppers
2 c. corn

2 c. tomato sauce
2 pkg. taco seasoning
2 c. shredded cheese, divided
2 c. cooked macaronies

Topping:
1 c. Aunt Jemima pancake mix
1⅓ c. milk

2 eggs
4 tsp. vegetable oil

Brown beef with onions. Add peppers and corn. Bring to a boil. Add tomato sauce and taco seasoning; cook 3-4 minutes. Add macaronies, then pour into a 9"x13" pan. Sprinkle with 1 cup cheese. Whisk together topping ingredients till large lumps disappear. Pour over beef mixture. Bake at 350° for 30-35 minutes. Top with remaining cheese and optional ingredients: sour cream and chopped cilantro. Serves 15 people.

Miss Sarah Mae Jantzi

Meats, Main Dishes

Taco Pie Casserole

pizza dough or crescent rolls
Velveeta cheese
1½ lb. hamburger
1 (15 oz.) can refried or chili beans
1½ c. pizza sauce
sour cream
taco sauce, opt.
shredded cheese
shredded lettuce
tomatoes
taco chips

Bake the dough on a 9"x13" pan for 10-15 minutes. Put a layer of Velveeta cheese on the crust. Mix fried hamburger, pizza sauce and beans and put on top of cheese. Bake until done. Top with rest of ingredients in order given.

Mrs. Ernest Sara Schrock

Taco Pie

Dough:
2 Tbsp. dry yeast
¾ c. warm water
½ c. sugar
1 tsp. salt
½ c. shortening
2 eggs
4 c. flour

Toppings:
taco flavored Doritos, divided
hamburger mixture
sour cream
grated cheese

Mix dough ingredients together and put in bottom of pie pans as you would for pies or you can use 2 round pizza pans. Mix fried hamburger with taco seasoning and taco sauce. Layer ingredients as listed: dough, Doritos, hamburger mixture, sour cream, other Doritos, grated cheese. Bake for 1½ hours at 325°. Serve with lettuce, tomatoes and salsa.

Mrs. David Verda Miller

Meats, Main Dishes

Deep Dish Taco Squares

1 lb. hamburger
1 med. onion, chopped
2 Tbsp. taco seasoning
1 c. chopped green peppers
2 tomatoes, sliced
1 c. sour cream
⅔ c. mayonnaise
¼ c. chopped onions
1 c. shredded cheese
pinch of salt
2 c. Bisquick
½ c. water

Fry hamburger, onions and taco seasoning. Then mix sour cream, mayonnaise, onions, cheese and salt; set aside. Mix Bisquick with water. Pat onto the bottom and partway up the sides of a 9"x13" baking pan. Pour the ground beef mixture onto the crust. Sprinkle with green peppers and tomatoes. Spoon the sour cream mixture on top. Lightly sprinkle with taco seasoning and bake at 350° for 25 minutes. Serve with salsa and enjoy. Delicious!

Mrs. Monroe Elsie Miller
Miss Dorcas Miller
Miss Julia Jantzi

Taco Squares

2 c. Bisquick or your own biscuit mix
½ c. cold water
2 lb. hamburger
1 qt. pizza sauce
1 c. sour cream
¾ c. mayonnaise
1½ c. shredded cheese
paprika

Mix Bisquick and water and press into a 9"x13" pan. Bake at 325° for 12 minutes. Fry hamburger and mix with pizza sauce. Put on top of baked crust. Next mix sour cream, mayonnaise and cheese; spread on top of meat. Sprinkle with paprika. Bake at 350° for 20-30 minutes or till bubbly at sides. Serves 15 people.

Mrs. Leon Christine Wagler

Meats, Main Dishes

BLT Pizza

pizza dough
Ranch dressing
mozzarella or provolone cheese
bacon
mayonnaise
lettuce
tomatoes

Prepare your favorite pizza dough and line pan. Put on a layer of Ranch dressing. Sprinkle with mozzarella or provolone cheese and plenty of fried, crumbled bacon. Bake till done. As soon as removed from oven, spread with mayonnaise. Layer on shredded lettuce and diced tomatoes. Enjoy!

Miss Ruth Miller

Barbecue Chicken Pizza

4 lg. chicken breasts
1 c. chopped green peppers
½ c. chopped onions
1 c. chopped ham
16 oz. mozzarella cheese
mustard
½ c. barbecue sauce
1 c. pizza sauce

Prepare your favorite pizza dough. Place in a 10"x15" pan. Cut chicken in bite-sized pieces and sautä chicken and onions in oil until chicken is tender. Spread on thin layer of mustard on dough. Combine barbecue sauce and pizza and spread evenly over mustard. Bake at 375° approximately 20 minutes, then spread chicken, ham, peppers and cheese over dough and bake an additional 15 minutes or until pizza dough is lightly browned on bottom. A unique and different pizza. Delicious! Serves 8-10 people.

Mrs. Clifford Rhoda Herschberger

The secret of happy living is not doing what you like, but to like what you do.

Meats, Main Dishes

Mexican Pizza

pizza crust
1 pt. sour cream
8 oz. cream cheese

1 lb. hamburger
2 c. salsa or pizza sauce
taco seasoning

Mix your favorite pizza crust. Put in pan and bake. Mix sour cream and cream cheese, then spread on crust. Mix salsa or pizza sauce with browned hamburger; season with taco seasoning. Spread on cream mixture. Top with: lettuce, tomatoes, onions, peppers, cheese, chips, etc.

Mrs. Kenneth Marilyn Otto

Stuffed Pizza

1 lb. sausage
3⅓ c. Bisquick mix
¾ c. cold water
3 c. mozzarella cheese, divided

2 c. pizza sauce
mushrooms
bacon
pepperoni

Heat oven to 450°. Grease a 9"x13" pan. Fry sausage, drain. Mix Bisquick with water. (can use own biscuit recipe.) Divide dough in 2 parts, one slightly larger. Roll large portion in bottom of pan and up sides. Sprinkle with 1 cup cheese, cover with ¾ cup sauce. Add meat and toppings. Cover with 1½ cups of cheese. Press bottom and top crust together to seal. Make small slits in top of crust. Spread crust with remaining sauce and cheese. Bake 22-25 minutes or until crust is golden. Serves 8-10 people.

Mrs. Reuben Marilyn Schrock

Meats, Main Dishes

Taco Pizza

Crust:
1 Tbsp. yeast
1⅓ c. warm water
1 tsp. sugar
1½ Tbsp. vegetable oil
½ tsp. salt
¼ tsp. oregano
⅛ tsp. garlic salt
3½ c. flour

Toppings:
1½ c. sour cream, approx.
1½-2 lb. hamburger or meat of your choice
1 pkg. taco seasoning
salsa
lettuce
tomatoes
shredded cheese

Mix together yeast, warm water, and sugar. In a mixing bowl combine yeast mixture, salt, seasonings, oil and flour. Let rise. Roll out dough on a large, greased cookie sheet. Bake at 375° for 8-10 minutes. Let cool a bit. Spread sour cream on crust. Fry hamburger and add taco seasoning. Spread on top of sour cream. Top with rest of ingredients in order given.

Miss Jolene Marie Kauffman

Upside Down Pizza

1½ lb. hamburger or sausage, fried
1 sm. onion
2 c. pizza sauce
½ tsp. garlic salt
¼ tsp. oregano
8 oz. mozzarella cheese
2 eggs
1 Tbsp. vegetable oil
½ tsp. salt
1 tsp. baking powder
1 c. milk
1 c. flour

Brown meat and onion. Add pizza sauce, garlic salt and oregano, Put in a 9"x13" pan and top with cheese. Beat and add the rest of the ingredients and pour on top of meat mixture. Sprinkle ½ cup Parmesan cheese on top if you like. Bake at 350° for 30 minutes or until lightly browned.

Mrs. Ernest Sara Schrock

Meats, Main Dishes

Zucchini Pizza

Crust:
4 c. shredded zucchini
4 eggs, beaten
⅓ c. flour
½ tsp. oregano
½ tsp. basil
¼ tsp. salt

Topping:
1 lb. hamburger or sausage
½ c. mushrooms
⅔ c. chopped onions
½ c. chopped green peppers
2 c. shredded mozzarella cheese
1 tsp. oregano
½ tsp. basil
2-3 med. tomatoes, peeled and chopped

Mix zucchini, eggs, flour, oregano, basil and salt. Spread evenly over the bottom of a greased 9"x13" pan. Bake at 400° for 8-10 minutes. Remove from oven and reduce heat to 350°. Sprinkle zucchini crust with mushrooms, onions, meat, peppers, cheese, oregano and basil. Cover with tomatoes. Bake at 350° for 25-30 minutes, or until cheese is bubbly. Serves 12 people.

Mrs. LaVern Linda Miller

Pepperoni Rolls

pizza crust
pizza sauce
pepperoni
ham
chips
peppers
onions
cheese

Using your favorite pizza crust or bread recipe, roll out and cover with pizza sauce, pepperoni, ham, chips, peppers, onions, cheese, etc. Whatever your family prefers. Roll up and seal edges and bake at 350° till done. You have to be careful that they are not doughy in the center. A family favorite.

Miss Deborah Ann Miller

Meats, Main Dishes

Taco Shells and Dressing

Shells:
1 egg
1½ c. water
1 c. flour
½ c. cornmeal
½ tsp. salt
¼ c. vegetable oil

Dressing:
¾ c. sugar
⅓ c. vinegar
1 tsp. salt
2 tsp. mustard
1 c. vegetable oil
2 tsp. celery seed
1 Tbsp. chopped onions

Combine shell ingredients and fry like pancakes. Mix dressing ingredients and beat till thick. Top hot shells with mashed potatoes, browned hamburger, diced lettuce and dressing. Delicious. Serves 8 people.

Miss Susanna Schrock

Cookies, Bars

Bar Cookies 146	Just Right Chocolate Chip Cookies 135
Best Ever Granola Bars 155	Little Debbie Cookies 138
Blueberry Buckle 147	Little Debbie Cookies 139
Blueberry Crumb Bars 146	Little Debbie Oatmeal Cookies 139
Blueberry Crumb Bars 147	Marshmallow Brownies 148
Butterscotch Delight Cookies 131	M&M Dream Bars 158
Butterscotch Dessert Cookies 132	Moist Brownies 148
Butterscotch Meringue Bars 150	Molasses Bars 158
Chewy Chocolate Bars (unbaked) 151	Molasses Cookies 140
Chocolate Chip Bars 150	Molasses Crinkle Cookies 140
Chocolate Chip Bars 151	Monster Cookie Bars 159
Chocolate Chip Cookies 133	Mud Hen Bars 159
Chocolate Chip Cookies 134	Oatmeal Butterscotch Cookies 140
Chocolate Chip Pudding Cookies 134	Oatmeal Chocolate Chip Cookies 141
Chocolate Chip Treasure Cookies 135	Oatmeal Chocolate Chip Cookies 141
Chocolate Chip Zucchini Bars 151	Peach Bars 160
Chocolate Peanut Butter Bars 152	Peanut Butter Brownies 160
Chocolate Revel Bars 153	Peanut Butter Oat Bars 161
Chocolate Surprise Bars 153	Peanut Butter Squares 161
Classic Chocolate Chip Cookies 133	Rhubarb Custard Bars 162
Coffee Bars 154	Snickerdoodles 142
Cookie Dough Brownies 154	Soft Buttermilk Cookies 131
Cowboy Cookies 136	Sour Cream Raisin Bars 163
Donut Bars 155	Sour Cream Raisin Bars 164
Five-Chip Cookies 132	Sour Cream Raisin Bars 165
Frosted Apple Squares 145	Spicy Sugar Cookies 143
Frosted Banana Bars 145	Swiss Roll Bars 165
Ginger Snaps 137	Texas Brownies 149
Granola Bars 156	Toll House Chocolate Chip Cookies 136
Granola Bars 156	Twinkies 166
Granola Bars 156	Twix Candy Bars 166
Granola Bars 157	Vanishing Oatmeal Sandwich Cookies . . . 142
Granola Chews 157	Whoopie Pies 143
Granola Cookies 137	Whoopie Pies 144
Holstein Cookies 138	

Cookies, Bars

Soft Buttermilk Cookies

3 c. sugar
2 c. butter, softened
4 eggs, beaten
1 Tbsp. vanilla
2 c. buttermilk

2 tsp. soda
4 tsp. baking powder
1 tsp. salt
6 c. flour

Frosting:
1 c. butter, lightly browned
¾ c. hot water

1 Tbsp. vanilla
9 c. powdered sugar

Cream butter and sugar. Add eggs and vanilla. Mix soda with buttermilk and add to the rest of ingredients. Mix well with flour, baking powder and salt. Chill. Drop by teaspoonfuls on greased and floured cookie sheet. Bake at 400° for 10 minutes or until done. Do not overbake. Frost while still warm.

Miss Wilma Fern Schrock

Butterscotch Delight Cookies

2½ c. sugar
2½ c. brown sugar
2 c. butter
5 eggs
2 Tbsp. vanilla
⅓ c. milk

2½ tsp. baking powder
1 Tbsp. soda
1 tsp. salt
5½ c. flour
5 c. quick oats

Mix sugars and butter. Add eggs, vanilla, milk, dry ingredients and oatmeal. Form into balls and press down a bit onto greased cookie sheet. Bake at 350° for 15 minutes. Yield: 6 dozen cookies.

Note: Don't over bake. They will be hard instead of soft and chewy if baked too long.

Miss Edna Mae Schrock

Cookies, Bars

Butterscotch Dessert Cookies

1½ c. brown sugar
½ c. butter
2 eggs
1 tsp. vanilla
1 tsp. soda

½ tsp. baking powder
2½ c. flour
½ tsp. salt
1 c. sour cream

Frosting:
5 Tbsp. butter, browned
1 tsp. vanilla

3 c. powdered sugar
¼ c. hot water

Bake at 400°. Frost cookies while still warm.

Mrs. Joseph Lucinda Miller

Five-Chip Cookies

1 c. butter
1 c. peanut butter
1 c. sugar
⅔ c. brown sugar, packed
2 eggs
1 tsp. vanilla
½ tsp. salt
2 tsp. soda

2 c. flour
1 c. oatmeal
⅔ c. butterscotch chips
⅔ c. milk chocolate chips
⅔ c. semi-sweet chocolate chips
⅔ c. peanut butter chips
⅔ c. vanilla chips

Cream butter, peanut butter and sugars. Add eggs and vanilla. Beat well. Add dry ingredients gradually, then oatmeal and chips. Bake at 350° for 8-10 minutes.

Miss Melissa Joy Otto

Classic Chocolate Chip Cookies

1⅓ c. butter or margarine
1⅓ c. butter flavored Crisco
1½ c. sugar
1½ c. brown sugar
4 eggs
4 tsp. vanilla

6 c. flour
2 tsp. soda
2 tsp. salt
1⅓ c. instant vanilla pudding
3 c. chocolate chips

Beat shortenings together until fluffy. Add both sugars, beat until well blended. Beat in eggs and vanilla. Add dry ingredients, stirring well. Stir in chocolate chips. Bake at 350° for 14-18 minutes. Longer baking time yields a crunchier cookie; less time, a chewy one. Yield: 5-6 dozen.

Note: Margaret uses 1 cup less flour. SueEllen uses ¾ teaspoon salt.

Miss SueEllen Miller
Miss Margaret Jantzi
Miss Miriam Miller

Chocolate Chip Cookies

1½ c. butter
1 c. shortening
4 eggs
1½ c. sugar
1½ c. brown sugar
4 tsp. vanilla

7-8 oz. instant vanilla pudding
2 tsp. salt
2 tsp. soda
6 c. flour
1 (12 oz.) pkg. chocolate chips

Mix well and bake at 350°. Do not overbake! This is our favorite! Yield: approximately 9 dozen cookies, when using a small cookie scoop.

Mrs. Clifford Rhoda Herschberger

Chocolate Chip Cookies

4 eggs
3 c. lard
4 c. brown sugar
1 c. sugar
3 c. milk
2 Tbsp. soda
2 Tbsp. baking powder
4 Tbsp. vanilla
4 Tbsp. maple, walnut or lemon flavoring
4½ tsp. salt
12 c. flour, or more
1½ c. chocolate chips

Mix together first 4 ingredients till fluffy then add the rest in order given. Bake at 350° till done.

Mrs. Jacob Elsie Mishler

Chocolate Chip Pudding Cookies

2½ c. brown sugar
2½ c. sugar
2½ c. butter
8 eggs
10 c. flour
4 tsp. soda
1 Tbsp. salt
4 tsp. vanilla
2 Tbsp. hot water
1 c. vanilla instant pudding
3 c. chocolate chips

Cream together sugars, butter and eggs. Then add flour, soda, salt, vanilla and water and mix well. Last, add instant pudding and chocolate chips. Bake at 350° for 8-10 minutes, or until done. Yield: 8-10 dozen.

Miss Lori Miller

If you walk with the Lord, you'll never be out of step.

Cookies, Bars

Chocolate Chip Treasure Cookies

1½ c. graham cracker crumbs
½ c. all-purpose flour
2 tsp. baking powder
1 can sweetened condensed milk
½ c. butter, softened
1⅓ c. flaked coconut
1 (12 oz.) pkg. milk chocolate chips
1 c. chopped nuts

Beat sweetened condensed milk and butter till smooth. Add rest of ingredients. Drop by rounded tablespoonfuls onto ungreased cookie sheet. Bake 9-10 minutes at 350° until lightly browned. Store loosely covered at room temperature.

Miss Cheryl DeAnn Otto

Just Right Chocolate Chip Cookies

3 c. butter
2 c. Crisco
3 c. sugar
3 c. brown sugar
8 eggs
8 tsp. vanilla
2⅔ c. instant vanilla pudding
4 tsp. salt
4 tsp. soda
12 c. flour
2 (12 oz.) pkg. chocolate chips

Cream together butter, shortening and sugars. Add eggs and vanilla, beat well. Mix in instant vanilla pudding. Add dry ingredients and chocolate chips. Mix well and bake at 350° until lightly brown and let set on cookie sheet for a little bit before taking off. Do not overbake.

Note: Marjorie uses Blue Bonnet margarine and butter flavored Crisco.

Mrs. Jerry Esther Schrock
Mrs. Ray Marjorie Wagler

Cookies, Bars

Toll House Chocolate Chip Cookies

2 c. butter flavored Crisco
1½ c. sugar
1½ c. brown sugar
2 Tbsp. vanilla
4 eggs

5 c. flour
2 tsp. soda
1 tsp. salt
2 c. chocolate chips

Mix in order given. Bake at 375° for 9-11 minutes.

Mrs. Reuben Marilyn Schrock

Cowboy Cookies

2 c. sugar
2 c. brown sugar
2 c. Crisco
2 tsp. soda
2 tsp. baking powder
1 tsp. salt

5 c. flour
4 c. oatmeal
2 c. chocolate chips
4 eggs
1 tsp. vanilla

Mix dry ingredients with Crisco. Add eggs, vanilla and chocolate chips. Drop on cookie sheet and flatten. Bake at 350°. Yield: 14 dozen cookies.

Miss Susie Eicher

Fear knocked on the door.
Faith opened it, and there
was no one there.

Cookies, Bars

Ginger Snaps

3 c. butter, softened
5 c. sugar
4 eggs
¾ c. molasses
1 c. buttermilk
8 tsp. soda

4 tsp. cinnamon
1 Tbsp. cloves
1 Tbsp. ginger
2 tsp. baking powder
12 c. flour

Cream sugar and butter. Add eggs and molasses. Dissolve soda in buttermilk. Mix well then add the flour and spices that have been mixed together. Chill dough and roll into small balls. Dip in sugar and bake approximately 12 minutes at 350°. These get hard if stored where it is cool.

Mrs. Ernest Sara Schrock

Granola Cookies

3½ c. butter
1 c. peanut butter
2 c. sugar
3 c. brown sugar
8 eggs
4 tsp. vanilla
2 tsp. wonder flavor
2 tsp. maple flavor
2 tsp. vanilla flavor
2 tsp. butter flavor
2 tsp. nut flavor

2 c. wheat flour
6 c. flour
4 tsp. soda
4 tsp. salt
4 tsp. baking powder
8 c. oatmeal
8 c. rice crispies
4 c. coconut
1 c. sunflower seeds
1 c. butterscotch chips

Mix in order given. Bake at 350°. This makes a large batch of cookies.

Mrs. Samuel Rachel Chupp

Holstein Cookies

½ c. butter, softened
¼ c. sugar
¾ c. brown sugar
1 tsp. vanilla
2 eggs

2½ c. flour
1 (12 oz.) pkg. chocolate chips
1 box vanilla or chocolate
   instant pudding

To make the two color cookies, make one batch cookie dough with vanilla instant pudding and one with chocolate instant pudding. Then take a little of each dough and roll together. Roll into white sugar before baking at 350°.

Miss Dorcas Miller

Little Debbie Cookies

2¼ c. butter
4½ c. brown sugar
6 eggs
1 Tbsp. vanilla
3 c. flour

2¼ tsp. soda
1½ tsp. salt
1 Tbsp. cinnamon
6 c. oatmeal

Filling:
2 eggs, beaten
2 c. powdered sugar

1 tsp. vanilla
1½ c. Crisco

Cream together butter and brown sugar, then add eggs and vanilla. Mix the dry ingredients together then add to butter mixture. Mix well. Drop by teaspoonfuls onto greased cookie sheet and bake at 350° until done. Filling: Mix together eggs, powdered sugar and vanilla. Add Crisco and mix until smooth. Put filling between 2 cookies. Yield: approximately 30 double cookies.

Miss Edna Mae Schrock

Cookies, Bars

Little Debbie Oatmeal Cookies

4½ c. butter, softened
9 c. brown sugar
12 eggs
6 c. flour
1½ Tbsp. soda

1 Tbsp. salt
2 Tbsp. cinnamon
2 Tbsp. vanilla
12 c. oatmeal

Filling:
5 Tbsp. Perma Flo
1½ c. milk

2 c. Crisco
8 c. powdered sugar

Mix in order given. Refrigerate overnight. Bake at 350°. When cool, put filling between two cookies. Filling: Cook Perma Flo and milk, cool; add Crisco and powdered sugar. Yield: approximately 100 small filled cookies.

Miss Denise Ann Kauffman

Little Debbie Cookies

3 c. butter
6 c. brown sugar
8 eggs
1 tsp. vanilla
1 Tbsp. soda

2 tsp. salt
4 tsp. cinnamon
1 tsp. nutmeg
8 c. oatmeal
4½ c. flour

Filling:
4 egg whites
2 c. Crisco
6 c. powdered sugar

6 Tbsp. flour
6 Tbsp. milk

Bake cookies at 350°. Filling: Cream together Crisco and powdered sugar; add to beaten egg whites. Add flour and milk. Put filling between 2 cookies.

Mrs. Joseph Lucinda Miller

Cookies, Bars

Molasses Cookies

3 c. vegetable oil
4 c. brown sugar
4 eggs
1⅛ c. molasses
8 tsp. soda
4 tsp. cinnamon
4 tsp. ginger
2 tsp. cloves
2 tsp. salt
9 c. flour

Roll balls in sugar. Bake at 350° for 12-15 minutes.

Mrs. Isaac Daisy Troyer

Molasses Crinkle Cookies

1½ c. shortening or vegetable oil
2 c. brown sugar
2 eggs
½ tsp. salt
½ c. molasses
4 tsp. soda
4½ c. flour
1 tsp. cloves
2 tsp. cinnamon

Mix the ingredients together in order given. Dough may be chilled or used right away. Shape into balls, then roll in sugar. Bake at 350° until set, but not hard. Yield: 2 dozen.

Miss Lovina Eicher

Oatmeal Butterscotch Cookies

2 c. shortening
2 c. sugar
2 c. brown sugar
4 eggs
2 tsp. vanilla
2 tsp. soda
2 tsp. salt
2 tsp. baking powder
3½ c. flour
5 c. oatmeal
2 c. butterscotch chips

Mix together shortening, sugars, eggs and vanilla. Add dry ingredients and butterscotch chips; mix well. Bake on greased cookie sheet at 350° until golden brown. Let stand a little before taking off cookie sheet.

Mrs. Jerry Esther Schrock

Cookies, Bars

Oatmeal Chocolate Chip Cookies

4 c. butter or margarine
6 c. brown sugar, packed
2½ c. sugar
10 eggs
⅔ c. milk
3 Tbsp. vanilla

8¼ c. all-purpose flour
5 tsp. soda
2½ tsp. salt
12½ c. quick oats
10 c. chocolate chips
5 c. chopped nuts

Heat oven to 375°. Beat butter and sugars until creamy. Add eggs, milk and vanilla. Beat well. Add flour, baking soda and salt, mix well. Stir in oats, chocolate chips and nuts. Bake 9-10 minutes for chewy cookies, or 12-13 minutes for crisp cookies. Yield: 12-15 dozen cookies.

Note: You can add 1½ cup peanut butter and add M&M's to taste. We replace chocolate chips for M&M's.

Miss Miriam Miller

Oatmeal Chocolate Chip Cookies

2 c. butter
½ c. sugar
1½ c. brown sugar
1⅓ c. instant vanilla pudding
4 eggs

2 tsp. soda
2½ c. flour
7 c. oatmeal
3 c. chocolate chips

Cream sugars and butter. Add eggs and beat well. Add pudding mix, flour and soda. Then stir in oatmeal and chocolate chips. Roll in balls and flatten. Bake on ungreased cookie sheet at 350° until golden brown. Do not overbake.

Mrs. Howard Ellen Schrock

Cookies, Bars

Vanishing Oatmeal Sandwich Cookies

2 c. butter
2 c. brown sugar
½ c. sugar
4 eggs
2 tsp. vanilla

3 c. flour
2 tsp. soda
1 tsp. salt
1 tsp. cinnamon
6 c. quick oats

Filling:
½ c. butter
½ c. shortening
milk

1 tsp. vanilla
powdered sugar

Beat the butter and sugars until creamy. Add the eggs and vanilla; beat well. Combine flour, soda, salt and cinnamon and add to sugar mixture. Stir in quick oats last. Mix well. Drop on an ungreased cookie sheet. Bake at 350° for 10 minutes. Cool, then put 2 cookies together with filling. To make filling, cream the butter and shortening. Add vanilla and powdered sugar to your liking. Milk will make it thinner so you can add more powdered sugar if you wish. Yield: 4 dozen sandwich cookies.

Mrs. Dennis Marilyn Hershberger

Snickerdoodles

2 c. shortening
3 c. sugar
4 eggs
5½ c. sifted flour

4 tsp. cream of tartar
2 tsp. soda
1 tsp. salt

Mix together shortening, sugar and eggs. Sift together flour, cream of tartar, soda and salt. Mix with the creamed shortening. Chill dough. Roll into balls the size of small walnuts. Roll in mixture of 4 teaspoons cinnamon and ¼ cup sugar. Place 2" apart on ungreased cookie sheets. Bake until lightly browned but still soft. These cookies puff up at first, then flatten out with crinkled tops. Bake at 400° for 8-10 minutes. Yield: approximately 4 dozen cookies.

Miss Marilyn W. Miller

Cookies, Bars

Spicy Sugar Cookies

1½ c. butter
2 c. sugar
2 eggs
½ c. honey
¼ c. milk
2 tsp. vanilla

5¼ c. flour
1 Tbsp. soda
1½ tsp. salt
1½ tsp. nutmeg
2 tsp. cinnamon

Cream together butter and sugar. Blend in rest of ingredients. Chill. Form into balls and dip in milk and white sugar. Bake at 350°.

Mrs. Joe Laura Hershberger

Whoopie Pies

1½ c. butter
3 c. sugar
3 eggs
¾ c. cocoa
1 Tbsp. soda

1 tsp. salt
6 c. flour, or more
1½ c. sour milk
1½ c. hot water
1 Tbsp. vanilla

Filling:
½ c. Crisco
½ c. butter
2 c. powdered sugar, or more

1 egg
2 Tbsp. vanilla
2 Tbsp. milk

Cream butter and sugar. Beat in eggs. Add rest of ingredients. Bake at 350°.

Miss Esther Miller

Cookies, Bars

Whoopie Pies

1½ c. butter or margarine
3 c. sugar
3 eggs
1 Tbsp. vanilla
1½ c. cocoa

6 c. flour
1 Tbsp. salt
1 Tbsp. soda
1½ c. sour milk or buttermilk
1½ c. hot water, not boiling

Filling:
3 egg whites, beaten
1½ c. Crisco
5 Tbsp. milk

1 Tbsp. vanilla
3 c. powdered sugar

Cream together butter and sugar. Add well beaten eggs and vanilla. Mix flour, cocoa and salt together and add alternately with sour milk, to first ingredients. Dissolve soda in hot water and add to mixture. Beat well, drop by teaspoon on greased cookie sheet. Bake 8 minutes at 375°. Filling: Cream Crisco, by adding a little of the stiffly beaten egg whites at a time. Alternately add milk, powdered sugar and vanilla. Spread between 2 cookies. Yield: 42 double cookies.

Mrs. Ernie Freeda Yoder

Frosted Apple Squares

4 c. flour
½ c. butter
1 c. lard
1 Tbsp. sugar
1½ tsp. salt
1 egg, beaten
1 Tbsp. vinegar

½ c. water
8-10 apples
1½ c. sugar
pinch of salt
3 Tbsp. flour
cinnamon
nutmeg

Icing:
1 c. powdered sugar

3-4 Tbsp. milk

Make a crumb mixture with flour, shortening, sugar and salt. Add beaten egg, vinegar and water. Roll out and place half of dough on a 10"x17" cookie sheet. Peel apples and slice thinly. Mix sugar, salt, flour, cinnamon and nutmeg; sprinkle over apples. Dot with butter. Roll remaining dough for top crust. Bake at 375° for 40-45 minutes. Frost while hot with powdered sugar icing.

Miss Denise Ann Kauffman

Frosted Banana Bars

½ c. butter or margarine
2 c. sugar
3 eggs
1½ c. or 3 med. mashed bananas

1 tsp. vanilla
2 c. all-purpose flour
1 tsp. soda
pinch of salt

Frosting:
½ c. butter, softened
8 oz. cream cheese

4 c. powdered sugar
2 tsp. vanilla

In a mixing bowl cream butter and sugar. Beat in eggs, bananas, and vanilla. Combine flour, and soda. Add to creamed mixture, and mix well. Pour in a greased 10"x15" pan. Bake at 350° for 25 minutes. Cool. Frost.

Miss Martha Troyer

Cookies, Bars

Bar Cookies

2 c. flour
1 c. sugar
1 c. brown sugar
1 tsp. salt
1 tsp. baking powder
1 tsp. soda

2 c. oatmeal
1 c. vegetable oil
1 tsp. vanilla
3 eggs
1 c. chocolate chips

Mix first 6 ingredients; stir in oatmeal. Add vegetable oil and mix. Combine vanilla and eggs. Add chocolate chips and stir well. Press dough into one 12½"x16½" cookie sheet. Bake at 350° for 20-30 minutes.
Note: Add butterscotch and chocolate chips for a good flavor.

Miss Rachel W. Miller

Blueberry Crumb Bars

Crust:
2½ c. flour
½ c. sugar

1 c. butter, softened
¼ tsp. salt

Topping:
1 c. quick oats
1 c. brown sugar

¼ tsp. baking powder

Mix and press crust into a 10"x15" jelly-roll pan. Spread 1 quart blueberry pie filling over crust. Mix topping crumbs and spread evenly on pie filling. Mixture will be crumbly and filling will not be completely covered. Bake at 350° for 35-40 minutes.
Note: Other kinds of pie fillings may be used.

Miss Miriam Miller

Cookies, Bars

Blueberry Crumb Bars

3½ c. flour
¾ c. sugar
1½ c. butter
¼ tsp. salt
1 qt. blueberry pie filling
1½ c. oatmeal

1½ c. brown sugar
1½ c. flour
½ tsp. baking powder
¼ tsp. soda
¾ c. butter

Mix first 4 ingredients. Press into greased 12"x16" cookie sheet. Spread blueberry pie filling on top. Mix last 6 ingredients into crumbs and sprinkle on top of pie filling. Bake at 350° for 30 minutes. Delicious with ice cream.

Miss Sarah Mae Jantzi

Blueberry Buckle

¾ c. sugar
¼ c. shortening
1 egg
½ c. milk

2 c. flour
2 tsp. baking powder
½ tsp. salt
2 c. fresh blueberries, drained

Topping:
1½ c. sugar
1 c. flour

1½ tsp. cinnamon
¾ c. butter, softened

Mix sugar, shortening and egg thoroughly. Stir in milk. Blend dry ingredients and stir in. Fold in berries just until blended. Spread batter into greased 9"x13" cake pan. Topping: Mix topping mixture and spread over batter. Bake at 350° for 45-50 minutes. (We use frozen blueberries instead of fresh blueberries.

Miss Mary Edna Miller

Cookies, Bars

Marshmallow Brownies

¾ c. shortening
1⅓ c. sugar
3 eggs
1⅓ c. flour
½ tsp. baking powder

2 Tbsp. cocoa
⅓ tsp. salt
1½ tsp. vanilla
¾ c. chopped nuts

Icing:
¾ c. brown sugar
⅓ c. water
3 Tbsp. cocoa

4 Tbsp. butter
1½ tsp. vanilla
2 c. powdered sugar

Mix in order given, put in a small jelly-roll pan and bake at 350°. Take out of oven and cover with miniature marshmallows. Put back in oven for 3 minutes. Icing: Boil all ingredients except powdered sugar for 3 minutes. Let cool. Add powdered sugar.

Mrs. Kenneth Marilyn Otto

Moist Brownies

1¼ c. flour
½ tsp. soda
¼ tsp. salt
¾ c. sugar
½ c. margarine

2 Tbsp. water
1 tsp. vanilla
2 eggs, beaten
10 oz. chocolate chips

In small saucepan, combine sugar, margarine and water. Bring just to a boil. Remove from heat. Add 1 cup chocolate chips, then add beaten eggs, flour, salt, soda and rest of chocolate chips. Put in a 9"x13" pan. Bake at 350° for approximately 20 minutes.

Miss Bethany Kay Otto

Texas Brownies

2 c. all-purpose flour
2 c. sugar
½ c. butter or margarine
½ c. shortening
1 c. strong brewed coffee or water

¼ c. dark cocoa
½ c. buttermilk
2 eggs
1 tsp. soda
1 tsp. vanilla

Frosting:
½ c. butter
2 Tbsp. dark cocoa
¼ c. milk

3½ c. powdered sugar
1 tsp. vanilla

In large mixing bowl, combine the flour and sugar. In heavy saucepan, combine butter, shortening, coffee or water and cocoa. Stir and heat to boiling. Pour boiling mixture over the flour and sugar in the bowl. Add the buttermilk, eggs, soda and vanilla. Mix well. Pour in well buttered 11"x17½" jelly-roll pan. Bake at 400° for 20 minutes. Frosting: While brownies bake prepare the frosting. In a saucepan, combine butter, cocoa and milk. Heat to boiling, stirring constantly. Mix in powdered sugar and vanilla. Pour warm frosting over brownies, spread. Cool and cut. Yield: 48 bars.

Note: If you don't have buttermilk, substitute 2 teaspoons vinegar or lemon juice, mixed into ½ cup milk.

Mrs. Ernie Freeda Yoder

When you speak, always remember that God is one of your hearers.

Butterscotch Meringue Bars

2¼ c. butter
2 c. brown sugar
1 Tbsp. vanilla
6 c. flour
1 tsp. salt

9 egg yolks
¾ tsp. soda
12 oz. butterscotch chips
3 c. coconut
1½ c. nuts

Topping:
9 egg whites, beaten stiff

2 c. brown sugar

Mix and press into 2 cookie sheets. Sprinkle butterscotch chips, coconut and nuts over each pan. Spread topping mixture over top. Bake at 350° for 35-40 minutes.
Note: Can use chocolate chips instead of butterscotch.

Miss Deborah Ann Miller

Chocolate Chip Bars

½ c. butter, melted
2 c. sugar
4 eggs
2 c. flour

2 tsp. baking powder
1 tsp. vanilla
1½ tsp. salt
2 c. chocolate chips

Mix together, then spread on greased cookie sheet. Bake at 350° for 25 minutes. Do not over bake.
Note: Sometimes we like to garnish with marshmallows and coconut. When removing from oven, put a layer of mini marshmallows over bars and return to oven for several minutes until they are easy to spread, using a knife (dipped in water) spread marshmallows and then sprinkle with the amount of coconut you desire.

Mrs. Ernest Sara Schrock

Cookies, Bars

Chocolate Chip Bars

1 c. butter, melted
½ c. vegetable oil
1½ c. brown sugar
1½ c. sugar
4 eggs
2 tsp. salt
2 tsp. baking powder
4½ c. flour
1 pkg. chocolate chips

Mix well in order given Put in cookie sheet. Bake at 350°-375° for 20-25 minutes until golden brown. Serves 24 people.

Mrs. Ernest Mary Ellen Miller

Chewy Chocolate Bars (unbaked)

1 c. peanut butter
3 c. unsweetened coconut
⅔ c. cocoa powder or melted chocolate
⅔ c. honey
1 tsp. salt
½ tsp. vanilla
½ c. flax meal
1 c. raisins
½ c. raw sunflower seeds

Mix and enjoy. Healthy energy bars. Use an 8"x8" pan.

Mrs. Kenneth Leanna Kauffman

Chocolate Chip Zucchini Bars

½ c. butter
½ c. vegetable oil
1¾ c. sugar
2 eggs
1 tsp. vanilla
½ c. sour milk
2½ c. flour
1 tsp. soda
½ tsp. salt
½ tsp. cinnamon
2 c. shredded zucchini
¼ c. cocoa
¾ c. chocolate chips, divided
¼ c. nuts

Cream butter, oil and sugar. Add eggs, vanilla and milk, then dry ingredients. Stir in zucchini and ¼ cup chocolate chips. Spread in greased 11"x17" pan. Sprinkle nuts and remaining ½ cup chocolate chips on top of batter. Bake at 350° for 40-45 minutes.

Miss Marietta W. Miller

Chocolate Peanut Butter Bars

¾ c. butter
¾ c. sugar
¾ c. brown sugar
2 eggs
½ c. peanut butter
¾ tsp. vanilla

¾ tsp. soda
1⅓ tsp. salt
1½ c. flour
1½ c. quick oats
1½ c. chocolate chips

Frosting:
1½ c. powdered sugar
½ c. peanut butter

6-8 Tbsp. milk

Cream butter and sugars. Add eggs, peanut butter, vanilla and dry ingredients. Pour batter into greased cookie sheet and bake at 350° for 25 minutes. Arrange 1½ cup chocolate chips over top to melt as soon as taken out of oven. Spread around evenly. For Frosting: Mix powdered sugar, peanut butter and milk. Drizzle this mixture over the top and swirl slightly. If you swirl too much it will look like chocolate frosting. Cut bars while slightly warm.

Miss Wilma Fern Schrock

Today I will let go and let God,
and then I will be on the path
of Joy and Peace.

Cookies, Bars

Chocolate Revel Bars

Dough:
1 c. butter
2 c. brown sugar
2 eggs
2 tsp. vanilla

2½ c. flour
1 tsp. soda
1 tsp. salt
3 c. oatmeal

Filling:
2 c. chocolate chips
1 c. milk

2 Tbsp. instant vanilla pudding
1 c. chopped nuts, opt.

Mix dough and press two-third of it in a greased 10"x15" pan. Filling: Beat together milk and instant vanilla pudding, bring to boiling and melt chocolate chips Add nuts, and spread on dough. Dot with remaining crumbs. Bake at 350° for approximately 20 minutes. Do not overbake.

Note: For filling you can substitute 1 can sweetened condensed milk, 2 tablespoons butter and 2 cups chocolate chips.

Mrs. Vernon Rachel Herschberger

Chocolate Surprise Bars

1½ c. brown sugar
6 c. oatmeal
1½ c. butter

2¾ c. chocolate chips
1½ c. peanut butter

Mix first 3 ingredients into crumbs. Press into 12"x16" cookie sheet. Bake at 350° for 15-20 minutes. Meanwhile melt chocolate chips with peanut butter. Spread over oatmeal crust while hot. Let cool to harden chocolate.

Miss Sarah Mae Jantzi

Cookies, Bars

Coffee Bars

2 eggs
2 c. brown sugar
1½ c. sugar
1 c. warm coffee
3 c. flour

1 c. vegetable oil
1 tsp. soda
1 tsp. vanilla
1 tsp. salt

Mix all ingredients together and spread onto a 10"x15" cookie sheet. Top with nuts and chocolate chips. Bake at 350° for 20-25 minutes.
Note: I like putting glaze on top when still warm.

Mrs. Clifford Rhoda Herschberger

Cookie Dough Brownies

1 c. vegetable oil
4 eggs
2 c. sugar
2 tsp. vanilla

1½ c. flour
½ c. cocoa
½ tsp. salt

Filling:
½ c. butter
¼ c. sugar
1 tsp. vanilla

½ c. brown sugar
2 Tbsp. milk
1 c. flour

Icing:
1 c. chocolate chips

¼ c. peanut butter

Pour into greased 9"x13" pan, and bake for 30 minutes at 350° or until done. Do not overbake. Cool completely. Filling: Mix all but flour well. Add flour, spread over brownies. Chill until firm. Icing: Melt chocolate chips and peanut butter; spread over filling.

Miss Melissa Joy Otto

Cookies, Bars

Donut Bars

1¾ c. warm water
1½ Tbsp. yeast
5 c. donut mix

Cinnamon/Sugar:
½ c. sugar
1 tsp. cinnamon

Frosting:
½ c. butter
1 c. brown sugar
¼ c. milk
1 tsp. vanilla
⅛ tsp. salt
2 c. powdered sugar

Mix water and yeast. Let rise a bit, then add donut mix. Spread in a large greased cookie sheet. Sprinkle cinnamon/sugar mixture on top of dough. Let rise 45 minutes. Bake at 350° till done. Frosting: Melt butter, brown sugar and milk. Cook for 2 minutes. Add vanilla, salt and powdered sugar. If too stiff, add more milk. Spread on top of bars while still warm.

Mrs. Gerald Betty Kauffman

Best Ever Granola Bars

4½ c. Rice Krispies
5 c. quick oats
1 c. coconut
1 pkg. graham crackers, crushed
1½ c. chocolate chips
1 c. raisins, opt.
1 c. butter, scant
¼ c. vegetable oil
¼ c. honey
½ c. peanut butter
1 tsp. vanilla
2 (10 oz.) pkg. mini marshmallows

In a large greased bowl, mix all the dry ingredients together. Melt butter over low heat; add oil, honey, peanut butter and vanilla; melt all together. Add marshmallows and stir until melted. Pour immediately over dry ingredients in bowl and mix. Pat into a well-greased 10"x15" cookie sheet. Cut into bars. Yield: 32 bars.

Mrs. Eldon Ray Denise Miller

Granola Bars

1 c. brown sugar
⅔ c. peanut butter
½ c. light corn syrup
½ c. butter, melted
2 tsp. vanilla

3 c. oatmeal
½ c. coconut
⅓ c. wheat germ
1 c. chocolate chips or raisins

Cream first 5 ingredients. Add the rest and mix well. Press into a 9"x13" pan. Bake at 350° for 20 minutes. For a sweet treat, eat with cappuccino.
Note: If I make these for supper, I have to first put away enough for lunches the next day or they'll be gone by then.

Mrs. Ernest Ray Inez Miller

Granola Bars

1½ lb. marshmallows
¼ c. butter
¼ c. vegetable oil
¼ c. honey
¼ c. peanut butter

9½ c. Rice Krispies
5 c. oatmeal
1½ c. raisins, opt.
1 c. chocolate chips

Melt butter and oil on low heat, add marshmallows and stir till melted. Turn off heat, add honey and peanut butter. In a large bowl, mix the remaining ingredients. Make a well in dry ingredients and pour in marshmallows, stir together. Spread on wax paper. Press and cool.

Mrs. Joe Laura Hershberger

Granola Bars

20 oz. marshmallows
¼ c. vegetable oil
¼ c. peanut butter
¾ c. butter

¼ c. honey
5 c. quick oats
4½ c. Rice Krispies
1 pkg. graham crackers, crushed

Melt the first five ingredients together. Remove from heat and add dry ingredients. Stir well. Spread on a greased 13"x18" cookie sheet.

Miss Maria Grace Schrock

Granola Bars

½ c. brown sugar
1 c. Karo
pinch of salt
2 c. peanut butter

2 c. quick oats
2 c. Rice Krispies
1 c. chocolate chips

Combine brown sugar, Karo and salt in a kettle. Bring to a boil. Remove from heat and stir in peanut butter, quick oats, Rice Krispies and chocolate chips. Press into two 9"x13" pans. Chill and cut into bars. Serves 20 people.

Note: Can add M&M's on top instead of mixing in chocolate chips. Very good!

Miss Rosetta Kay Wagler

Granola Chews

½ c. brown sugar
1 Tbsp. water
¼ c. molasses or honey

½ c. chunky peanut butter
2½ c. granola

Combine brown sugar, water and molasses in a saucepan. Heat until bubbles form around the edge of the pan, then add peanut butter. Next add granola. If I have granola that's old or don't like, I use that. Mix carefully then press into a greased 9"x9" pan.

Miss Verna Kay Miller

M&M Dream Bars

2 c. oatmeal
1½ c. flour
1 tsp. soda
1 c. butter or margarine

1 c. brown sugar
1 can sweetened condensed milk
½ c. peanut butter
1 c. M&M's

Mix oatmeal, flour, soda, margarine and brown sugar until coarse. Reserve 1 cup crumbs. Press remaining mixture on cookie sheet. Bake 12 minutes at 375°. Don't cool. Mix sweetened condensed milk with peanut butter. Spread on crust. Top with crumbs and M&M's. Bake for 15 minutes. Enjoy!

Miss Rosetta Kay Wagler

Molasses Bars

14 c. Seal of Minnesota flour
4 c. sugar
1 tsp. salt
1 lb. margarine, room temp.
1 pt. molasses

5 eggs, beaten
3 Tbsp. soda
½ c. boiling water
2 sm. bags chocolate chips

In a 13-quart stainless steel mixing bowl, put in flour, sugar and salt. Mix well. Work in margarine with your hands. Make a well in the mixture and add molasses, eggs and hot water, which has the soda mixed into and chocolate chips. Shape into a 1" thick roll, the length of the cookie sheet. Flatten with fingers till ½" thick and 1¾" wide. Brush top with beaten egg for a glaze. Bake at 350° for 13 minutes. Cut with spatula, then let set on pan 2 minutes before removing. Yield: 7-8 dozen.

Mrs. Ernie Freeda Yoder

Monster Cookie Bars

½ c. butter, melted
1½ c. peanut butter
¾ c. sugar
1¼ c. brown sugar
3 eggs
4 c. oatmeal

1 tsp. Karo
2 tsp. soda
¾ c. M&M's
1½ c. chocolate chips
1 tsp. vanilla

Mix in order given and put on a cookie sheet. Bake at 350° for 15-20 minutes.

Miss Rosetta Kay Wagler

Mud Hen Bars

½ c. shortening
1 c. sugar
1 egg
2 eggs, separated
1½ c. flour
¼ tsp. salt

1 tsp. baking powder
1 c. brown sugar
1 c. chocolate chips
1 c. mini marshmallows
1 c. nuts

Cream shortening and sugar. Beat in whole egg and two egg yolks. Sift flour, baking powder and salt together. Combine the two mixtures, blend thoroughly. Spread batter in 9"x13" pan. Sprinkle nuts, chocolate chips and marshmallows over the batter. Beat the 2 egg whites until stiff. Fold in brown sugar and spread over top of batter. Preheat oven to 350° and bake for 30-40 minutes.

Miss Edna Mae Schrock

Peach Bars

Crust:
1¼ c. butter, softened
¾ c. sugar
¾ tsp. vanilla

pinch of salt
3 c. flour
1 c. nuts, opt.

Filling:
16 oz. cream cheese
1½ c. sugar
3 eggs

1½ tsp. vanilla
4½-5 c. fresh, chopped peaches

Mix crust ingredients and put in large cookie sheet. Bake at 325° for 15-20 minutes. Mix filling and spread on top of crust. Sprinkle cinnamon on top of filling. Bake at 375° for 25-30 minutes.

Mrs. Gerald Betty Kauffman

Peanut Butter Brownies

2 c. sugar
1½ c. brown sugar
½ c. butter
1 c. peanut butter
6 eggs
1 tsp. vanilla

4 c. flour
1½ tsp. baking powder
1½ tsp. salt
½ c. nuts, opt.
1 c. chocolate chips, for top

Cream sugars, butter and peanut butter. Add eggs and vanilla, then add dry ingredients and mix well. Press into 2 cookie sheets. Sprinkle chocolate chips over top and put in oven for 1 minute or till chocolate chips are soft. Take a knife and swirl chocolate chips then put back in oven. Bake at 325° for 20 minutes.

Mrs. Wilbur Wilma Miller

Peanut Butter Oat Bars

⅔ c. butter, melted
¼ c. peanut butter
1 c. brown sugar, packed

¼ c. light corn syrup
¼ tsp. vanilla
4 c. quick oats

Topping:
1 c. milk chocolate chips
½ c. butterscotch chips

⅓ c. peanut butter

In a mixing bowl combine the butter, peanut butter, brown sugar, corn syrup and vanilla; gradually stir in oats. Press into a greased 9"x13" pan. Bake at 400° for 12-14 minutes or until edges are golden brown. Cool. Topping: Melt chips and peanut butter in a saucepan over low heat. Stir until blended; spread over warm bars. Cool completely; refrigerate for 2-3 hours before cutting.
Note: This recipe does not contain flour.

Miss SueEllen Miller

Peanut Butter Squares

1 c. butter, melted
1¾ c. powdered sugar
1¾ c. peanut butter

1⅔ c. or 1 pkg. crushed graham crackers
1 (12 oz.) pkg. chocolate chips

Mix first 3 ingredients, add crushed crackers. Pat and press in 9"x13" pan. Put in freezer 10 minutes. Melt chocolate chips and pour over peanut butter mixture. Cool and cut in small squares. Delicious!

Miss Lyndora Kay Miller

Rhubarb Custard Bars

Crust:
1 c. all-purpose flour
¼ c. brown sugar
1 c. butter

Filling:
1½ c. sugar
7 Tbsp. all-purpose flour
3 eggs, beaten
½ c. milk
½ c. cream
5 c. finely chopped fresh or frozen rhubarb

Topping:
8 oz. cream cheese
½ tsp. salt
½ c. sugar
8 oz. Cool Whip

Crust: Make crumbs like pie dough and press into greased 9"x13" pan. Bake at 350° for 10 minutes. Filling: Mix and pour over hot crust. Bake at 350° for 40-45 minutes or until custard is set. Topping: Mix and spread over top of cooled custard.

Mrs. David Verda Miller

Every sunrise is a new message from God,
And every sunset – His signature.

Sour Cream Raisin Bars

Crumbs:
1 c. butter
1 c. brown sugar
2 c. flour
2 c. quick oats

1 tsp. soda
1 tsp. baking powder
¼ tsp. salt

Filling:
4 egg yolks
2 c. sour cream
1½ c. raisins

1 c. sugar
1 Tbsp. cornstarch

Mix crumb ingredients together; mixture will be crumbly. Set aside 2 cup crumbs. Put the rest in a 9"x13" pan. Bake at 350° for 15 minutes or until light brown. Filling: Combine ingredients in a saucepan. Bring to a boil and cook for 3 minutes stirring constantly. Pour over baked crust. Sprinkle 2 cups of crumbs over filling. Return to top oven shelf for 15 minutes or until light brown. Serves 16 people.

Miss Cathy Wagler

Cookies, Bars

Sour Cream Raisin Bars

Crumbs:
1¾ c. oatmeal
1¾ c. flour
½ c. brown sugar
½ c. sugar
1 c. butter

1 tsp. soda
1 tsp. baking powder
¼ tsp. salt
1 tsp. vanilla

Filling:
4 egg yolks
1 Tbsp. cornstarch or
  2 Tbsp. flour

1 c. sugar
1 c. raisins
2 c. sour cream

Mix crumbs together then pat two-third of the crumbs in a 9"x13" pan. Bake 15 minutes. (Not longer or they'll be hard.) Cool. Put filling together and bring to a boil, stirring often. Pour filling over baked crumbs and cover with remaining crumbs. Bake at 350° for 20 minutes.

Miss SueEllen Miller

Sour Cream Raisin Bars

- 2 c. raisins
- 1 c. water
- 1 c. brown sugar
- 1 c. butter or ½ butter and ½ lard
- 1 tsp. soda
- 1¾ c. flour
- 1½ c. quick oats
- 1½ c. sour cream
- 1 c. sugar
- 3 egg yolks or 2 whole eggs
- 2½ Tbsp. Perma Flo
- 1 tsp. vanilla

Cook raisins in water for 10 minutes. Cool and drain. Mix next 5 ingredients. Put half of crumbs in the bottom of a 9"x13" pan and bake 7 minutes at 350°. In medium saucepan heat sour cream, sugar, eggs and Perma Flo. Stir constantly until thick and pudding-like. Then add vanilla and raisins. Spoon onto baked crust and sprinkle remaining crumbs on top. Bake at 350° for 30 minutes.

Note: Shredded apples may be substituted for cooked raisins and you have delicious apple bars. If you have milk that has gone sour, it works well for this recipe instead of sour cream. I use up to 2 cups of sour milk.

Mrs. Samuel Rachel Chupp

Swiss Roll Bars

- 8 oz. cream cheese
- 1 c. powdered sugar
- 1 c. marshmallow creme
- 8 oz. Cool Whip
- ½ c. butter
- 12 oz. chocolate chips

Bake a chocolate cake on a cookie sheet. Your favorite, or use a cake mix. Beat cream cheese and powdered sugar, add marshmallow creme and stir, then add Cool Whip. Spread onto cooled cake. Melt together butter and chocolate chips, stir well. Spread evenly onto filling. Serves 20-24 people.

Mrs. William Miriam Yoder

Cookies, Bars

Twinkies

1 box yellow cake mix
1 box instant vanilla pudding
½ c. vegetable oil

1 c. water
4 eggs, beaten

Filling:
3 egg whites, beaten
1 Tbsp. vanilla
1½ c. Crisco

3 Tbsp. flour
3 Tbsp. milk
4 c. powdered sugar

Mix everything together and put into 2 well greased 10"x15" pans. Bake at 350° for 20 minutes. Cool. Frost one sheet pan. Flip other one on top of frosted one. Cut and put in tight container. Filling: Beat egg whites till stiff, add vanilla, milk and sugar. Cream shortening and add to mixture.
Note: You may need to add more powdered sugar to filling.

Miss Gloria Faith Schrock

Twix Candy Bars

club crackers
½ c. margarine
1 c. graham cracker, crumbs
¾ c. brown sugar

½ c. sugar
⅓ c. milk
1 c. chocolate chips
¾ c. peanut butter

Line a 9"x13" pan with crackers. Melt together margarine, graham crackers, sugar and milk. Cook 5 minutes. Pour over club crackers. Add another layer of club crackers. Melt chocolate chips and peanut butter. Spread on top of crackers. Cool and cut in bars. Yield: 24-1½"x 3" bars.

Miss Lyndora Kay Miller

Cakes Frostings

Cakes, Frostings

Angel Food Cake 169	Homemade Chocolate Cake 174
Apple Cake 169	Hot Fudge Sundae Cake 179
Best-Ever Chocolate Cake 171	Hot Sauce for Apple Cake 169
Brown Sugar Frosting (for maple twists) . . 188	Hummingbird Cake 179
Buttermilk Cake 170	Lava Cake 180
Buttermilk Chocolate Cake 171	Lazy Wife Cake 180
Butter Pecan Cake with Icing 172	Mahogany Cake 181
Caramel Icing 188	Maple Nut Angel Food Cake 182
Chocolate Bean Cake (gluten free) 172	Mint Chocolate Cake 174
Chocolate Cake 173	Mint Chocolate Cake 175
Chocolate Frosting 189	Oatmeal Cake 183
Chocolate One Minute Frosting 189	Oatmeal Cake 184
Chocolate Snack Cake 173	Peanut Butter Cake 184
Coco Cola Cake 175	Peanut Butter Cake 185
Cookies and Cream Cake 176	Pumpkin Tasty Cake 185
Cowboy Cake 176	Raw Apple Cake 170
Creamy Butter Frosting 189	Shoo-Fly Cake 186
Decorating Frosting 190	Strawberry Heart Cake 186
Fast Fixing Fruit Cake 177	Strawberry Shortcake 187
Gingerbread Cake 177	Texas Sheet Cake 187
Graham Streusel Cake 178	Zucchini Chocolate Cake 188
Ho-Ho Cake 178	

Angel Food Cake

2 c. egg whites
pinch of salt
¾ tsp. cream of tartar
¾ c. sugar

1 tsp. vanilla
1 c. flour
1 c. sugar
¼ c. Jell-O

Have egg whites at room temperature. Beat egg whites, salt, and cream of tartar together until stiff adding ¾ cup sugar a little at a time while beating. Sift together flour and 1 cup sugar 3 times. Fold in vanilla, Jell-O and sifted flour and sugar a little at a time with a scraper. Put in angel food pan. Bake at 350° for 45 minutes.

Mrs. Ray Marjorie Wagler

Apple Cake

3 c. shredded apples
1½ c. sugar
2 eggs

1½ c. flour
2¼ tsp. soda

Mix apples with sugar. Set aside until dissolved. Add eggs and beat well. Add flour and soda. Pour into 9"x13" cake pan and bake at 350° until done.

Miss Susie Eicher
Miss Margaret Jantzi

Hot Sauce for Apple Cake

¾ c. brown sugar
¾ c. sugar
3 Tbsp. flour

1½ c. water
⅓ c. butter
½ tsp. vanilla

Mix sugars and flour. Add water and butter. Bring to a boil while stirring constantly. Boil until thickened and pour on warm cake.

Miss Susie Eicher

Cakes, Frostings

Raw Apple Cake

2 eggs
½ c. vegetable oil
2 c. sugar
2 tsp. vanilla
2 c. flour

2 tsp. cinnamon
1 tsp. salt
2 tsp. soda
4 c. shredded apples

Crumbs:
1 Tbsp. butter, melted
2 Tbsp. flour

½ c. brown sugar
2 tsp. cinnamon

Combine eggs and oil. Beat until foamy. Add sugar and beat. Mix in dry ingredients. Add apples last. Put in a 9"x13" pan. Sprinkle crumbs on top. Bake at 350° for 45 minutes.

Mrs. Joe Laura Hershberger

Buttermilk Cake

3 c. flour
2 c. sugar
½ tsp. salt
¾ c. butter or lard

2 eggs
1½ c. buttermilk
1 tsp. soda
1 tsp. cinnamon

Mix flour, sugar, salt and butter. Set aside 1 cup of crumbs. To the rest add eggs, buttermilk, soda and cinnamon. Mix well. Pour in a 9"x13" pan. Spread the cup of crumbs on top. Bake at 350° for approximately 40 minutes.

Mrs. Wilbur Wilma Miller

Best-Ever Chocolate Cake

3 c. flour
2 c. sugar
6 Tbsp. cocoa
2 tsp. soda
1 tsp. salt

2 c. water
⅔ c. vegetable oil
2 tsp. white vinegar
2 tsp. vanilla

Fluffy Chocolate Frosting:
1 c. cold milk
1 pkg. instant chocolate pudding mix

8 oz. frozen whipped topping, thawed

Combine the first 5 ingredients. Add the water, oil, vinegar and vanilla. Beat for 1 minute. Pour into a greased 9"x13" baking pan. Bake at 350° for 40-45 minutes. Cool. Frosting: Beat the milk and pudding mix for 2 minutes. Beat in whipped topping. Spread over cake.

Note: This cake does not contain eggs.

Mrs. Delbert Martha Schrock

Buttermilk Chocolate Cake

2½ c. flour
2 c. sugar
1 tsp. baking powder
2 tsp. soda
½ tsp. salt

½ c. cocoa
1 c. vegetable oil
2 eggs
1 c. buttermilk

Mix dry ingredients. Stir in oil, eggs, buttermilk, and water, mixing after each wet ingredient. Last of all, beat with a wire whip. Pour batter into a greased 9"x13" cake pan. Bake at 350° for 45 minutes.

Note: A substitute for buttermilk is 1 tablespoon vinegar mixed with 1 cup milk.

Miss Rachel W. Miller

Cakes, Frostings

Butter Pecan Cake with Icing

butter pecan cake mix
8 oz. cream cheese
¾ c. brown sugar
8 oz. whipped topping

¼ c. margarine
1½ c. brown sugar
1 c. sour cream

Mix cake as directed, then bake and let cool. Mix cream cheese and ¾ cup brown sugar. Then add whipped topping and put on cake. Melt the butter and 1½ cup brown sugar, but do not boil. Add sour cream to this, let cool and put on top and enjoy.
Note: This can be baked in round pans, or jelly-roll pan, however you wish.

Mrs. Kenneth Marilyn Otto

Chocolate Bean Cake (gluten free)

1½ c. cooked beans, pinto or black
5 eggs, divided
1 Tbsp. vanilla
½ tsp. salt

6 Tbsp. butter
1 tsp. stevia powder, scant
6 Tbsp. baking powder
½ tsp. soda
1 Tbsp. water

Frosting:
4 oz. cream cheese, softened
8 oz. Cool Whip

stevia

Rinse and drain cooked beans. Mash beans with potato masher or blender. Mix beans, 3 eggs, vanilla and salt. Blend until smooth. In a mixing bowl mix butter and stevia, then add last 2 eggs, beat until smooth. Add remaining four ingredients and bean mixture. Beat 2 minutes. Bake in a 9"x 9" pan at 350° for 30 minutes or until toothpick comes out clean. Do not go by finger testing or tapping. It will not feel done when it is. Frosting: Mix and spread on cake.

Miss Verna Kay Miller

Cakes, Frostings

Chocolate Cake

2 c. flour
2 c. sugar
⅔ c. cocoa
2 tsp. soda
2 tsp. baking powder
½ tsp. salt

2 eggs
1 c. milk
⅔ c. vegetable oil
1 tsp. vanilla
1 c. brewed coffee

Mix dry ingredients together. Add rest of ingredients and stir well. Bake at 350° till done.

Mrs. Leroy Barbara Weaver

Chocolate Snack Cake

3 c. flour
2 c. sugar
5 Tbsp. cocoa
1 tsp. salt
2 tsp. baking powder

½ tsp. soda
1 c. vegetable oil
2 c. milk or water
1 tsp. vanilla

Mix all together at once. Beat 100-150 beats. Bake at 350° for 20 minutes in half-sheet pan.

Miss Sharon Miller

If your knees knock, kneel on them.

Cakes, Frostings

Homemade Chocolate Cake

3 c. flour
2 c. sugar
⅓ c. cocoa
2 tsp. soda
1 tsp. salt

2 c. water
¾ c. vegetable oil
2 tsp. vanilla
2 tsp. vinegar

Frosting:
3 oz. cream cheese, softened
¼ c. butter, softened
2 c. powdered sugar
⅓ c. cocoa

dash of salt
3 Tbsp. milk
½ tsp. vanilla

In a mixing bowl combine first 5 ingredients. Add the water, oil, vanilla and vinegar. Mix well. Batter will be thin. Pour into a greased 9"x13" pan. Bake at 350° for 25-30 minutes or until toothpick comes out clean. Cool before serving. Serves 18-20 people.

Mrs. William Miriam Yoder

Mint Chocolate Cake

1 chocolate cake mix

Frosting:
½ c. butter, softened
2 c. powdered sugar
1 Tbsp. water

½ tsp. peppermint extract
3 drops green food coloring

Topping:
1½ c. milk chocolate chips
6 Tbsp. butter, softened

¼ tsp. peppermint extract

Prepare cake batter according to package directions. Pour into a greased 10"x15" baking pan. Bake at 350° for 25-30 minutes. Cool. Combine the frosting ingredients until smooth. Spread over cooled cake. Topping: Melt chocolate chips and butter, stir in extract. Spread over frosting. Refrigerate until set.

Miss Marilyn Schrock

Cakes, Frostings

Mint Chocolate Cake

1 chocolate cake mix

Mint Frosting:
½ c. butter, softened
3 c. powdered sugar
1 Tbsp. milk, or as needed
1 tsp. peppermint flavoring or
    4-6 drops peppermint oil
green food coloring

Chocolate Topping:
½ c. butter
1 lb. chocolate chips

Put a chocolate cake in a 12"x17" sheet cake pan. Bake at 350°. Cool. Chocolate Topping: Melt together on low heat and spread on top of mint frosting. Put mint frosting on cooled cake, then add chocolate topping.

Miss Kristina Wagler

Coca Cola Cake

2 c. sugar
1 c. Coca Cola, classic
½ c. shortening
2 eggs
1 tsp. soda
2 c. flour
⅓ c. butter
¼ c. cocoa
½ c. buttermilk
1 tsp. vanilla

Frosting:
⅓ c. butter
3 Tbsp. cocoa
⅓ c. Coca Cola, classic
1 c. chopped pecans
1 c. marshmallows
1 lb. powdered sugar

Sift flour and sugar. In a saucepan blend Coca Cola, butter, shortening and cocoa together, bring to a boil. Remove from heat; add the flour mixture and eggs. Beat with mixer until well blended. Add buttermilk, soda and vanilla. Mix well. Pour in 9"x13" pan. Bake at 350° for 40 minutes. Frosting: In saucepan blend butter, Coca Cola and cocoa. Bring to a boil. Remove from heat and add marshmallows, nuts and powdered sugar. If too thick, add more Coca Cola.

Miss Verna Kay Miller

Cakes, Frostings

Cookies and Cream Cake

1 white cake mix
½ c. cookies and cream instant pudding
4 eggs, beaten
½ c. vegetable oil
1 c. water
½ c. crushed oreo cookies

Filling:
½ c. cookies and cream instant pudding
1 c. milk, scalded and cooled
8 oz. cream cheese
½ c. sugar
12 oz. Cool Whip
½ c. crushed oreo cookies

Mix cake ingredients together and bake in 2 round cake pans; cool. Split each cake and put filling in between and on top. Filling: Beat instant pudding and milk. In another bowl, mix cream cheese and sugar. Fold in Cool Whip and cookies. Last add instant pudding mixture.

Mrs. Perry Delores Herschberger

Cowboy Cake

Crumbs:
2 c. brown sugar
2 c. flour
½ c. shortening

Cake:
1 c. sour milk
1 tsp. soda
1 egg
2 tsp. vanilla
½ tsp. salt

Crumbs: Mix all ingredients. Reserve ⅔ cup. Dissolve soda in the sour milk. Add crumbs, except ⅔ cup. Add the rest of the ingredients. Mix all together and bake in a cake pan. Sprinkle the ⅔ cup of crumbs on top of the cake before baking. Bake at 325° for 30 minutes.

Miss Dorcas Miller

Cakes, Frostings

Fast Fixing Fruit Cake

1 box yellow cake mix
¼ c. vegetable oil
2 eggs
½ c. water
1 can pie filling

Pour oil into a 9"x13" pan. Tilt pan to cover bottom. Put dry cake mix, eggs and water into pan, on top of oil. Stir with fork, until blended for 2 minutes. Scrape sides and spread batter in pan. Spoon pie filling over batter and marbleize with knife. Bake at 350° for 35-45 minutes. Store cake loosely covered. Good with brown sugar and cinnamon on top.

Note: For best results, it is important to stir the batter in pan as stated.

Miss Susan Miller

Gingerbread Cake

½ c. butter
½ c. sugar
1 c. maple syrup or molasses
½ tsp. ginger
½ tsp. cinnamon
2 tsp. soda
2½ c. flour
1 c. boiling water
2 eggs, well beaten
1 qt. pie filling

Cream butter and sugar; add molasses. Mix in dry ingredients and boiling water with soda. Add eggs last. In a greased 9"x13" cake pan, spread pie filling on the bottom. Pour cake batter on top. Bake at 325° for 40-45 minutes or until done. A delicious cake dessert. Eat with ice cream or milk. Serves 12 people.

Miss Miriam Miller

Cakes, Frostings

Graham Streusel Cake

2 c. graham cracker crumbs
¾ c. chopped nuts, opt.
¾ c. brown sugar, packed
1¼ tsp. cinnamon
¾ c. butter, melted

1 yellow cake mix
¼ c. vegetable oil
3 eggs
1 c. water

Vanilla Glaze:
1 c. powdered sugar
vanilla

1-2 Tbsp. water

Mix graham cracker crumbs, nuts, brown sugar, cinnamon and melted butter. Set aside. Reserve. Blend cake mix, oil, eggs and water. Beat well. Pour half of the batter into a 9"x13" pan. Sprinkle with half of the crumb mixture. Spread remaining batter evenly over crumb mixture. Sprinkle with remaining crumb mixture on top of batter. Bake at 350° for 45-50 minutes. Cool. Drizzle cake with vanilla glaze.

Mrs. Reuben Marilyn Schrock

Ho-Ho Cake

1 chocolate cake mix

Frosting:
8 oz. cream cheese
8 oz. Cool Whip

2 c. powdered sugar

Glaze:
½ c. butter

1 c. chocolate chips

Bake cake according to box or recipe instructions. Mix frosting well and spread on cooled cake. In double boiler melt together butter and chocolate chips. Cool to spreading consistency and spread on top of frosting. Cut cake while chocolate is still warm.

Mrs. Vernon Rachel Herschberger

Hot Fudge Sundae Cake

2 c. flour
1½ c. sugar
3 Tbsp. cocoa
4 tsp. baking powder
½ tsp. salt
1½ c. milk

2 tsp. vanilla
¼ c. vegetable oil
1½ c. nuts, opt.
¾ c. cocoa
2 c. brown sugar
3¼ c. hot water

Mix first 5 ingredients. Add milk, vanilla and vegetable oil. Mix well and add nuts. Pour in ungreased 9"x13" pan. Mix cocoa and brown sugar and spread on batter. Pour hot water on top of this. Bake at 350° for 40 minutes. Let cool 20 minutes before serving. Serve with ice cream.

Mrs. Joseph Lucinda Miller

Hummingbird Cake

3 c. flour
2 c. sugar
1 tsp. salt
1 tsp. soda
1 tsp. cinnamon
3 beaten eggs

1½ c. vegetable oil
1½ tsp. vanilla
1½ c. crushed pineapple
1½ c. mashed bananas
1 c. chopped nuts

Frosting:
8 oz. cream cheese
¼ c. butter

2 c. powdered sugar

Mix dry ingredients in bowl. Mix eggs and oil and add to dry ingredients. Add vanilla, bananas, pineapples and nuts. Don't over beat while mixing. Pour in 9"x13" pan and bake at 350° for 24-30 minutes until toothpick inserted comes out clean.

Mrs. Kenneth Leanna Kauffman

Cakes, Frostings

Lava Cake

- 4 oz. Bakers semi sweet baking chocolate
- ½ c. butter
- 1 c. powdered sugar
- 2 eggs
- 2 egg yolks
- 6 Tbsp. flour

Preheat oven to 425°. Grease 4 custard cups and place on baking sheet. Melt chocolate and butter until melted and stir with wire whisk until chocolate is completely melted. Stir in sugar until well blended. Then add eggs, egg yolks and flour. Divide batter between custard cups. Bake 13-14 minutes. Carefully take a knife around cake to loosen. Put cakes on dessert dishes. We serve with a scoop of ice cream, drizzled with chocolate syrup, and topped with maraschino cherries. Serves 8 people.

Miss Cheryl DeAnn Otto

Lazy Wife Cake

- 3 c. pastry flour
- ¼ tsp. salt
- 2 tsp. soda
- 2 c. sugar
- 2 tsp. baking powder
- ¼ c. cocoa
- 2 tsp. vanilla
- ¾ c. vegetable oil
- 2 Tbsp. vinegar
- 2 c. cold water

Sift the above ingredients into a 9"x13" ungreased cake pan. Mix with fork. Make 3 holes in dry ingredients. Into one put the vanilla, the next oil, and into the third, vinegar. Pour water over everything. Mix with a fork. Do not beat. Bake at 350° for 30-40 minutes.

Miss Rosanna Jantzi

Cakes, Frostings

Mahogany Cake

2 c. flour
2 c. sugar
2½ tsp. soda
½ tsp. salt
2 Tbsp. cocoa

2 eggs
⅔ c. sour cream
1 tsp. vanilla
½ c. margarine, melted
1 c. hot water

Filling:
1 (6 oz.) can milnot
½ c. pecans
5½ Tbsp. butter

1 Tbsp. flour
1 c. sugar
4 egg yolks

Frosting:
½ c. cocoa, scant
½ c. shortening
1 tsp. vanilla

6 Tbsp. milk
½ c. chopped nuts or coconut
3 c. powdered sugar

Mix dry ingredients, add eggs, sour cream and vanilla. Add melted butter and hot water. Put cake in three layers. Filling: Cook in double boiler for approximately 1 hour. Spread between layers of cake. Cover with frosting.

Mrs. Kenneth Marilyn Otto

Cooked up excuses usually sound half baked.

Keep your words soft and sweet – you never know when you'll have to eat them.

Cakes, Frostings

Maple Nut Angel Food Cake

2 c. egg whites
1 tsp. vanilla
1 tsp. maple flavoring
½ tsp. salt
2 tsp. cream of tartar

1 c. sugar
½ c. brown sugar
1½ c. cake flour
1 c. brown sugar
½ c. nuts

Frosting:
½ c. powdered sugar, heaping
8 oz. cream cheese

1½ c. whipped cream

Glaze:
1 c. water, divided
¾ c. brown sugar
pinch of salt
1-2 Tbsp. Perma Flo

¾ tsp. Knox gelatin
1 Tbsp. butter
1 tsp. maple flavoring

Beat first 5 ingredients together until quite stiff. Gradually add—2 tablespoon at a time—white sugar and ½ cup brown sugar and beat till stiff. Sift flour, 1 cup brown sugar and nuts together and fold in. Put in tube pan and bake about 50 minutes at 300°. After it is baked, let cool. Remove from pan and cut in half; lift top half off on another plate. Frost both halves and then drizzle on glaze. Frosting: Mix powdered sugar and cream cheese well and fold in whipped cream. Glaze: Heat brown sugar and ¾ cup water and pinch of salt. Thicken with ¼ cup water and Perma Flo. (It should be quite thin and syrupy yet. If too thick use less Perma Flo). Add Knox gelatin, (which has been dissolved in water) after it is removed from heat but still hot and stir well. Add butter and maple flavoring. Cool before drizzling over cake.

Mrs. Jacob Elsie Mishler

Cakes, Frostings

Oatmeal Cake

1¾ c. boiling water
1½ c. oatmeal
¾ c. butter
1½ c. brown sugar
1½ c. sugar
3 eggs

2¼ c. flour
1½ tsp. nutmeg
1½ tsp. cinnamon
1½ tsp. soda
¾ tsp. salt

Coconut Topping:
1 c. brown sugar
1 c. chopped nuts
1½ c. coconut

¼ c. butter, melted
⅓ c. cream
1½ tsp. vanilla

In small bowl mix boiling water and oatmeal. Set aside. In big bowl cream sugars and butter, add eggs. Beat well. Then add oatmeal mixture and rest of ingredients. Bake in a 9"x13" pan for 30 minutes. Remove from oven and immediately top with coconut topping. Brown in broiler.

Miss Sarah Mae Jantzi

Cakes, Frostings

Oatmeal Cake

1¼ c. boiling water
1 c. quick oats
½ c. butter
1 c. sugar
1¼ c. brown sugar
1 tsp. vanilla

2 eggs
1½ c. flour
1 tsp. soda
½ tsp. salt
¾ tsp. cinnamon
¼ tsp. nutmeg

Topping:
½ c. butter, melted
1 c. brown sugar
1 c. coconut

¼ c. cream
¾ c. chopped nuts

Put oats and butter in a bowl, pour boiling water over it. Let stand 20 minutes. Add sugars, eggs and vanilla and stir well. Mix dry ingredients and add to the batter. Pour in a greased 9"x13" pan. Bake at 350° for 35 minutes or until a toothpick inserted comes out clean. Mix topping and spread over cake and toast very lightly in broiler.

Miss Rose Elaine Schrock

Peanut Butter Cake

1 c. brown sugar
1 c. sugar
1 tsp. salt
2 tsp. soda
2 tsp. baking powder
1 c. peanut butter

¾ c. vegetable oil
1 Tbsp. vanilla
2 eggs
3 c. flour
2 c. milk

Mix first 9 ingredients. Alternately add milk and flour. Mix well. Bake in a 9"x13" cake pan at 350° for 30 minutes or until done in the middle.

Miss Susanna Schrock

Peanut Butter Cake

2¼ c. flour
1 c. peanut butter
½ c. butter
2 c. brown sugar
1 c. milk

3 eggs
1 tsp. baking powder
½ tsp. soda
1 tsp. vanilla
¾ c. chocolate chips

Peanut Butter Frosting:
3 c. powdered sugar
⅓ c. peanut butter

⅓ c. milk

Mix together and bake in a 9"x13" pan at 350° for 35-40 minutes. Can also be baked on a cookie sheet. Frosting: Beat until smooth. May need more milk. Serves 15-20 people.

Mrs. William Miriam Yoder

Pumpkin Tasty Cake

4 eggs
2 c. sugar
¾ c. vegetable oil
2 c. flour

1 tsp. salt
2 tsp. soda
2 tsp. cinnamon
2 c. pumpkin

Filling:
¾ c. butter
1½ lb. powdered sugar

12 oz. cream cheese
1½ tsp. vanilla

Cream eggs and sugar. Add oil and beat. Mix together remainder of dry ingredients and add to batter alternately with pumpkin. Mix well. Divide batter evenly into 2 jelly-roll pans. (Line pans with wax paper). Bake at 350° until cake springs back lightly to the touch. Cool. Filling: Beat together butter and cream cheese. Add powdered sugar and vanilla, and whip until fluffy. Spread filling onto one cake then place second cake right side up on top of filling. These are nice to freeze.

Miss Cheryl DeAnn Otto

Cakes, Frostings

Shoo-Fly Cake

4 c. flour
¾ c. shortening
2 c. brown sugar
1 tsp. salt

1 c. molasses
1 Tbsp. soda
2 tsp. vanilla
2 c. boiling water

Mix first 4 ingredients. Take out 1 cup of crumbs and reserve for top. To the rest of the mixture, add molasses, soda and vanilla. Stir lightly, then add boiling water and mix well. Put into a large cake pan, since this is a large cake. Sprinkle remaining crumbs on top. Bake at 300° for 1 hour.

Mrs. Samuel Rachel Chupp

Strawberry Heart Cake

1 box white cake mix
1 pkg. strawberry Jell-O
3 Tbsp. flour
⅓ c. vegetable oil
4 eggs

1 pkg. frozen, sweetened strawberries, thawed
½ c. cold water
½ c. butter, softened
5-5½ c. powdered sugar

Combine cake mix, Jell-O and flour. Beat in oil and eggs. Drain strawberries, reserving ½ cup syrup for frosting. Add berries and water to batter; mix well. Divide batter between 2 (1 square and 1 round) waxed paper lined 8" baking pans. Bake at 350° for 30-35 minutes. Cool for 10 minutes then remove from pans to cool completely. Combine butter and reserved syrup. Gradually add sugar; beat until fluffy. Place square cake diagonally. Cut round cake in half. Frost cut sides and place against the top two sides of square cake, forming a heart. Frost sides and top of cake. Decorate with red hots around the edge.

Miss Marilyn Schrock

Strawberry Shortcake

2 c. flour
4 tsp. baking powder
¾ tsp. salt
1 Tbsp. sugar

½ c. shortening
⅔ c. milk
1 egg, beaten

Topping:
½ c. sugar
½ c. flour

3 Tbsp. butter

Combine first 5 ingredients, then add milk and beaten egg. Pat onto a cookie sheet, then mix topping and spread on top. Bake at 350° for approximately 20 minutes.

Miss Marietta W. Miller

Texas Sheet Cake

½ c. cocoa
1 c. shortening
1 c. water
2 c. flour
2 c. sugar

2 eggs
½ c. sour milk
1 tsp. soda
1 tsp. vanilla

Frosting:
¼ c. shortening
½ c. cocoa
1 tsp. vanilla

6 Tbsp. milk
3 c. powdered sugar

Bring cocoa, water and shortening to boil.. Add eggs. Mix in rest of ingredients. Bake on cookie sheet at 350° for 20 minutes or until done. Spread frosting on cake while cake is warm.
Leanna would add ½ cup chopped nuts or coconut.

Miss Esther Miller
Mrs. Kenneth Leanna Kauffman

Cakes, Frostings

Zucchini Chocolate Cake

½ c. margarine
½ c. vegetable oil
1¾ c. sugar
2 eggs
½ c. buttermilk or sour milk
2 c. grated zucchini
2½ c. flour
¼ c. cocoa
½ tsp. baking powder
1 tsp. soda
½ tsp. cinnamon
½ tsp. cloves
1 c. chocolate chips

Beat well. Sprinkle chocolate chips on top. Bake at 350° for 40-45 minutes. Very moist.

Mrs. Reuben Marilyn Schrock

Brown Sugar Frosting (for maple twists)

½ c. butter
1 c. brown sugar
¼ tsp. salt
¼ c. cream
powdered sugar

Stir butter and brown sugar in a kettle over low heat till melted. Add salt and cream and bring to a boil. Boil for 1 minute. Cool and add powdered sugar till desired consistency.

Mrs. Leon Cristina Wagler

Caramel Icing

1 c. butter
1 c. brown sugar
½ c. milk or cream
4½ c. powdered sugar

Boil butter, brown sugar and milk or cream until smooth. Add powdered sugar while warm and beat well.
Note: May need more powdered sugar.

Mrs. Eldon Ray Denise Miller

Chocolate Frosting

1 c. sugar
¼ c. cocoa
¼ c. clear jel

1 c. boiling water
dash of salt

Boil until thick. Add a little butter and vanilla.

Miss Susie Eicher

Chocolate One Minute Frosting

¼ c. butter
1 c. sugar
¼ c. cocoa

¼ c. milk
½ tsp. vanilla

Mix all together and cook for 1 minute. Let cool until just right to spread. This is enough for one 9"x13" cake.

Miss Rachel W. Miller

Creamy Butter Frosting

1 c. sugar
⅓ c. flour

1 c. milk
½ c. butter

Mix well in saucepan. Add milk, stirring constantly until mixture boils. Boil for 1 minute, then add butter and chill. Can use some less butter.
Note: This frosting is not as sweet as powdered sugar frosting.

Mrs. Howard Ellen Schrock

Cakes, Frostings

Decorating Frosting

2 c. butter
1½-2 c. Crisco
½ c. water

your choice of flavoring
4 lb. powdered sugar

Beat together butter and Crisco then add flavoring and water a little at a time and beating between every time you add water. Then add powdered sugar a little at a time. Beat until nice and fluffy. You may need to add more or less powdered sugar. This makes a good size batch.

Note: I like to use a 12 volt cordless drill with a salsa master beater tip to make fluffier frosting.

Miss Verna Kay Miller

Desserts

Desserts

Apfel Crisp. 193	Hot Fudge Pudding. 204
Apple Dumplings 193	Ice Cream 227
Apple Goodie. 194	Ice Cream Sandwiches. 228
Baby Pearl Tapioca 218	Jeweled Jell-O Dessert. 216
Baked Apples. 194	Lemon Cream Pudding. 205
Banana Split Dessert 221	Maple Nut Ice Cream or
Basic Vanilla Pudding 207	Cookies and Cream Ice Cream 227
Blueberry Pudding. 196	Mocha Tapioca 220
Butterscotch Sauce. 199	Orange Slush 218
Butterscotch Tapioca. 219	Oreo Cookie Pudding 215
Cherry Cobbler 196	Oreo Pudding 214
Cherry Sundae Pie. 200	Oreo Pudding 224
Chocolate Dessert 200	Peach Cobbler 197
Chocolate Mocha Angel Food Ice Box. . . 220	Peaches and Cream Dessert. 206
Chocolate Peanut Supreme 201	Pearl Tapioca Pudding. 218
Corina's Oreo Pudding 214	Peppermint Cheesecake. 223
Country Ice Cream 226	Pretzel Fruit Pizza 208
Creamy Mocha Frozen Dessert 221	Pretzel Salad 209
Crumb Mix for Crunches 197	Pumpkin Dessert. 209
Date Pudding 202	Pumpkin Dessert Squares 210
Delicious Rhubarb Dessert 197	Pumpkin Yummy. 210
Easy Ice Cream 227	Quick Apple Dessert 195
Faye's Moon Cake 203	Quick Ice Cream 228
Fresh Fruit Salad 217	Rhubarb Torte. 198
Frozen Cheesecake. 222	Rhubarb Torte. 199
Frozen Cheesecake. 222	Rice Krispie Ice Cream Pie 225
Frozen Orange Dessert 223	Slush 217
Frozen Peanut Butter Dessert 225	Snow Cream 228
Frozen Peanut Butter Pie. 224	Strawberry Cream 211
Frozen Yogurt. 229	Strawberry Shortcake. 211
Frozen Yogurt. 229	Sweet Cream Cones. 212
Fruit Pizza 207	Tapioca 219
Fruit Slush 217	Three Layer Jell-O Pudding. 216
Grandma's Apple Dumplings 195	Toffee Coffee Blizzards 226
Grapenut Pudding. 203	Two in One Dessert. 202
Grape Salad 215	Vanilla Pudding. 206
Heavenly Hash Dessert 204	Yogurt Parfait Dessert 213

Desserts

Apfel Crisp

1 Tasse Mehl
¾ Tasse Haferflocken
1 Tasse Brauner Zucker

1 TL Canela
½ Tasse Butter

Sosze:
1 Tasse Zucker
2 EL Maisstärke

1 Tasse Wasser
1 TL Vanille

Mache zu Krümel und shütte die Hälfte davon in eine 9"x13" Backform. Schütte 4 Tassen klein geschnittene Äpfel darüber. Sosze: Koch die sosze bis dick. Giesze über die Äpfel und streue die übrigen Krümel darüber. Backe bis goldbraun.
Note: This is a recipe we discovered in Mexico. Enjoy the challenge of decoding the German language.

Mrs. Dennis Marilyn Hershberger

Apple Dumplings

8-10 med. baking apples

Dough:
3 c. flour
1 c. shortening
½ tsp. salt

3¾ tsp. baking powder
¾ c. milk

Sauce:
1½ c. brown sugar
2 c. hot water

¼ c. butter
½ tsp. cinnamon

Peel apples and cut in halves. Roll out dough and cut in squares. Place half an apple in each square fold edges up and press dough lightly around apple. Place in baking dish. Pour sauce over them and bake. Serve warm with rich milk. Serves 6 people.

Mrs. Isaac Daisy Troyer

Desserts

Apple Goodie

1½ c. sugar
pinch of salt
2 Tbsp. flour

1 tsp. cinnamon
1½ qt. shredded apples
1 c. water

Crumbs:
1 c. brown sugar
¼ tsp. soda
⅔ c. butter

1 c. oatmeal
1 c. flour
⅓ tsp. baking powder

Combine apple mixture in 9"x13" pan. Smooth out and sprinkle with crumbs. Bake at 350° for 30-45 minutes.

Miss Susie Eicher

Baked Apples

peeled and sliced apples
1 c. brown sugar
1 c. sugar

2 Tbsp. flour
water

Crumbs:
2 c. flour
1 c. sugar

½ c. butter.

Fill a 9"x13" pan with peeled and sliced apples. Take sugars and flour and mix with a small amount of water. Pour over apples. Crumbs: Mix flour, sugar and butter thoroughly. This mixture will be crumbly. Spread over top of apple mixture and bake at 375° until apples are tender. Serve with milk and cream.

Miss Cheryl DeAnn Otto

Grandma's Apple Dumplings

3 c. flour
1 Tbsp. baking powder
1½ tsp. salt

½ c. butter
1⅛ c. milk

Sauce:
1½ c. water
1½ c. brown sugar
1½ Tbsp. flour

¾ tsp. salt
½ tsp. cinnamon

Mix first 4 ingredients until crumbly. Add milk. Mix, then roll on floured surface to ¼"-⅜"thick. Spread with butter, cinnamon, brown sugar and chopped apples. Roll up and cut into 1½" slices. Place in 9"x13" pan, and cover with the sauce. Sauce: Combine all ingredients and boil together for 3 minutes. Pour over dumplings. Bake at 350° for 45 minutes. Serves 12 people.

Mrs. Nelson Ruth Miller

Quick Apple Dessert

6 shredded apples
8 coarsely broken graham crackers

¾ c. chocolate chips
½ c. coconut
12 oz. Cool Whip

Mix all together. Serves 10 people.

Mrs. Kenneth Leanna Kauffman

It's often not a slow metabolism that makes us put on weight, but a fast fork.

Desserts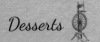

Blueberry Pudding

1 angel food cake mix   fresh blueberrries

Filling:
8 oz. cream cheese   1 pkg. vanilla pudding
½ c. powdered sugar   12 oz. Cool Whip
1 can sweetened condensed   fresh blueberries
   milk

Cube angel food cake, mix together filling in order given. Place cubed cake, filling, then blueberries in a bowl, ending with blueberries on top. Looks pretty in a clear bowl. Serves 30 people.

Miss Denise Ann Kauffman

Cherry Cobbler

Cherry Mixture:
1 qt. cherries   ¾ c. sugar
4 Tbsp. miniature tapioca,   3 c. water
   heaping   ¼ c. Jell-O

Dough:
1½ c. flour   ½ tsp. salt
2 tsp. baking powder   ¼ c. shortening
2 Tbsp. sugar   ½ c. milk, or less

Pour cherry mixture into a 9"x13" baking pan. Shape dough into small round patties and put on top of cherries. Bake at 350° for 45 minutes. Cool. Very good with ice cream. Serves 10 people.

Note: Susie uses 4 cups water.

Miss Susie Eicher
Miss Julia Jantzi

Desserts

Crumb Mix for Crunches

10 c. quick oats
10 c. brown sugar
10 c. flour
4 tsp. baking powder

5 c. margarine, softened
1 Tbsp. soda
1 Tbsp. baking powder
1 tsp. salt

Mix all ingredients together with hands and keep in airtight container. How to use: Put 1 quart sweetened thickened fruit (of your choice) in bottom of 9"x13" glass pan. Spread 3½ cups of crumbs over top. Pat down and bake at 350° for 30-35 minutes. Serve with milk. Fresh fruit can be used too. Yield: 30 cups.

Mrs. Ernie Freeda Yoder

Delicious Rhubarb Dessert

4 c. fresh or frozen rhubarb
⅔ c. sugar
1 (3 oz.) box strawberry Jell-O

1 yellow cake mix, dry
2 c. cold water

Put into a 9"x13" pan in layers in order given. Do not stir. Bake at 350° for 45 minutes. Can be served with whipped cream or ice cream.

Mrs. Samuel Rachel Chupp

Peach Cobbler

1½ c. flour
1½ c. sugar
¾ tsp. baking powder
1⅛ c. milk

5 Tbsp. butter
2¼ c. diced peaches
½ c. sugar

Melt butter in a 9"x13" cake pan at 350°. Then add dough mixture made from the first 4 ingredients. Mix the peaches and ½ cup sugar together and let stand while you are melting the butter and mixing the dough. Put this on top of dough mixture. Bake at 350° until edges are brown and cobbler is done in the middle. Serve with milk.

Mrs. Ray Marjorie Wagler

Desserts

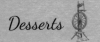

Rhubarb Torte

Crust:
¾ c. butter
2 c. flour

2 Tbsp. sugar

Custard:
6 eggs yolks
1 c. cream or milk
2 c. sugar

7 Tbsp. flour
¼ tsp. salt
5 c. chopped rhubarb

Meringue:
6 egg whites
¾ c. sugar
¼ tsp. salt

1 tsp. vanilla
¼ tsp. cream of tartar

Mix crust ingredients until crumbly. Pat into a 9"x13" pan. Bake at 350° for 10 minutes. Beat egg yolks and milk; add sugar, flour and salt. Stir in rhubarb. Pour over crust. Bake at 350° for 45 minutes or until custard is set. Meringue: Beat egg whites until stiff. Gradually add rest of ingredients. Spread over custard layer. Bake at 350° for 15 minutes. Serves 20 people.

Miss Esther Miller

Desserts

Rhubarb Torte

Crust:
1 c. flour
½ c. butter
2 Tbsp. sugar
pinch of salt

Sauce:
2¼ c. rhubarb
1¼ c. sugar
⅓ c. milk
2 Tbsp. flour
3 egg yolks

Meringue:
3 egg whites
¼ tsp. cream of tartar
6 Tbsp. sugar

Crust: Mix and press into 8"x10" pan. Bake at 325° for 20-25 minutes. Sauce: Combine ingredients in saucepan; cook until thick, then pour into baked crust. Meringue: Beat egg whites and add cream of tartar, and sugar. Spread over rhubarb mixture. Brown in oven for 10-15 minutes.

Mrs. Eldon Ray Denise Miller

Butterscotch Sauce

½ c. butter
1 c. sugar
1 c. brown sugar
2 c. milk
2 egg yolks
3 Tbsp. clear jel
1 c. water
½ tsp. salt
vanilla
maple flavoring

Melt butter; add sugars and stir till slightly brown, approximately 5 minutes. Add milk. Make a paste with egg yolks, clear jel and water and add to the rest. Bring to a boil. Boil until thickened; add flavorings and salt.

Mrs. Howard Ellen Schrock

Desserts

Cherry Sundae Pie

1⅓ c. crushed cornflakes
3 Tbsp. sugar
⅓ c. butter, softened

1 qt. vanilla ice cream
1 (21 oz.) can cherry pie filling

Heat oven to 375°. Mix cornflake crumbs, sugar and butter thoroughly. Press mixture firmly and evenly against bottom and sides of a 9" pie pan. Bake 8-10 minutes. Cool thoroughly. Just before serving, fill crust with scoops of ice cream; top with pie filling. Serves 6 people.

Mrs. Delbert Martha Schrock

Chocolate Dessert

2 c. flour
1 Tbsp. baking powder
1 tsp. salt
1 c. sugar

2 Tbsp. cocoa
1 c. milk
2 tsp. vanilla
¼ c. butter

Sauce:
2 c. brown sugar
4 c. boiling water

1 c. cocoa
2 Tbsp. butter

Mix flour, baking powder, salt, sugar and cocoa. Stir in milk, vanilla and butter. Spread in a greased 9"x13" pan. Mix sauce and pour over batter. Bake at 350°. Serve with whipped cream or vanilla ice cream.

Mrs. Kenneth Marilyn Otto

Chocolate Peanut Supreme

Crust:
⅓ c. butter
½ c. chunky peanut butter
24 sq. graham crackers, crushed
½ c. sugar

Pudding:
4 c. milk, divided
1 c. sugar
½ tsp. salt
½ c. cocoa
¼ c. cornstarch
2 Tbsp. butter
2 tsp. vanilla
Cool Whip

Crust: Melt together butter and peanut butter. Add graham crackers and sugar. Mix well and press into a 9"x13" pan. Pudding: Bring 3½ cups milk, sugar, salt and cocoa to a boil, mix cornstarch with ½ cup milk. Stir into cocoa mixture to thicken. Add butter and vanilla. Pour on top of crust. Top with Cool Whip.

Mrs. Eldon Ray Denise Miller

Desserts

Date Pudding

1 c. chopped dates
1 tsp. soda
1½ c. boiling water
1½ c. sugar
3 Tbsp. butter

2 eggs
1½ c. flour
½ tsp. baking powder
1 c. chopped nuts

Sauce:
1 c. brown sugar
½ c. butter, browned
1 egg yolk
1 Tbsp. flour, heaping

½ c. corn syrup
⅛ tsp. salt
½ c. water

Combine dates, soda and boiling water; let stand 5 minutes. Cream sugar and butter; add eggs, then rest of ingredients. Pour in a greased 9"x13" pan and bake at 325° for 45 minutes. Sauce: Combine all ingredients; cook and stir until thickened. Remove from heat; add 1 teaspoon vanilla. Cut cake in small squares. Layer in bowl: cake, sauce and whipped topping. Serves 15-20 people.

Miss Edna Mae Schrock

Two in One Dessert

1 cake mix

1 qt. pie filling

Cornstarch Pudding:
4 c. milk, divided
2 egg yolks
⅓ c. cornstarch
¾ c. sugar

½ tsp. salt
1 Tbsp. butter
1 tsp. vanilla

Mix cake mix according to instructions. Divide cake batter into two 9"x13" pans and bake according to instructions. Cornstarch Pudding: Heat 3½ cups milk. Mix dry ingredients, egg yolks and ½ cup milk. Stir into hot milk, stirring constantly until it boils and thickens. After allowing cake and pudding to cool, pour pudding on 1 cake. Spread evenly and top with your favorite pie filling. Serves 20 people.

Mrs. Vernon Rachel Herschberger

Desserts

Faye's Moon Cake

Crust:
1 c. water
½ c. butter
1 c. flour
4 eggs

Pudding:
2 boxes instant vanilla pudding
8 oz. cream cheese

Toppings:
Cool Whip
chocolate sauce

Crust: Mix water and butter. Bring to a boil. Add flour, all at once, and stir rapidly until mixture forms a ball. Cool a little. Beat in eggs, one at a time, beating well. Spread on an ungreased cookie sheet. Bake at 400° for 30 minutes. Cool. Mix pudding according to directions, first mixing some of the milk with the cream cheese. Blend well, spread on crust. Top generously with Cool Whip and drizzle with Hershey's chocolate sauce. Serves 16 people.

Note: Instead of using instant vanilla pudding we usually just make our own cornstarch pudding.

Miss Cathy Wagler

Grapenut Pudding

4 c. milk, divided
1 c. brown sugar
⅓ c. cornstarch
2 eggs
1 tsp. vanilla
½ tsp. maple flavoring
1 c. raisins
1 c. grapenuts
8 oz. Cool Whip

Heat 3½ cups milk until hot. Mix sugar, cornstarch, eggs and ½ cup milk; add to the hot milk. Bring to a boil. Remove from heat, and add flavorings. Cool and add raisins, grapenuts and Cool Whip.

Miss Martha Troyer

Desserts

Heavenly Hash Dessert

1 angel food cake
1 (12 oz.) pkg. chocolate chips
4 eggs, separated
1 tsp. vanilla
½ tsp. salt
2½ c. whipped cream

Melt chocolate chips over low heat. Beat egg yolks and add to chocolate. Add beaten egg whites, vanilla, salt and whipped cream. Cut angel food cake into small pieces and mix everything together. Yield: approximately 4-5 quarts.

Note: Can mix 2 tablespoons coffee with ½ cup boiling water and add to melted chocolate chips.

Miss Marietta W. Miller

Hot Fudge Pudding

Cake:
2 c. flour
4 Tbsp. butter, softened
1 c. milk
2 tsp. baking powder
1¼ c. sugar
¼ c. cocoa
2 tsp. vanilla
¾ tsp. salt

Sauce:
3⅓ c. water
¾ tsp. salt
1¼ c. sugar
¼ c. cocoa
4 Tbsp. butter

Cake: Mix all ingredients and spread in a greased 9"x13" pan. Mix sauce ingredients and boil in a saucepan for 5 minutes. Pour sauce over unbaked cake and bake at 350° for 50 minutes. Serve warm with ice cream or whipped topping. Serves 20 people.

Miss Cathy Wagler

Desserts

Lemon Cream Pudding

Crust:
1½ c. flour
¾ c. butter
½ c. chopped pecans

Second Layer:
8 oz. cream cheese
¾ c. sugar
8 oz. Cool Whip

Pudding:
3 c. sugar
¾ c. cornstarch
4 c. water
6 eggs, beaten
4 Tbsp. butter
¾ c. frozen lemonade concentrate

Crust: Mix flour, butter and chopped pecans. Press into 9"x13" pan and bake at 375° for 15 minutes. Second layer: Combine ingredients and put on top of baked crust. Pudding: Combine sugar, cornstarch and water; boil one minute. Add eggs and boil for another minute. Remove from heat and add butter and frozen lemonade concentrate. Cool a little, then pour over cream cheese mixture.

Miss Rosanna Jantzi

Swallow your pride occasionally, it is non-fattening.

Desserts

Peaches and Cream Dessert

Dough:
3 Tbsp. butter, softened
¾ c. flour
1 tsp. baking powder
1 box instant vanilla pudding
1 egg
½ c. milk
1 (15 oz.) can sliced peaches, drained, or fresh peaches

Filling:
8 oz. cream cheese
3 Tbsp. peach juice
½ c. sugar

Topping:
1 Tbsp. sugar
½ tsp. cinnamon

Combine all dough ingredients except peaches and mix well. Pat dough on bottom sides of a greased 9" square baking pan. Put peaches on top of dough. Combine filling ingredients and spread on peaches. Topping: Mix sugar and cinnamon; sprinkle on top. Bake at 350° for 30-35 minutes or until crust is browned. Serves 12-15 people.

Mrs. Joe Lorene Miller

Vanilla Pudding

3 qt. milk, divided
1 c. sugar
2 eggs
5 egg yolks
1 tsp. salt
1 c. flour
⅔ c. therm flo
1 tsp. vanilla
4 Tbsp. butter, opt.

Heat 2½ quarts milk and sugar to the scalding point. To the rest of the milk, add eggs, salt, flour and therm flo. Beat well and stir into hot milk. Keep stirring until it cooks for 2-3 minutes. Remove from heat and add vanilla and butter if desired. Cool. You can use this pudding to make peanut butter pie or pudding by layering it with peanut butter crumbs and Cool Whip. One recipe will fill two 9"x13" pans with pudding.

Mrs. Dennis Marilyn Hershberger

Desserts

Basic Vanilla Pudding

4 c. milk, divided
½ c. sugar
⅓ c. cornstarch
½ tsp. salt
1 Tbsp. butter
1 tsp. vanilla
2 eggs yolks

Heat 3½ cups milk to scalding. Make thickening with dry ingredients, beaten egg yolks and ½ cup cold milk. Pour into hot milk and stir until it thickens. Add vanilla and butter.

Note: To use for pie filling, add a little more cornstarch. For chocolate pie filling, add 2 rounded tablespoons cocoa.

Mrs. Nelson Ruth Miller

Fruit Pizza

Crust:
1 yellow cake mix
¾ c. butter flavored Crisco
2 Tbsp. milk
1 egg

Filling:
8 oz. cream cheese
1 c. powdered sugar
12 oz. whipped topping

Glaze:
1 c. pineapple juice or water
¾ c. water
2 Tbsp. Perma Flo, rounded
⅔ c. sugar

Mix crust ingredients together and press into jelly-roll pan. Bake at 325° for 12 minutes. Do not overbake. When cool, spread filling on top of crust. Add any fruit of your choice on top of filling. Glaze: Bring ingredients to a boil. Spread glaze on top of fruit.

Note: We like to use orange juice instead of pineapple juice. When using water we add Jell-O for flavor and color. A Sunday evening special.

The Bunch of Six

Desserts

Pretzel Fruit Pizza

Crust:
2½ c. finely crushed pretzels
⅔ c. brown sugar
1 c. butter

Filling:
8 oz. cream cheese
powdered sugar
1 can sweetened condensed milk
1 tsp. ReaLemon
3 c. whipped topping

Fruit:
strawberries, grapes, apples, mandarin oranges, etc.

Crust: Combine pretzels and sugar, cut in softened butter. Press into a 10"x15" pan. Bake at 350° for 10 minutes. Cool. Filling: Combine cream cheese with some powdered sugar, add sweetened condensed milk, ReaLemon and topping. Spread over the crust. Chill well then spread with fresh fruit. No glaze needed. The best. Serves 15-20 people.
Note: SueEllen uses a 9"x13" pan.

Miss SueEllen Miller
Mrs. William Miriam Yoder

Christ has no place in your life
unless He has first place.

Desserts

Pretzel Salad

Base:
1 c. broken pretzels
½ c. margarine, melted
½ c. sugar

Center:
8 oz. cream cheese, softened
8 oz. Cool Whip
½ c. sugar

Topping:
1 can crushed pineapple
¼ c. sugar
2 Tbsp. cornstarch

Base: Combine ingredients and press into bottom of pan. Center: Combine ingredients and put on pretzel layer. Topping: Drain pineapple. Combine syrup with sugar and cornstarch. Cook until clear. When cool, mix with pineapple. Put on top of salad.

Mrs. David Verda Miller

Pumpkin Dessert

Crust:
3 c. graham cracker crumbs
½ c. brown sugar
⅔ c. butter, melted
¼ tsp. salt

Filling:
1 c. pumpkin
1 c. brown sugar
1 tsp. cinnamon
¼ tsp. salt
⅛ tsp. nutmeg
8 oz. Cool Whip
1 qt. vanilla ice cream, softened

Mix and put half of crumbs in a 9"x13" pan, keeping the other half to put on top. Filling: Mix filling together, adding ice cream last. Pour over crumb mixture, smoothing out evenly. Sprinkle with remaining crumb mixture and freeze overnight. Very smooth and delicious!

Miss SueEllen Miller

Desserts

Pumpkin Dessert Squares

Crust:
1½ c. whole wheat flour
1 c. sugar
2 tsp. baking powder
½ tsp. salt
½ c. butter, melted
1 egg

Filling:
2 eggs
16 oz. pumpkin
½ c. brown sugar
2½ tsp. pumpkin pie spice
⅔ c. milk

Topping:
1 c. reserved crumbs
¼ c. sugar
1 tsp. cinnamon
2 Tbsp. butter
chopped, nuts, opt.

Crust: Mix first 4 ingredients. Reserve 1 cup for topping. Add butter and egg to the rest of the flour mixture. Spread into a greased 9"x13" pan. Filling: Combine eggs, pumpkin, brown sugar, pumpkin pie spice and milk. Pour over crust. Topping: Combine reserved crumbs with sugar, cinnamon and butter and nuts. Sprinkle over filling. Bake at 350° for 45-50 minutes. May be served with whipped topping or ice cream.

Mrs. Ernest Ray Inez Miller

Pumpkin Yummy

2½ c. pumpkin
1 c. brown sugar
2 tsp. cinnamon
½ tsp. ginger
¼ tsp. nutmeg
3 eggs
1 can evaporated milk
1 yellow cake mix
¾ c. butter, melted

Combine first 5 ingredients. Beat in eggs and milk until mixture is smooth. Pour into a 9"x13" pan. Sprinkle dry cake mix over the pumpkin mixture and drizzle melted butter over cake mix. Bake at 350° for 50 minutes. Cool and serve with whipped cream or Cool Whip. Serves 15 people.

Mrs. Steven Katie Jantzi

Desserts

Strawberry Cream

2 c. milk, divided
1 Tbsp. plain gelatin
1 tsp. vanilla

½ c. sugar
1-3 c. frozen strawberries

Put 1 cup milk in blender with the gelatin and let soak. Heat 1 cup milk till hot and add to the cold milk. Blend well. Add the rest of the ingredients and blend well. Let set in the refrigerator for 15-20 minutes or overnight till set, then serve.

Note: Also good with canned strawberries

Mrs. Jacob Elsie Mishler

Strawberry Shortcake

2 c. flour
4 tsp. baking powder
¾ tsp. salt
1 Tbsp. sugar

⅓ c. shortening
⅔ c. milk
1 egg, beaten

Topping:
½ c. sugar
½ c. flour

3 Tbsp. butter

Mix first 5 ingredients then add milk and egg. Put in 9"x9" pan, then add topping. Put in oven. Bake at 350° for 30 minutes. Top with fresh strawberries and Cool Whip.

Note: We like to fix our own individual pieces in our plate, it's easier to put away the leftovers and it doesn't get so soggy.

Miss Verna Kay Miller

Desserts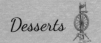

Sweet Cream Cones

2 c. cold milk
2 boxes instant pudding, any flavor
8 oz. Cool Whip, divided
10 ice cream cone cups

Pour milk into a large bowl. Add pudding mix. Stir well. Add 2 cups Cool Whip. Spoon into cone cups. Top with leftover Cool Whip. Put into freezer at least 3 hours before serving. May top with sprinkles if desired. Serves 10 people.

Mrs. Leroy Barbara Weaver

He who would not fall into sin
must not sit at the door of temptation.

Desserts

Oreo Cookie Pudding

12 oz. Cool Whip
2 boxes instant vanilla pudding
3 c. milk
8 oz. cream cheese

½ c. butter
1 c. powdered sugar
1 tsp. vanilla
Oreos

Mix pudding and milk and add Cool Whip. Mix together rest of ingredients and add to pudding mixture. Crush Oreo cookies and put on top and bottom.

Mrs. David Verda Miller

Grape Salad

Bottom Layer:
1⅓ c. grape Jell-O
2 c. hot water

2 c. cold water

Top Layer:
8 oz. cream cheese, softened
1 c. sour cream
1½ c. powdered sugar

1 tsp. lemon juice
Cool Whip
4-6 lb. grapes

Bottom Layer: Mix and pour into a 9"x13" pan and let set. Top Layer: Cream together cream cheese, sour cream, powdered sugar and lemon juice. Fold in Cool Whip and grapes. Spread on top of chilled set Jell-O. Also works for other fruit.

Miss Deborah Ann Miller

Desserts

Jeweled Jell-O Dessert

Crust:
1½ c. crushed graham crackers
½ c. brown sugar
½ c. butter, melted

Jell-O:
3 oz. strawberry Jell-O
3 oz. grape Jell-O
3 oz. orange Jell-O
3 oz. lime Jell-O
1 c. pineapple juice
¼ c. sugar
3 oz. lemon Jell-O
2 c. Cool Whip

Crust: Mix all ingredients and press into a 9"x13" pan. Set aside. Dissolve first 4 Jell-Os separately in 1 cup boiling water each. Add ½ cup cold water to each and pour into 8"x8" pans. Let set. Meanwhile bring pineapple juice to boil. Add sugar and lemon Jell-O. Stir well then let cool till partially set. Fold in Cool whip. Cut Jell-O into small cubes and gently mix with pineapple mixture. Pour on top of crumbs. Refrigerate until set.

Miss Sarah Mae Jantzi

Three Layer Jell-O Pudding

½ c. of three different
  flavors Jell-O
2 c. boiling water, divided
8 oz. cream cheese
1 c. sugar
1½ c. sour cream
16 oz. Cool Whip

Dissolve each flavor Jell-O in ⅔ cup boiling water. Let water and Jell-O cool until partly set. Mix the cream cheeese, sugar, sour cream and Cool Whip together. Add 2⅔ cups of cream cheese mixture to each kind of Jell-O. Pour layers on top of each other according to your choice. Fills a 9"x13" pan.

Mrs. Steven Katie Jantzi

Desserts

Fresh Fruit Salad

8 c. apples
8 c. peaches
1½ c. grapes
4 bananas

Sauce:
1½ c. orange juice
½ c. water
1 tsp. vanilla
1½ c. sugar
½ c. miraclear

Mix orange juice according to directions on can. Mix sauce ingredients. Cook until thickened. Cool. Add to fruit.

Mrs. Kenneth Marilyn Otto

Fruit Slush

2 c. sugar
3 c. hot water
3 c. peaches
1 (20 oz.) can crushed pineapple
6 oz. frozen orange juice concentrate

Combine sugar and hot water. Cool and add the rest of the ingredients to the syrup. Freeze. Thaw to icy slush before serving, very refreshing!

Miss Wilma Fern Schrock

Slush

2 c. sugar
3 c. water
8 oz. frozen orange juice
6 bananas, sliced
1 (20 oz.) can crushed pineapple

Boil together sugar and water then cool. Add orange juice, bananas and crushed pineapple. Freeze. Eat partly thawed.
Note: I usually add sliced red seedless grapes and a little more orange juice.

Mrs. David Verda Miller

Desserts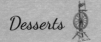

Orange Slush

3 (12 oz.) cans frozen orange juice
7 c. water
1 (20 oz.) can crushed pineapple
1 c. sugar

Stir together and freeze. Serve when a little slushy.

Miss Lovina Eicher

Baby Pearl Tapioca

7 c. water
1½ c. tapioca
pinch of salt
1 c. sugar
3 oz. Jell-O
Cool Whip
fruit

Bring water to a boil. Slowly add tapioca. Cook 10-12 minutes. Stir occasionally. Take off stove and cover tightly for 5 minutes. Then add sugar and Jell-O. Cool. Add Cool Whip and fruit.

Mrs. Jerry Esther Schrock

Pearl Tapioca Pudding

3 c. pearl tapioca
18 c. water, divided
1½ c. sugar, or to taste
1½ c. Jell-O or to taste
1 c. whipped topping

Soak tapioca in 4 cups water for 2 hours. Heat rest of water to a boil. Combine and cook till clear or soft. Add sugar and Jell-O. Cool, then add whip topping and fruit of your choice. Serves 25 people.

Miss Rosanna Jantzi

Desserts

Tapioca

2 qt. water
1½ c. sugar
⅛ tsp. salt
1 c. tapioca

1 c. Jell-O
1 box instant vanilla pudding
Cool Whip

Heat water, sugar and salt until boiling. Slowly add tapioca while stirring. Boil slowly, stirring constantly until clear. Remove from heat, then add Jell-O, mixed with instant pudding. Cool; add Cool Whip before serving.
We like this best without fruit, except when using strawberry Jell-O we add a quart of strawberries.

Miss Wilma Fern Schrock

Butterscotch Tapioca

6 c. boiling water
1 tsp. salt
1½ c. pearl tapioca
2 c. brown sugar
2 eggs, beaten
½ c. sugar

1 c. milk
½ c. butter, browned
1 tsp. vanilla
whipped topping
bananas
Snickers

Cook water, salt and tapioca for 15 minutes. Add brown sugar, and cook till done. Stir often. Mix together eggs sugar and milk; add to tapioca mixture. Cook until it bubbles. Add browned butter and vanilla. Cool, then add whipped topping, bananas and diced Snicker candy bars. Double this recipe to fill a fix and mix bowl. I put in one can Rich's topping for a double batch.

Mrs. Ray Marjorie Wagler

Desserts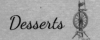

Mocha Tapioca

6 c. water
1 tsp. salt
1½ c. tapioca
2 c. brown sugar
2 eggs, beaten
¼ c. cornstarch
1 c. milk

½ c. sugar
¼ c. cocoa
2 Tbsp. instant coffee
24 oz. Cool Whip
mini chocolate chips or
  toffee bits, opt.

Cook water, salt and tapioca together till tapioca is clear, stirring frequently. Add brown sugar. Mix eggs, cornstarch, milk, sugar, cocoa and instant coffee. Stir into tapioca; bring to a boil, then remove from heat and cool. Mix in Cool Whip and chocolate chips or toffee bits. 1½ batches fills a 5 quart bucket.

Mrs. Wilbur Wilma Miller

Chocolate Mocha Angel Food Ice Box

½ c. boiling water
2 tsp. instant coffee
4 c. milk
2 boxes instant vanilla pudding

½ c. Nesquik
24 oz. Cool Whip
1 angel food cake

Add coffee to boiling water, then cool. Mix milk, instant pudding, and Nesquik. Then add cooled coffee. Fold in Cool Whip. First put a layer of pudding, then angel food cake, then pudding. Refrigerate till ready to serve. Can also be frozen.

Mrs. Ervin Ella Miller

Creamy Mocha Frozen Dessert

1 Tbsp. hot water
2 Tbsp. instant coffee granules
1 c. Oreo cookie crumbs
¾ c. chopped pecans, divided
¼ c. butter, melted

16 oz. cream cheese
1 can sweetened condensed milk
½ c. chocolate syrup
8 oz. whipped topping

Dissolve coffee in hot water; set aside. In a mixing bowl, combine Oreo crumbs, ½ cup pecans and butter. Put in a 9"x13" pan. In another bowl beat cream cheese until fluffy. Blend in coffee mixture, milk and chocolate syrup. Fold in whipped topping and spread over crust. Garnish with remaining pecans and additional cookie crumbs. Freeze. A rich dessert. Serves 15 people.

Note: Christina uses 2 teaspoons instant coffee instead of 2 tablespoons.

Mrs. Leon Christina Wagler
Miss Miriam Miller

Banana Split Dessert

graham cracker crumbs
2-3 bananas
½ gallon neapolitan ice cream
1 c. chopped walnuts
½ c. butter

2 c. powdered sugar
1 c. chocolate chips
1 can evaporated milk
1 tsp. vanilla
1 pt. whipping cream

Cover bottom of a 11"x15" pan with graham cracker crumbs. Reserve one cup crumbs. Slice bananas and layer over crust. Slice ice cream ½" thick. Sprinkle nuts over ice cream. Freeze until firm. Melt butter, powdered sugar, chocolate chips and evaporated milk. Cook mixture until thick and smooth, stirring constantly. Remove from heat, and add vanilla. Cool chocolate mixture then pour over ice cream. Freeze until firm. Whip cream until stiff. Spread over chocolate layer and top with reserved crumbs. Store in freezer. Remove about 10 minutes before serving. Will keep for several weeks.

Mrs. Ervin Ella Miller

Desserts

Frozen Cheesecake

2 c. graham cracker crumbs
3 Tbsp. sugar
¼ c. butter, melted
16 oz. cream cheese
1 tsp. vanilla
½ c. sugar
1 can sweetened condensed milk
8 oz. Cool Whip

Mix first 3 ingredients and press in a 9"x13" pan. Mix rest of ingredients well and put on top of crumbs and freeze. Put any kind of fruit filling on top before serving.

Mrs. Gerald Betty Kauffman

Frozen Cheesecake

Crust:
2 pkg. graham crackers, crushed
¾ c. butter, melted
6 Tbsp. brown sugar

Filling:
16 oz. cream cheese
1 c. sugar
4 eggs, beaten
1 c. whip topping
1 tsp. vanilla

Mix crust and press into a 9"x13" pan. Mix softened cream cheese and sugar, slowly add beaten eggs. Add whipped topping and vanilla. Freeze. Take out of freezer a bit before serving. Serve with thickened strawberries.

Miss Wilma Fern Schrock

Before me as behind, God is and all is well.

Desserts

Peppermint Cheesecake

Crust:
15-20 crushed Oreo cookies
¼ c. butter, melted

Filling:
1 can sweetened condensed milk
8 oz. cream cheese
8 oz. sour cream
12 oz. Cool Whip
3 drops peppermint flavoring
5 lg. crushed candy canes

Crust: Mix together Oreo cookies and butter. Put in a 9"x13" pan. Mix filling in order given. Reserve 2 tablespoons crushed candy canes for the top. Pour filling on cookies, top with remaining candy canes. Freeze. Serves 15 people.

Miss Denise Ann Kauffman

Frozen Orange Dessert

Crumbs:
2 c. flour
½ c. brown sugar
1 c. pecans
1 c. butter, melted

Filling:
32 oz. Cool Whip
16 oz. cream cheese
½ c. powdered sugar
8 egg whites
¼ c. sugar
2 pkg. orange Kool-Aid
2 (20 oz.) cans crushed pineapple, drained
pinch of salt

Crumbs: Mix all ingredients. Put in pan and bake at 350°. Stir often. Crumble part of this into 9"x13" pan and save the rest for the top. Filling: Add softened cream cheese to Cool Whip and powdered sugar. Beat egg whites. When foamy, add sugar, and beat till stiff. Add beaten egg whites to whipped topping mixture and whip together. Add Kool-Aid, pineapple and salt. Freeze. Yield: 1½ pans.

Mrs. Joe Laura Hershberger

Desserts

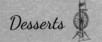

Oreo Pudding

1 lg. pkg. Oreo cookies
12 oz. Cool Whip

½ gal. vanilla ice cream, softened

Crush the cookies. Put some in the bottom of a 9"x13" pan. Reserve ⅔ cup for the top. Mix the rest of the crumbs with the other ingredients and pour in pan. Put crumbs on top and freeze. Take out of freezer a bit before serving.

Mrs. Ernest Sara Schrock

Frozen Peanut Butter Pie

Crust:
1¾ c. butter, melted
1½ Tbsp. sugar

2 pkg. crushed grahams

Filling:
8 oz. cream cheese
2 c. powdered sugar
⅔ c. peanut butter

1 c. milk
9 oz. Cool Whip

Press crust into 2 pie pans or a 9"x13" pan. For Filling: Mix cream cheese, powdered sugar and peanut butter. Add milk and Cool Whip and pour onto the crust. Freeze.

Miss Mary Edna Miller

Desserts

Frozen Peanut Butter Dessert

2 c. graham cracker crumbs
2 Tbsp. sugar
¼ c. butter, melted
8 oz. cream cheese

2 c. powdered sugar
⅔ c. peanut butter
1 c. milk
16 oz. Cool Whip

Combine first 3 ingredients and press ⅔ of mixture into bottom of a 9"x13" pan. Reserve rest of crumbs for top. Beat cream cheese, powdered sugar and peanut butter until smooth. Slowly add milk, blending well into mixture. Fold in Cool Whip, then pour over crust. Sprinkle remaining crumbs on top. Freeze.

Miss Edna Mae Schrock

Rice Krispie Ice Cream Pie

8 c. Rice Krispies
2 c. peanut butter

1 gal. ice cream

Mix Rice Krispies and peanut butter, then press in four 9" pie pans or two 9"x13" pans. Fill with ice cream. Now drizzle with chocolate or caramel topping or anything you like with ice cream.

Mrs. Ervin Ella Miller

We make a living by what we get,
We make a life by what we give.

Desserts

Toffee Coffee Blizzards

¼ c. sugar
1 Tbsp. cornstarch, rounded
1 Tbsp. instant coffee
1 Tbsp. butter
1¼ c. milk, divided
1 tsp. vanilla

1 can sweetened condensed milk
2 c. Rich's topping
12 Oreo cookies
12 oz. English Heath toffee bits
caramel and chocolate syrup

In a saucepan heat 1 cup milk to the boiling point. In the meantime, combine sugar, cornstarch and coffee. Mix in ¼ cup milk and slowly add to hot milk, stirring constantly. Bring to a boil and boil 1 minute or until thickened. Remove from heat and add vanilla and butter. Cool completely and add sweetened condensed milk. Whip the topping and fold into pudding. Add Heath bits. Crush cookies into a 10" pie plate. Pour pudding mixture over cookies. Swirl with caramel and chocolate syrup. Freeze overnight or longer. A great make-ahead dessert. A favorite

Mrs. Clifford Rhoda Herschberger

Country Ice Cream

4 eggs
2 c. sugar
5 c. milk, divided
4 c. cream

4½ tsp. vanilla
½ tsp. salt
1⅓ c. instant vanilla pudding

Beat eggs for 5 minutes. Beat in sugar and 1 cup milk until thick. Add rest of milk and cream, vanilla and salt. Sprinkle pudding on top and beat in. This will fill a 6-quart freezer. Other flavor pudding may be used instead of vanilla. Very good!

Mrs. Howard Ellen Schrock

Desserts

Easy Ice Cream

1 qt. cream
5 eggs
1½-2 c. brown sugar
1⅓ c. instant vanilla pudding
maple flavoring
pecans, opt.

Beat cream and eggs; add sugar. Put in rest of ingredients. Pour into 1½ gallon ice cream can and fill with milk to desired amount. Put in pecans when almost done freezing. Serves 15-20 people.

Mrs. Nelson Ruth Miller

Ice Cream

3 eggs
¾ c. sugar
½ c. sweetened condensed milk
½ tsp. salt
1 tsp. vanilla
3 c. sweet cream or milk

This is a simple recipe to use in 1-quart freezer. Alter ingredients to suit your taste. Sometimes I add mint flavor and chocolate chips. Green food coloring is optional. Serves 4-6 people.

Miss Susanna Schrock

Maple Nut Ice Cream or Cookies and Cream Ice Cream

1 qt. cream
2 boxes instant vanilla pudding
5 eggs
1 tsp. vanilla
1½ c. brown sugar
1½ tsp. maple flavoring,
pecans, opt.

Maple Nut Ice Cream: Beat cream and eggs. Add instant pudding and rest of ingredients. Put in freezer can and fill with milk to about 3½" from the top. Add pecans after partly froze or just add while serving. Cookies and Cream: Don't add maple flavoring. Instead add ¾ cup brown sugar, ¾ cup white sugar and Oreo cookies when partly frozen. Yield: 1 gallon.

Mrs. Ray Marjorie Wagler

Desserts

Quick Ice Cream

5 eggs, beaten
3½ c. sugar, divided
3 c. cream
1 tsp. salt
1½ tsp. vanilla

¾ c. instant clear jel
1 box instant vanilla pudding
1 Tbsp. plain gelatin
1 c. milk

Add 1 cup sugar to beaten eggs and beat until lemon colored. Add cream, salt and vanilla. In separate bowl mix 2½ cups sugar, clear jel and instant pudding. Add clear jel mixture to milk and cream mixture. Soak gelatin in milk and melt. Add gelatin mixture to the rest. Pour in 6-quart freezer can and add extra milk and/or cream until can is ¾ full. Serves approximately 20 people.

Mrs. Monroe Elsie Miller

Ice Cream Sandwiches

3 eggs, separated
½ c. sugar

1 c. cream
½ tsp. vanilla

Beat egg yolks until light. Add sugar and beat well. Beat egg whites until stiff. Whip the cream and fold everything together. Line a pan with graham crackers and top with the above mixture; put another layer of crackers on top of this. Freeze either in the freezer, or outside overnight in 0° weather.

Miss Marilyn W. Miller

Snow Cream

2 c. cream
2 eggs
1 c. brown sugar

½ tsp. salt
1 tsp. maple or vanilla flavoring
fluffy snow

Whip the cream. Whip eggs till fluffy. Beat in sugar, salt and flavoring. Mix cream and egg mixture together. Stir in light fluffy snow till it's thick like ice cream. Serves approximately 8 people.

Mrs. Jacob Elsie Mishler

Desserts

Frozen Yogurt

1 c. sugar
1½ qt. milk
2 eggs
2 qt. vanilla yogurt

2 boxes instant vanilla pudding
2 c. whipped cream
2 c. pie filling, your choice

Heat sugar in milk; cool. Combine the rest of ingredients. Add milk mixture. Freeze in ice-cream freezer. Very good! Serves 14-16 people.

Mrs. Clifford Rhoda Herschberger

Frozen Yogurt

9 c. homemade yogurt
4 c. cream
1 can sweetened condensed milk

4 c. chopped strawberries or peaches, sweetened

Mix everything together and put in 6-quart ice cream freezer. Freeze and enjoy. You may also substitute other fruit.

Mrs. Wilbur Wilma Miller

Be faithful in small things,
because it is in them,
that your strength lies.

Prayer Answered

I asked for strength that I might achieve;
He made me weak that I might obey.
I asked for health that I might do greater things;
I was given grace that I might do better things.
I asked for riches that I might be happy;
I was given poverty that I might be wise.
I asked for power that I might have the praise of men;
I was given weakness that I might feel the need of God.
I asked for all things that I might enjoy life;
I was given life that I might enjoy things.
I received nothing that I asked for, all that I hoped for,
My prayer was answered.

Pies

Pies

Apple Cream Pie 234	Pecan Pie. 247
Butterscotch Pie 236	Pecan Pie. 247
Butter Tarts. 237	Pie Crusts (large recipe). 233
Chocolate Chiffon Pie. 238	Pie Dough 233
Chocolate Mocha Pie. 240	Pie Dough 233
Chocolate Pie. 238	Pumpkin Bob Andy Pie. 247
Chocolate Pie Filling. 239	Pumpkin Pie 248
Cornstarch Pie Filling 241	Pumpkin Pie 248
Crumb Pie. 242	Pumpkin Pie 249
Custard Pie 242	Pumpkin Pie 249
Dutch Apple Pie .234	Pumpkin Pie 250
Fruit Topped Custard Pie 243	Pumpkin Pie 250
Ground Cherry Pie 244	Pumpkin Pie 251
Lemon Cream Cheese Pie 245	Pumpkin Pie 251
Lemon Pie. 244	Shoestring Apple Pie 235
Lemon Pie Filling 245	Simple Cream Pie 241
Lemon Pie Filling 245	Sour Cream Cherry Pie 237
Makes It's Own Crust Coconut Pie. 240	Special Apple Pie .236
Our Favorite Apple Pie 235	Strawberry Pie. 252
Our Favorite Custard. 243	Strawberry Pie Filling 252
Peach Cream Pie .246	White Chocolate Pie 239
Pear Pie 246	Whole Wheat Pie Dough. 234
Pecan Pie 246	

Pies

Pie Dough

1½ lb. shortening
8¾ c. flour
1 tsp. baking powder
1½ c. cold water

Mix shortening, flour and baking powder until crumbly. Add cold water and mix only until well blended. Yield: approximately 14 crusts.
Note: Use plenty of flour to roll out dough.

Mrs. Jerry Esther Schrock

Pie Dough

3 lb. can Crisco shortening
5 lb. bag all-purpose flour
¾ Tbsp. baking powder
3 c. cold water

Save 3 cups of the flour for rolling out the crusts. Mix first 3 ingredients with a chopper until crumbly. Add cold water and mix. Some can be frozen for later use. Use plenty flour to roll out the crusts. Yield: approximately 10 double crust pies.

Mrs. Ernest Mary Ellen Miller

Pie Crusts (large recipe)

1 (3 lb.) can Crisco
5 lb. Gold Medal flour or pie crust flour
1 Tbsp. salt
1 Tbsp. baking powder
½ c. sugar

Mix altogether until crumbly. For 1 heaping cup of mix, add 2 tablespoons water. This recipe makes around 20 crusts then I stack them with wax paper in-between and put 4 or so in a bag and freeze. It is so handy to just pull out of the freezer. These always go fast and it's hard to keep on hand. Yield: 18-20 crusts.
Note: I often use lard instead of Crisco.

Mrs. Samuel Dorothy Miller

Pies

Whole Wheat Pie Dough

3½ c. whole wheat flour
¾ tsp. salt
½ tsp. baking powder
1 Tbsp. sugar

1 c. lard
1 egg, beaten
1 Tbsp. vinegar
½ c. cold water

Mix dry ingredients, add lard, and rest of ingredients. Yield: 4 pie crusts.

Mrs. Wilbur Wilma Miller

Apple Cream Pie

2 c. shredded apples
2 eggs, well beaten
2 Tbsp. flour, rounded

1½ c. sugar
5 Tbsp. water
1 unbaked pie crust

Peel and shred apples. Beat eggs; add sugar, flour, and water. Last stir in apples. Pour into an unbaked pie crust. Sprinkle cinnamon on top of filling, then bake at 425° for 10 minutes. Turn oven to 300° for 25-30 minutes or until knife inserted in middle of pie comes out clean. Serves 6 people.

Mrs. Ernie Freeda Yoder

Dutch Apple Pie

3 c. diced apples
1 c. sugar
2 Tbsp. rich milk

½ tsp. cinnamon
1 Tbsp. flour
2 Tbsp. butter, melted

Crumbs:
½ c. brown sugar
⅓ c. butter

¾ c. flour

Mix together and put in an unbaked pie shell. Put crumbs on top and bake at 400° for 10 minutes, then at 350° till done.

Note: One recipe filling is a little scant for a 9" pie. For 4 pies: 5 x filling and 3 x crumbs was about right.

Mrs. Gerald Betty Kauffman

Chocolate Pie Filling

6 c. milk
2½ c. sugar
6 Tbsp. Perma Flo, rounded
6 Tbsp. cocoa, rounded
1 tsp. salt
4 eggs, beaten
2 Tbsp. butter
1 Tbsp. vanilla

Heat milk to boiling. While milk is heating, mix dry ingredients and add some milk and the eggs. Mix well and add to the boiling milk. Bring to a boil, then add butter and vanilla. Pour into two baked pie shells and top with Cool Whip. Serves 12 people.

Miss Wilma Fern Schrock

White Chocolate Pie

8 oz. cream cheese
1 can sweetened condensed milk
1½ c. cold water
2 boxes white chocolate instant pudding
2 c. Cool Whip

Mix the cream cheese and sweetened condensed milk till smooth. In a separate bowl, mix the cold water and instant pudding. Mix the 2 mixtures together well and add the Cool Whip. Put in baked pie shell. Let set. Put a layer of Cool Whip on top and sprinkle with heath toffee bits or other candy bar of your choice. Yield: 1 pie.

Mrs. Gerald Betty Kauffman

Pies

Chocolate Mocha Pie

1 Tbsp. gelatin
¼ c. cold water
1 Tbsp. cocoa
1 tsp. instant coffee
⅛ tsp. salt

¾ c. sugar
1¼ c. milk
1 c. cream
1 tsp. vanilla
nuts, opt.

Soak gelatin in water. Mix cocoa, coffee, salt and sugar in saucepan. Add milk, bring to a boil, stirring constantly. Remove from heat and stir in gelatin. Cool till slightly thickened. Beat the cooked mixture until smooth. Whip the cream, add vanilla and fold into cooked mixture. Pour into a 9" baked pie crust and top with nuts.

Mrs. Wilbur Wilma Miller

Makes It's Own Crust Coconut Pie

4 eggs, beaten
1¾ c. sugar
½ c. flour
¼ c. butter, melted

2 c. milk
1½ c. coconut
1 tsp. vanilla

Beat eggs real well then add the rest of ingredients except coconut and beat again. Add coconut and pour in a 10" pie pan. We like a cake pan better. Double the recipe for a 9"x13" pan. Bake at 350° for 45 minutes, or just until center is set. Don't overbake or it will be more like a cake.

Note: A special family favorite. It is good when still a little warm.

Mrs. Ernest Sara Schrock

Cornstarch Pie Filling

6 c. milk, divided
1⅓ c. sugar
5 Tbsp. cornstarch, rounded
2 Tbsp. flour, rounded
¾ tsp. salt
6 egg yolks
2 Tbsp. butter
1 Tbsp. vanilla

Heat 5½ cups milk. While milk is heating mix dry ingredients and add ½ cup milk and the egg yolks. Mix well and slowly pour into the milk and stir till it boils. Add butter and vanilla. Cool. We prefer cornstarch and not other thickener. Yield: 2 pies or a 9"x13" pan of pudding.

Note: We use this recipe for peanut butter or coconut pie. Sometimes we make this with a little less sugar and serve warm with brown sugar and nutmeg sprinkled on top of each serving.

Mrs. Ernest Sara Schrock

Simple Cream Pie

1 c. sugar
½ c. butter
2 c. milk
¼ c. Perma Flo
1 tsp. vanilla
nutmeg

Melt sugar and butter over low heat. Add milk, but save enough to mix with Perma Flo. Add Perma Flo mixture and cook until thick, stirring constantly. Remove from heat and add vanilla. Pour into a baked pie shell. Sprinkle nutmeg on top. Yield: 1 pie.

Mrs. Samuel Rachel Chupp

Pies

Crumb Pie

1½ c. brown sugar
1½ c. sugar
2 eggs

3 c. water
3 Tbsp. flour
2 tsp. vanilla

Crumbs:
3 c. flour
1½ c. brown sugar
½ c. lard

¾ tsp. soda
1½ tsp. cream of tartar

Put in baked pie crust. Brown crumbs in broiler. Then put on top of filling. Yield: 3 pies.

Mrs. Kenneth Marilyn Otto

Custard Pie

14 eggs
1 Tbsp. vanilla

2 c. sugar
8 c. milk

Beat well in order given. Pour into 4 pie crusts. Sprinkle nutmeg on top. Bake at 400° for 12 minutes, then at 325° until custard is set. Serves 24 people.

Mrs. Ernest Mary Ellen Miller

Pies

Our Favorite Custard

2 Tbsp. butter, browned
2 c. milk
½ c. brown sugar
½ c. sugar
1 Tbsp. flour, heaping
½ tsp. salt
½ tsp. cinnamon
2 eggs, separated
½ c. pumpkin or squash

Brown butter in a 4 quart kettle. Add milk and heat till almost boiling. Mix together brown sugar, white sugar, flour, salt and cinnamon. Blend in egg yolks and pumpkin or squash. Stiffly beat the egg whites. Mix milk and egg whites alternately into pumpkin mixture. Pour into an unbaked pie shell. Bake at 400° for 10 minutes, then at 350° for 20-25 minutes more. Do not overbake, just until barely set. For custard: pour into a 9"x9" pan. Set into a larger pan with hot water to bake. It might take longer to bake than pie. You can omit butter and reduce sugar. Serves 8 people.

Miss Miriam Miller

Fruit Topped Custard Pie

2½ c. milk
2 eggs
½ c. sugar
½ tsp. salt
2 Tbsp. flour
¾-1 cup fresh or frozen fruit

Heat milk to scalding, (do not boil). In another bowl, beat eggs. Add sugar, salt and flour; beat again. Gradually add hot milk to this mixture while beating at the same time. Pour into baked 9" pie shell, then sprinkle with fruit such as blackberries, blueberries, raspberries, etc. Bake at 350° for 35-40 minutes or until edge is set and center is "jiggly." Serves 6 people.

Mrs. Perry Delores Herschberger

Pies

Ground Cherry Pie

1 c. ground cherries, heaping
2 c. water
½ c. sugar
¼ tsp. salt
½ tsp. lemon juice
¼ c. Perma Flo

Bring ground cherries, water, sugar, salt and lemon juice to a boil. Dissolve Perma Flo in small amount of water and add to ground cherries. Stir till thick. Pour into 1 unbaked pie crust and put top crust on. Bake.

Mrs. Wilbur Wilma Miller

Lemon Pie

4½ c. water
12 egg yolks
1⅛ c. lemon juice
3¼ c. sugar
¾ c. Perma Flo
1 Tbsp. salt

Meringue:
12 egg whites
1 c. sugar
¼ tsp. salt
1 tsp. vanilla
¼ tsp. cream of tartar

Heat water, egg yolks and lemon juice until almost boiling. Mix dry ingredients and add to mixture. Bring to a boil, stirring constantly. Add 6 tablespoons butter. Cool. Pour in baked pie shell. For Meringue: Beat egg whites until stiff, gradually add rest of ingredients. Spread on pie and bake until lightly browned. Yield: 4 pies.

Miss Esther Miller

Worry is interest paid on trouble before it is due.

Pies

Lemon Pie Filling

4 c. water
1 Tbsp. butter
½ tsp. salt
1¾ c. sugar
5 eggs, separated

⅔ c. Perma Flo
1 c. water
½ c. lemon Jell-O
½ c. ReaLemon
1 Tbsp. lemon flavor

Boil the first 4 ingredients together. Beat the egg yolks in a different bowl, add the Perma Flo and water. Stir together. Then stir slowly into boiling mixture with a whisk. When thickened, add the last 3 ingredients. Beat egg whites for on top. Brown whites in toaster.

Mrs. Ray Marjorie Wagler

Lemon Pie Filling

6¾ c. water
1¼ c. sugar
¾ c. brown sugar

¾ c. lemon juice
1 c. clear jel
6 egg yolks

Bring water to a boil. Beat together rest of ingredients and add to boiling water. Stir until it bubbles. Yield: approximately 3 pies.

Miss Susie Eicher

Lemon Cream Cheese Pie

6 oz. box lemon pudding
¾ c. sugar
1 Tbsp. Perma Flo
3½ c. water

3 egg yolks
8 oz. cream cheese
2¼ c. Cool Whip
2 c. powdered sugar

Mix first 3 ingredients then add water and egg yolks. Cook mixture until thick, stirring constantly. Put a wax paper on top and cool. Mix together cream cheese, Cool Whip and powdered sugar. After the lemon mixture had cooled, add the cream cheese mixture. Yield: 2 pies.

Mrs. LaVern Linda Miller

Pies

Peach Cream Pie

1 (9") baked pie shell
4 or more lg. fresh peaches, sliced
1 egg
1 c. sugar
¼ c. flour
½ tsp. vanilla
1 c. cream

Spread peach slices all over the bottom of unbaked pie shell. Beat egg. Mix sugar and flour and beat in. Blend vanilla and cream. Pour over the peaches and sprinkle with cinnamon, if desired. Bake 10 minutes at 400°, then at 350° until done.

Miss Cheryl DeAnn Otto

Pear Pie

2 c. water
⅓ c. Perma Flo
¾ c. sugar
3 Tbsp. butter
½ tsp. lemon juice
1 box lemon Jell-O
2 c. fresh or frozen chopped pears

Heat water. Mix Perma Flo, sugar and Jell-O; add to boiling water. Stir till it looks clear. Then add butter, lemon juice and pears. Pour in a baked pie shell then top with Cool Whip.

Note: Can also use for strawberry pie. Use strawberry Jell-O instead of lemon and strawberries instead of pears.

Mrs. Ervin Ella Miller

Pecan Pie

6 eggs, beaten
2 c. dark Karo
1 c. light Karo
2 tsp. vanilla
4 Tbsp. butter, melted
2 Tbsp. flour
½ tsp. salt
2 c. pecans

Beat eggs then add rest of ingredients except for the pecans. Pour in two 9" pie crusts, then add 1 cup pecans to each pie. This recipe isn't so sweet. Bake at 350° for 45-50 minutes.

Mrs. Ray Marjorie Wagler

Pecan Pie

12 eggs
2 c. sugar
2 tsp. salt
1⅓ c. butter, melted
4 c. corn syrup
4 c. pecan halves

Preheat oven to 370°. Beat eggs, sugar, salt, butter and corn syrup together with a beater. Line pie shell bottom with pecans, then fill with filling. Bake 40-50 minutes or until set and pastry is nicely browned. Cool or serve slightly warm with ice cream, if desired. Yield: 4 pies.

Mrs. Samuel Dorothy Miller

Pecan Pie

9 eggs, beaten
3 c. Karo
3 c. brown sugar
3 Tbsp. butter
1½ tsp. salt
1 Tbsp. vanilla
9 Tbsp. milk
3 c. pecans, divided

Beat eggs, add Karo, sugar, melted butter, salt, vanilla and milk. Mix real well. Pour mixture into 3 pie shells. Put 1 cup pecans on top of each pie. Bake at 450° for 10 minutes. Reduce to 350° till set. Very good. Yield: 3 pies. Serves 18 people.

Mrs. Delbert Martha Schrock

Pumpkin Bob Andy Pie

¾ c. brown sugar
1 c. sugar
¼ c. flour
1 tsp. cinnamon
½ tsp. cloves
1 tsp. salt
1 Tbsp. butter, softened
1 c. pumpkin
4 eggs, separated
3½ c. milk

Mix first 6 ingredients, add butter, pumpkin, beaten egg yolks and milk. Last of all fold in stiffly beaten egg whites. Pour into 2 unbaked pie shells. Bake at 450° for 10 minutes, then reduce heat to 350° and bake till done, another 40-45 minutes.

Mrs. Wilbur Wilma Miller

Pies

Pumpkin Pie

2 Tbsp. butter
2 c. rich milk
½ c. brown sugar
½ c. sugar
1 Tbsp. flour, heaping
¼ tsp. salt
several dashes of cinnamon
½ c. pumpkin or squash
2 eggs, separated

Brown butter; add milk and heat to scalding. Mix sugars, flour, salt and cinnamon. Add pumpkin and egg yolks, mix well. Beat egg whites until stiff. Fold half the hot milk into sugar mixture, then egg whites, and rest of milk. Bake at 375° for approximately 35 minutes or just until set. Yield: 1 pie.

Note: If you want to bake custard without the crust, set in a pan of hot water to bake.

Miss Bethany Kay Otto

Pumpkin Pie

1 c. pumpkin
1 Tbsp. flour
1 tsp. cinnamon
1 tsp. allspice
½ c. sugar
½ tsp. salt
½ tsp. vanilla
1 c. hot milk
2 eggs, beaten

Mix first 7 ingredients, then add hot milk. Last of all add the beaten eggs. Pour in unbaked pie crust and bake approximately 45-60 minutes. Yield: 1 pie.

Mrs. Wilbur Wilma Miller

Pumpkin Pie

1 c. brown sugar, packed
2/3 c. bread flour
1 Tbsp. cinnamon
1 tsp. allspice
1/2 tsp. cloves
1/2 tsp. nutmeg
3/4 tsp. salt
2/3 c. pumpkin
5 1/3 c. milk, divided
6 eggs, separated

Mix first 7 ingredients then add pumpkin, egg yolks and 1 cup milk. Heat 4 1/3 cup milk, then add to batter and stir well. Beat egg whites till stiff then beat in last. Pour into two 9" pie crusts. Bake at 400° till golden brown.

Mrs. Joe Laura Hershberger

Pumpkin Pie

2 c. brown sugar
2 c. sugar
2 c. cooked pumpkin
12 eggs, separated
2 tsp. vanilla
1/4 tsp. salt
1/2 c. flour, rounded
4 tsp. cinnamon
12 c. milk

Mix sugars and pumpkin together in a large 13-quart bowl. Add the beaten egg yolks, vanilla and salt. Stir in flour and cinnamon. Have most of the milk heated to warm before adding to mixture. Add beaten egg whites last. Put into six 9" pie crusts and bake at 400° for 10 minutes. Reduce heat to 350° and finish baking till browned.

Mrs. Joe Lorene Miller

Pies

Pumpkin Pie

2 c. pumpkin
½ c. sugar
½ c. brown sugar
2 c. milk
½ c. cream

2 eggs, separated
2 Tbsp. flour
1½ tsp. pumpkin pie spice
¼ tsp. salt

Beat egg yolks and milk. Add all the rest of ingredients except egg whites. Mix well. Beat egg whites until stiff, beat into pumpkin mixture. Bake at 425° for 15 minutes. Reduce temperature to 350° for 35 minutes or until done. Yield: 2 pies.

Mrs. Nelson Ruth Miller

Pumpkin Pie

5 eggs, separated
1½ c. brown sugar
1 c. sugar, divided
4 c. milk
4 c. pumpkin

¼ c. flour, heaping
1 tsp. salt
1 tsp. cinnamon
1 tsp. nutmeg
1 tsp. ginger

Separate the eggs and stiffly beat the egg whites. Put half of the white sugar in the whites. Heat milk to scalding. Mix all together adding egg whites last. Bake at 400° for 10 minutes then turn oven down to 350° and bake till done. Yield: 3 pies. Serves 18 people.

Mrs. Isaac Daisy Troyer

A pound of patience you must find,
Mixed well with loving words so kind.
Drop in two pounds of helpful deeds,
And thoughts for other peoples' needs.
A peck of smiles will make the crust,
Then stir and bake it well, you must.
And now I ask that you may try,
A piece of my sunshine pie.

Pumpkin Pie

1 c. flour
½ c. sugar
4 c. pumpkin
4 c. brown sugar
12 eggs, separated

2 tsp. pumpkin pie spice
2 tsp. cinnamon
1 tsp. salt
10 c. creamy milk

Mix flour and white sugar; set aside. Mix pumpkin and brown sugar. Separate eggs and beat whites, adding last. Add egg yolks to pumpkin, then add spices and flour/sugar mixture and blend well. Then add milk and beat well and beat in egg whites. Bake at 450° for 10 minutes, then turn down to 325° for approximately an hour or until pies are set. Yield: 6 pies.

Mrs. Jerry Esther Schrock

Pumpkin Pie

1 c. pumpkin, mashed
2 eggs, separated
1 Tbsp. flour, rounded
½ tsp. cinnamon

½ tsp. allspice
¾ c. brown sugar
2 c. milk

Beat egg whites and add last. Heat milk to scalding. Pour into 9" pie shell. Bake at 400° for 10 minutes. Reduce to 350° and bake 30-35 minutes more or until finished. Serves 6-8 people.

Mrs. Jacob Elsie Mishler

Pies

Strawberry Pie Filling

1½ c. sugar
½ c. clear jel
3 c. water

½ c. strawberry Jell-O
strawberries

Bring 2 cups water and sugar to a boil. Mix clear jel and rest of water. Add strawberry Jell-O to boiling water mixture, then thicken with clear jel. Cook until clear and thickened. I like to refrigerate filling overnight. This always turns out good. When cool, add plenty of sliced strawberries. Yield: 3 pies.

Mrs. Ray Marjorie Wagler

Strawberry Pie

1 c. sugar
¼ c. clear jel
1 c. water
½ tsp. salt
½ tsp. red food coloring

2 Tbsp. light Karo
3 Tbsp. strawberry Jell-O
1½ c. strawberries
whipped topping

Cook first 6 ingredients together. Save part of water to mix with clear jel. Add strawberry Jell-O after removing from stove. Then add 1½ cup strawberries. Pour in baked pie shell. When cool, top with whipped topping.

Mrs. Kenneth Marilyn Otto

Candies Snacks

Candies, Snacks

Butter Brickle Bars 255	Mound Bars 259
Cheddar Snack Mix 266	No Bake Protein Balls 260
Chex Muddy Buddies 256	Party Mix 265
Cinnamon Popcorn 256	Party Mix 265
Cornflake Candy 256	Peanut Butter Balls 260
Cornflake Candy 257	Peanut Butter Candies 260
Cracker Mix 264	Peanut Butter Candy Squares 261
Creamy Caramels 255	Peanut Butter Fudge 259
Crispy Caramel Corn 255	Peanut Butter Squares 261
Crunch Candy Bars 257	Pizza Bites 262
Crunchy Peanut Bark 257	Plantation Crunch 262
Finger Jell-O 262	Reese's Peanut Butter Treats 261
Frozen Candy Bars 258	Seasoned Pretzels 266
Holiday Fudge 258	Seasoned Pretzels 266
Holiday Fudge 258	Taffy Candy 264
Laffy Taffy 263	White Chocolate Cereal Snack 263
Mint Patties 259	White Trash 263
Mocha Truffles 267	

Candies, Snacks

Butter Brickle Bars

saltine crackers
1 c. butter
1 c. brown sugar
1½ c. chocolate chips

Place a single layer of saltine crackers on a cookie sheet. Cook butter and brown sugar for 3 minutes. Pour over crackers and bake at 400° for 5 minutes. Remove from oven and sprinkle with chocolate chips. Wait for 2 minutes, then spread chocolate chips evenly over butter and sugar layer. Cool and cut into pieces. This is a simple, sweet, delicious snack.

Miss Rachel W. Miller

Creamy Caramels

1 c. sugar
1 c. butter
1 c. light corn syrup
1 can sweetened condensed milk
1½ tsp. vanilla

Combine sugar, corn syrup and butter in a 3-quart saucepan. Bring to a boil, stirring constantly. Boil slowly for 4 minutes without stirring. Remove from heat and add sweetened condensed milk. Bring to soft ball stage. (238°). Stir constantly. Remove from heat; add vanilla. Pour into greased 9"x13" pan. Cool. Cut and enjoy.

Miss Maria Grace Schrock

Crispy Caramel Corn

8 qt. popped corn
2 c. brown sugar
½ c. light Karo
1 c. butter
1 tsp. salt
½ tsp. soda
1 tsp. vanilla

Boil the brown sugar, Karo, butter and salt for 5 minutes. Take off burner; add soda and vanilla. Pour over popcorn and mix well. Pour into pan and bake at 250° for 1 hour. Stir several times during baking.

Miss Esther Miller
Mrs. Leon Christine Wagler

Candies, Snacks

Cinnamon Popcorn

8 oz. popped snacks
1 c. butter
½ c. Karo
1 c. red hots

Mix butter, Karo and red hots in saucepan. Boil 5 minutes. Stirring occasionally. Pour over popcorn and mix thoroughly. Put in pans and bake at 250° for 1 hour. Pour on wax paper and break apart.

Mrs. Gerald Betty Kauffman

Chex Muddy Buddies

9 c. Chex cereal
¼ c. butter
1 c. semisweet chocolate chips
½ c. peanut butter
1 tsp. vanilla
1½ c. powdered sugar

Measure Chex into large bowl; set aside. Heat butter, chocolate chips and peanut butter in 1-quart saucepan over low heat. Stir frequently until melted. Remove from heat. Stir in vanilla. Pour chocolate mixture over cereal. Stir until evenly coated. Pour into a clean brown grocery bag or ziploc bag and add powdered sugar. Fold top shut and shake until well coated. Yield: 9 cups.

Miss Dorcas Miller
Miss Lyndora Kay Miller

Cornflake Candy

1 c. cream
1 c. sugar
1 c. Karo
2 Tbsp. butter
3 c. peanuts
1 c. Rice Krispies
5 c. cornflakes

Cook first 4 ingredients to soft ball. Pour over peanuts and cereal. Pour into a 9"x13" greased pan. Cool. Cut into squares and serve.

Miss Lovina Eicher

Candies, Snacks

Cornflake Candy

1 c. sugar
1 c. Karo
1 c. peanut butter
6 c. cornflakes

Bring sugar and Karo to a boil. Add peanut butter. Pour over cornflakes. Stir till well mixed. Drop by teaspoon on wax paper. Let cool. Serves 12 people.

Miss Leah Miller

Crunch Candy Bars

2 c. chocolate chips
½ c. peanut butter
2 c. cornflakes or Rice Krispies

Melt chocolate chips then add peanut butter and cereal. Drop by teaspoonfuls on wax paper. Chill. Store in cool place.

Miss Verna Kay Miller

Crunchy Peanut Bark

2 lb. almond bark
1 c. peanut butter
3 c. Rice Krispies
2 c. dry roasted peanuts
2 c. miniature marshmallows

Melt almond bark, then add peanut butter and stir until smooth. Take off burner and add rest of ingredients. Drop by heaping tablespoonfuls onto wax paper or divide between two greased 9" square pans. Let cool or set for at least 1 hour.

Miss Jolene Marie Kauffman

Success is liking yourself, liking what you do, and liking how you do it.

Candies, Snacks

Frozen Candy Bars

ripe bananas
peanut butter
granola cereal

Mash bananas and add other ingredients according to your taste. Put into sandwich bags or wrap in pieces of plastic wrap, flatten, and freeze.

Note: This is a good way to use bananas that are becoming too ripe. It is also a refreshing and nourishing summer treat.

Mrs. Samuel Rachel Chupp

Holiday Fudge

4 c. sugar
1⅔ c. evaporated milk
½ c. butter
1 pt. marshmallow creme
12 oz. chocolate coating or chips
1 tsp. vanilla
1 c. nuts

Cook sugar, milk and butter to soft ball or (235°). Remove from heat and add marshmallow creme, chocolate, vanilla and nuts. Beat till chocolate pieces are melted and blended. Pour into a greased 9"x13" pan.

Miss Rosanna Jantzi

Holiday Fudge

4 c. sugar
1 can evaporated milk
½ c. butter
1 c. nuts
1 pkg. marshmallows
1¾ c. chocolate chips
1 tsp. vanilla

Cook sugar, milk and butter to soft ball. Remove from heat and add the rest of the ingredients. Stir until chocolate and marshmallows are melted. Pour into a 9"x13" pan and let it get hard. Yield: approximately 2¼ lb.

Miss Lovina Eicher
Miss Susie Eicher

Candies, Snacks

Peanut Butter Fudge

1 c. cream
2 c. sugar
½ c. peanut butter

3 c. mini marshmallows
1 tsp. vanilla

In a 3 qt. saucepan mix together the cream and sugar. Boil over medium heat till soft ball stage (225°-235°) or until it forms a firm ball when dropped into cold water. Add peanut butter and mix well. Add marshmallows and vanilla. Pour in a buttered 9"x9" pan. Cut when cooled a little. Enjoy.

Miss Rose Elaine Schrock

Mint Patties

2½ lb. powdered sugar
8 oz. cream cheese
4 Tbsp. butter

1½ tsp. peppermint extract
a couple drops green food coloring

Mix all the ingredients together. Shape into balls and press down. Dip into chocolate coating.

Miss Mary Edna Miller
Miss Kristina Wagler

Mound Bars

2 c. graham cracker crumbs
2 Tbsp. brown sugar
½ c. butter, melted

1 can sweetened condensed milk
7 oz. coconut
6 oz. chocolate chips

Combine the first 3 ingredients and press into a 9"x13" cake pan. Mix sweetened condensed milk with coconut. Spread over cracker crumb mixture. Bake at 350° for 15 minutes. Remove from oven and spread the chocolate chips on top. Return to oven until chocolate chips spread out easily.

Miss Wilma Fern Schrock

Candies, Snacks

No Bake Protein Balls

1 c. dry milk or protein powder
1 c. honey
1 c. peanut butter
3 c. Rice Krispies

Mix all ingredients together. Roll in balls, or press in 9"x9" pan. You can dip the balls in melted chocolate, or spread melted chocolate on top of a 9"x9" pan.

Miss Verna Kay Miller

Peanut Butter Balls

2 lb. peanut butter
1 c. butter, softened
6 c. powdered sugar
16 oz. almond bark, chocolate

Mix powdered sugar, peanut butter and butter. Shape into small balls and chill. Meanwhile, melt chocolate in heavy saucepan or double boiler. Dip chilled balls into chocolate. Chill again. If you have leftover chocolate use it to coat pretzels, graham crackers, or Ritz crackers.

Miss Sarah Mae Jantzi

Peanut Butter Candies

½ c. peanut butter
1 c. dry powdered milk
½ c. honey
¾ c. coconut or crushed nuts

Combine all ingredients in a bowl and stir until well blended. Pat into a buttered 8"x8" pan. Chill and cut into squares. You can also form the dough into small balls and roll into coconut or crushed nuts, then chill.

Mrs. Jacob Elsie Mishler

Peanut Butter Candy Squares

3 c. powdered sugar
1½ c. graham cracker crumbs
1 c. crunchy peanut butter
1 c. butter, melted
2 c. chocolate chips

Mix first 4 ingredients well; press into a buttered 9"x13" pan. Melt chocolate chips and spread on top. Chill until firm. Cut into small squares. These squares can be frozen.

Miss Leah Miller

Peanut Butter Squares

1 c. butter, melted
1¾ c. powdered sugar
1¾ c. peanut butter
1⅔ c. graham cracker crumbs
12 oz. milk chocolate chips

Mix first 3 ingredients; add cracker crumbs. Press in 9"x13" pan. Put in freezer for 10 minutes. Melt chocolate chips and pour over peanut butter mixture. Cool and cut in small squares. Delicious!

Mrs. Gerald Betty Kauffman

Reese's Peanut Butter Treats

3 c. peanut butter
1 c. butter, melted
1 c. brown sugar
1 tsp. vanilla
5 c. powdered sugar

Topping:
1½ c. chocolate chips
2 Tbsp. butter

Mix together the first 4 ingredients. Add the powdered sugar. Put into jelly-roll pan. Chill. Topping: Melt butter and chocolate chips together. Spread on top of the chilled mixture. This is a yummy "no-bake" recipe for hot summer days.

Miss Dorcas Miller

Candies, Snacks

Finger Jell-O

4 c. boiling water
1 c. Jell-O
2 tsp. unflavored gelatin
1 pkg. Kool-Aid
½ c. sugar

Mix all together except water. Pour in boiling water and mix quickly until dissolved. Stir 5 minutes. Chill.

Miss Dorcas Miller

Pizza Bites

10 slices American cheese
40 slices pepperoni
40 Ritz snack crackers

Cut each cheese slice into 4 pieces. Place crackers on cookie sheet, top with cheese and a slice of pepperoni. Bake at 300° for 10 minutes or until warm. A child pleasing snack!

Miss Marlys Renae Kauffman

Plantation Crunch

1 lb. white chocolate
2 Tbsp. peanut butter
½ c. Spanish peanuts
2 c. Rice Krispies

Melt chocolate and peanut butter in top of double boiler over boiling water. Mix peanuts and cereal in bowl. Pour melted mixture over nuts and cereal. Stir carefully to combine, then spread ¼" thick on wax paper lined cookie sheet. When cool break into pieces. Yummy!

Mrs. Ernie Freeda Yoder

Candies, Snacks

White Trash

4 c. Crispix cereal
1 c. mini pretzels
1 c. peanuts
1 lb. M&M's
1 lb. almond bark

Mix all ingredients except almond bark in large bowl. Melt almond bark and pour over all ingredients. Pour onto waxed paper and let cool.

Miss Bethany Kay Otto

White Chocolate Cereal Snack

2 c. Rice Chex
2 c. pretzels
2 c. Fruit Loops
1 lb. white chocolate

Mix cereals and pretzels. Melt chocolate and pour over mixture. Stir well. Spread on buttered cookie sheets to cool. Break apart after it is dry.

Miss Melissa Joy Otto

Laffy Taffy

3½ c. sugar
1 c. water
1 c. Karo
¼ c. butter
¼ tsp. cream of tartar

Mix together and bring to a boil. Stir slowly (it turns sugary if stirred too fast). Test with cold water into firm ball. Pour into buttered pie pans. Add flavor and color to taste, when it is ready to pull.

Miss Susan Miller

Candies, Snacks

Taffy Candy

4 c. sugar
2 c. cream
1 Tbsp. gelatin
¼ c. cold water
1 Tbsp. paraffin
2 c. Karo

Combine all ingredients and boil until it forms a hard ball in cold water when dropped from a teaspoon or 250° on the candy thermometer. Pour onto 2 well buttered cookie sheets. When cool enough to handle, start pulling. Once ivory color is obtained, pull into a long thin rope and cut to desired length pieces with kitchen scissors.

Miss Cathy Wagler

Cracker Mix

5 different kinds of crackers
1 bag pretzels
1 bag Bugles
1 box Corn Chex
1 c. Orville Redenbacher popcorn oil
1 pkg. Hidden Valley Ranch dressing mix

Mix the popcorn oil and the ranch dressing mix together. Put the rest of the ingredients in a garbage bag, then add the oil mixture and mix. Store in an airtight container.

Miss Cheryl DeAnn Otto

It's how you deal with failure that determines how you achieve success.

Party Mix

14 oz. box Corn Chex
12 oz. box Rice Chex
12 oz. box Kix
15 oz. Cheerios
10 oz. box chicken crackers

16 oz. cheese curls
16 oz. bag pretzels
14 oz. bag Bugles
30 oz. peanuts
16 oz. cashews

Sauce:
3 c. butter
3½ Tbsp. Worcestershire sauce
3 Tbsp. season all
2 tsp. salt

1 Tbsp. sour cream and onion powder
a few shakes garlic powder
a few shakes Accent

Mix everything together except sauce. Combine sauce ingredients together in a 2-quart saucepan and heat until butter is melted. Mix well into other mixture. Divide into 2 large roasters and bake at 250° for 1 hour, stirring every 15 minutes.

Miss SueEllen Miller

Party Mix

6 oz. pkg. pretzel sticks
1 box Rice Chex
1 box Cheerios
1 lb. peanuts
1 c. butter

3 Tbsp. Worcestershire sauce
1½ tsp. garlic salt
1½ tsp. celery salt
1½ tsp. onion salt
2 tsp. Lawry's salt

Combine pretzels, Chex, Cheerios and peanuts in large roaster. Melt butter, stir in sauce and salts. Pour over dry ingredients very gradually and mix thoroughly. Cover and bake for 1 hour or until you think it tastes right. Sometimes we add 1 package crunchy cheese curls, after it is baked.

Mrs. Ernest Sara Schrock

Candies, Snacks

Seasoned Pretzels

1 c. vegetable oil
3 Tbsp. cheddar cheese powder
3 Tbsp. sour cream and onion powder
1 lb. pretzels

Mix together oil and seasonings. Pour over pretzels. Mix thoroughly. Bake at 250° for 30 minutes, stirring often. Let cool and enjoy.

Miss Denise Ann Kauffman

Seasoned Pretzels

1 c. vegetable oil
½ tsp. garlic salt
½ tsp. lemon pepper
1 Tbsp. dill weed
1 pkg. Hidden Valley Ranch mix or ½ c. sour cream and onion powder
30 oz. pretzels

Mix oil, garlic salt, lemon pepper, dill weed and ranch mix; pour over pretzels. Let set a few hours, then they are ready to eat.

Mrs. Joseph Lucinda Miller

Cheddar Snack Mix

3 c. Chex
3 c. peanuts
3 c. pretzels
3 c. crackers
3 Tbsp. cheddar cheese powder
3 Tbsp. sour cream and onion powder
2 Tbsp. Ranch dressing mix
½ c. vegetable oil, no substitute

Mix first 4 ingredients. You may substitute anything you want. Set aside. Mix last 4 ingredients and pour over dry ingredients. Stir well and bake in a roaster at 250° for 1 hour or until crisp. Stir every 15 minutes. You can also use cookie sheets but must watch carefully to avoid burned snacks. Yield: 12 cups.

Miss Clara Mae Miller

Candies, Snacks

Mocha Truffles

12 oz. milk chocolate chips
8 oz. cream cheese, softened
1½ Tbsp. instant coffee
1 tsp. water

Melt chocolate chips in double boiler. Combine instant coffee and water. Add cream cheese and coffee to melted chocolate chips; mix brew. Chill until mixture is firm enough to shape into balls. Chill again. Dip in chocolate. Serve to mocha lovers!

Miss Edna Mae Schrock

Send Them With A Prayer

There was a toddler who cried for his breakfast,
There was a youngster singing for joy,
There were braids to put up for wee lady,
And trousers to be found for small boy.
There were lunches to pack in a minute,
There were toys underfoot everywhere,
Yet amid all this turmoil a mother,
Sent her children to school with a prayer.

'Twas this prayer that glowed forth from the children,
As they happily entered the school,
'Twas this prayer that caused hearts to be softened,
To desire to follow each rule.
Tho' the teacher was feeling discouraged,
And sinking in waves of despair,
Her spirits were lifted because a mother,
Sent her children to school with a prayer.

Prayer is a lowly, community service,
Unseen by neighbors and friends,
It's a precious community service,
Whose rewards shall be great in the end.
There is power and strength and protection,
From idleness, pride and care,
There is LOVE in the schools where mothers,
Send their children to school with a prayer.

Canning Freezing

Canning, Freezing

Apple Barbecue Sauce 290	Jerky 281
Apple Butter 271	Ketchup. 291
Apple Pie Filling .277	Kosher Dill Pickles 273
Bacons. 283	Mom's Chili 298
Banana Pickles. 272	Our Favorite Sausage. 286
Barbecued Peppers. 273	Peach Pie Filling .278
Barbecue Sauce 289	Peach Pie Filling .279
Barbecue Sauce 289	Pineapple-Orange Fruit to Can 279
Bologna. 284	Pizza Hut Pizza Sauce 294
Bread and Butter Pickles 272	Pizza Hut Sauce. .294
Brine for Liver and Steaks 282	Pizza Sauce 293
Canned Cheeseburger Soup. 295	Pizza Sauce 295
Canning Beef Chunks 280	Pork Bologna. 284
Canning Fruit 276	Raspberry Pie Filling. 279
Chili Sauce. 288	Refried Beans. 287
Chili Sauce. 292	Salsa. 275
Chili Soup 297	Sausage 285
Chili Soup 297	Sausage Seasoning 285
Chili Soup 298	Sausage Seasoning 285
Chunky Chicken or Turkey Soup 296	Smoked Turkey Thighs 283
Chunky Soup. 296	Smokey Honey Barbecue Sauce. 290
Cucumber Relish .274	Strawberry Jam 271
Curing Meats turkey, ham, bacon, etc. . . .282	Stuffed Sausage 286
Easy Peach Jam 271	Sweet Baby Ray Barbecue Sauce 288
Freezing Strawberries. 280	Sweet Pickle Relish 275
Fruit Slush 278	Thank You Pie Filling 280
Garlic Dill Pickles 273	Thick and Spicy Pizza Sauce 293
Grape Sauce. 278	To Cure Ham. 281
Green Tomato Relish. 274	To Freeze Broccoli or Cauliflower 272
Heinz Ketchup. 291	Venison Bologna .287
Homemade Ketchup 292	

Apple Butter

4 gal. apples
6 lb. sugar
1 gal. corn syrup

1 Tbsp. cinnamon, rounded
2 tsp. nutmeg

Wash and cut up apples in fourths or slices. Put 4 gallon apple slices in 20-quart kettle. Spread sugar on top of apples, then corn syrup on top of that. Sprinkle with cinnamon and nutmeg. Let stand overnight. Cook slowly with lid on kettle for 3 hours. Put through victorio strainer. Put in jars and cold pack 10 minutes. Can use zucchini instead of apples but cook with lid off and cook till you have only half the amount. This won't be pulpy enough to put through victorio strainer. We use a cone strainer. Yield: 9-10 quarts.

Mrs. Monroe Elsie Miller

Easy Peach Jam

7 c. peaches
5 c. sugar

1 (20 oz.) can crushed pineapple
6 oz. Jell-O

Chop peaches fine in salsa master. Mix in sugar and pineapple; bring to boil on high heat. Turn heat down and simmer for 20 minutes. Then add orange or peach Jell-O. Put in jars and seal.

Mrs. Nelson Ruth Miller

Strawberry Jam

½ c. instant clear jel
6 c. sugar, divided
1 c. dutch jel, heaping

6 c. mashed strawberries
2¼ c. water

Mix clear jel and 1 cup sugar. Add 5 cups sugar to the strawberries and mix well. Combine the 2 mixtures. Mix the dutch jel and the water. Stir into the strawberries. Freeze. Yield: 3 quarts.

Mrs. Dennis Marilyn Hershberger

Canning, Freezing

To Freeze Broccoli or Cauliflower

Cut cauliflower or broccoli into 1½"-2" pieces. Put in boiling water for 3-5 minutes. Then put in cold water for a little bit. Dry and cool on towel. Put in bags or containers to freeze.

Mrs. Joe Lorene Miller

Banana Pickles

cucumbers
3 c. sugar
1 c. vinegar
1 c. water
1 tsp. salt
1 tsp. celery seed
1 tsp. mustard seed
1 tsp. turmeric

Peel big cucumbers. Scoop out seeds. Cut in spears and pack in jars. Cover with vinegar mixture. Cold pack 5 minutes. Syrup fills 2 quarts.

Mrs. Steven Katie Jantzi

Bread and Butter Pickles

1 tsp. celery seed
1 tsp. mustard seed
1 tsp. salt
3 c. water
3 c. vinegar
6 c. sugar
1 tsp. turmeric

Put first 3 ingredients in bottom of a quart jar then fill with sliced pickles. Heat water, vinegar, sugar and turmeric until dissolved then pour over pickles. Close jars and cold pack for 5 minutes. Yield: 5-6 quarts.

Miss Edna Mae Schrock

Canning, Freezing

Garlic Dill Pickles

9 c. sugar
6 c. water
6 c. vinegar
6 Tbsp. salt
1½ Tbsp. dry mustard
1½ Tbsp. turmeric

Bring the above mixture to a boil. Fill jars with pickles; add 1 head dill, and 1 clove garlic. Pour hot syrup over pickles. One batch of syrup is about right for 10 quart pickles. Put in hot water bath. Bring to a boil. Remove from hot water at once.

Mrs. Leroy Barbara Weaver

Kosher Dill Pickles

1 tsp. dry mustard
½ tsp turmeric
1 tsp. minced garlic, rounded
2 tsp. dill seed or weed
½ tsp. black pepper
1 grape leaf or powdered alum

Brine:
1 qt. vinegar
3 qt. water
½ c. salt

Slice cucumbers lengthwise or use small whole ones. Stuff jars full and measure spices into each jar. Then pour boiling hot brine over it. Put grape leaf on top before closing. Makes enough brine for approximately 8 quart of pickles. Cold pack like regular pickles.

Mrs. Jacob Elsie Mishler

Barbecued Peppers

Sauce:
2 c. sugar
1 pt. vinegar
1 c. vegetable oil
26 oz. ketchup

Slice peppers; pack in jars. Top jars of peppers with a half garlic clove and ½ teaspoon oregano. Add boiling sauce. Cold pack for 5 minutes.

Miss Deborah Ann Miller

Cucumber Relish

10 c. ground cucumbers
4 c. ground onions
2 c. ground green peppers
1 c. ground red peppers
3 c. sugar

2½ c. vinegar
½ c. cornstarch
5 tsp. salt
2 tsp. celery seed
½ tsp. turmeric

Combine cucumbers, onions, peppers, sugar and vinegar. Let stand a few hours. Mix cornstarch with a small amount of water. Add the rest of ingredients and mix with ground mixture. Put into pint jars. Process in boiling water bath for 10 minutes.

Note: We like to mix this with salad dressing to make tartar sauce for fish or chicken breast.

Mrs. Nelson Ruth Miller

Green Tomato Relish

1 gal. chopped green tomatoes
6 green bell peppers
6 red bell peppers
6 hot peppers

1 lg. head cabbage
1 qt. coarsely chopped onions
½ c. salt

Syrup:
½ gal. cider vinegar
3 lb. sugar
1 tsp. celery seed

1 tsp. ground cloves
1 tsp. ginger
1 tsp. cinnamon

Wash vegetables, put through food chopper using the medium blade. Add salt. Allow mixture to stand overnight. Drain well. Bring syrup ingredients to a boil. Add vegetables and boil for 30 minutes. Place in sterile jars and seal. Yield: approximately 14 pints.

Mrs. Perry Delores Herschberger

Sweet Pickle Relish

- 4 c. ground cucumbers
- 3 green peppers
- 2 lg. onions
- 1 Tbsp. salt
- 3 c. sugar
- 2¼ c. vinegar
- ¼ tsp. turmeric
- ¼ tsp. black pepper

Grind cucumbers, peppers and onions. Add salt. Let stand overnight. Drain and add rest of ingredients in order. Boil 5 minutes, then put in jars. Makes about 5-6 pints.

Note: Thicken a little with clear jel or Perma Flo.

Miss Susie Eicher

Salsa

- 20 lg. tomatoes
- 4 chopped onions
- 3 green peppers
- 5 or more hot peppers
- 2 Tbsp. salt
- 1 Tbsp. pepper
- 3 Tbsp. sugar
- 1½ tsp. cumin
- 1 Tbsp. garlic powder
- 1 Tbsp. chili powder
- 5 Tbsp. cornstarch or Perma Flo
- ½ c. vinegar
- 1 c. tomato sauce

Combine all ingredients. Cook for 10-15 minutes, then cold pack for 20 minutes. Yield: 8 pints.

Mrs. David Verda Miller

Come unto me all ye that perform and do your best and are depressed and I will give you rest.

Canning, Freezing

Canning Fruit

Cherries:
8 c. pitted cherries
12 c. water
½ tsp. salt
5 c. sugar, scant

1 Tbsp. butter
1 tsp. almond flavoring
1½ c. Perma Flo*
2 c. Perma Flo

Raspberries or Blackberries:
6 c. raspberries or blackberries
5 c. water
¼ tsp. salt

1½ c. sugar
1 c. Perma Flo,*
1½ c. Perma Flo

Blueberries:
8 c. blueberries
10 c. water
¼ tsp. salt
5 c. sugar

1 Tbsp. butter
1 Tbsp. lemon juice
1½ c. Perma Flo*
2 c. Perma Flo

Grapes:
8-9 c. grapes
10 c. water
½ tsp. salt
5 c. sugar

1 Tbsp. butter
1½ c. Perma Flo*
2 c. Perma Flo

Peaches:
6 qt. sliced peaches
3 c. water
6 c. sugar

3 c. pineapple juice
½ c. Jell-O, opt.
1¾ c. Perma Flo

Rhubarb:
8 qt. chopped rhubarb
6 qt. water
10 c. sugar

1¼ c. Jell-O
4 c. Perma Flo*

Blueberries and Cherries: Heat water, salt and sugar almost to boiling, then add fruit and other ingredients. When almost boiling, add Perma Flo mixture and bring to a boil again. Fill jars and hot water bath for 10 minutes. *Raspberries or Blackberries:* Thicken sauce, then add berries last. Hot water bath for 10 minutes. *Grapes:* Boil first 4 ingredients till grapes are soft, then strain through food mill. Return juice to heat and add butter.

Bring almost to boiling, then thicken with Perma Flo mixture. Stir well while bringing to a boil again. Hot water bath for 10 minutes. *Peaches:* Bring water, pineapple juice and sugar to a boil. (Or omit pineapple juice and double the amount of water). Add Perma Flo mixture, and boil till thick. If desired, add orange and/or pineapple Jell-O, or you can use ½ can of orange juice concentrate. Cool slightly, then add sliced peaches and mix well. Do not fill jars to the neck, because they will easily overflow when canning. Hot water bath for 20 minutes. Yield: 7 quarts. This is very handy when preparing fruit pizza, mixed fruit, etc. It is also good as is in lunch buckets or with other meals. Another option is adding pineapple chunks to your peaches. *Rhubarb:* Rhubarb may be chopped and soaked in soda water overnight to remove some of the tartness. Drain water and put rhubarb into a large stockpot, along with fresh water and sugar. Boil till soft. Thicken with Perma Flo mixed with water. Turn off heat and add Jell-O. Stir till dissolved. Yield: approximately 13 quarts. Fill jars and hot water bath for 10 minutes.

    Note: *Perma Flo with a star is for regular table use. Perma Flo without a star is thicker for pudding and pie filling. Always mix Perma Flo or Miraclear or other thickener with an equal or greater amount of water before adding to other ingredients.

Mrs. Samuel Rachel Chupp

Apple Pie Filling

6 qt. chopped apples
5 c. apple juice
5 c. water, divided
¾ c. lemon juice

4 c. sugar
1½ c. Perma Flo
1 Tbsp. cinnamon

    Peel and slice apples. In 14-quart or larger kettle heat apple juice, 2½ cups water and lemon juice. Mix dry ingredients together, add 2½ cups cold water, then add to hot juice. Stir until boiling. Add apples; mix well, and fill jars. Process in boiling water for 25 minutes. Yield: 7 quarts.

Mrs. Nelson Ruth Miller

Fruit Slush

4 c. sugar
6 c. hot water
12 oz. frozen orange juice concentrate
6 bananas, mashed
2 (20 oz.) cans crushed pineapple
6 c. fresh mashed peaches

Mix water and sugar until dissolved. Mix orange juice and 1½ cup cold water, then add to water and sugar mixture. Add pineapple, bananas and peaches. Freeze in any size containers you wish. Allow to thaw until slushy before serving.

Mrs. Jerry Esther Schrock

Grape Sauce

1 qt. pure grape juice
1 qt. water
1½ c. sugar
1 c. Perma Flo

Bring grape juice, water and sugar to a boil in a 4 quart kettle. Mix Perma Flo with 1 cup warm water and stir into juice. Cook until it thickens.

Mrs. Ernest Mary Ellen Miller

Peach Pie Filling

12 c. sugar
1 (46 oz.) can pineapple juice
6 c. water
1 can frozen orange juice conc.
1 tsp. salt
4 c. Perma Flo
4 c. water
12 qt. sliced peaches

Heat first 5 ingredients to boiling, then add Perma Flo which has been dissolved in water. Boil till thick. Cool slightly, then add peaches and mix well. Cold pack 20 minutes. Yield: approximately 17 quarts.

Note: Can use only about 2½ c. Perma Flo. This will not be thick enough for pie but is good to use for canned or fresh fruit. Can also use this glaze for mixed fruit such as apples, bananas, pineapple, grapes, etc.

Mrs. Wilbur Wilma Miller

Peach Pie Filling

6 qt. sliced fresh peaches
5¼ c. cold water
1¾ c. lemon juice
2¼ c. Perma Flo

5 c. sugar
20 oz. crushed pineapple
1 c. orange Jell-O

Peel and slice peaches. In 14-quart or larger kettle, heat water and lemon juice. Mix together Perma Flo, sugar and 3½ cup water. Add to hot water, stir until boiling. Add orange Jell-O and mix. Add peaches and pineapple, mix well. Fill jars and process immediately in boiling water for 25 minutes.
Note: If not processed immediately it will be thin.

Mrs. Nelson Ruth Miller

Pineapple-Orange Fruit to Can

1 gal. crushed pineapple
2 gal. water
4 lb. sugar
2½-3 lb. Perma Flo

1 gal. mandarin oranges
1 gal. peaches
24 oz. orange or apricot Jell-O

Heat pineapple, water and sugar to boiling. Add Perma Flo mixed with 1 quart water. Bring to boil again and add other fruit and Jell-O. Put in jars and cold pack for 15 minutes. Adds a nice variety to your canning shelves. Is good on cheesecakes or with fruit mix as a fruit glaze.

Mrs. Monroe Elsie Miller

Raspberry Pie Filling

8 c. raspberries
7½ c. water

4 c. sugar
2 c. Perma Flo

Bring raspberries, water and sugar to a boil. Gradually stir in Perma Flo mixture. Bring to a boil again. Put in jars and cold pack 10-15 minutes.
Note: When canning to use as fruit, use only 1 cup Perma Flo.

Mrs. Gerald Betty Kauffman

Thank You Pie Filling

10 c. water
4 c. sugar
2 c. Therm Flo
2 c. water

1 c. Jell-O
2 tsp. vanilla
½ c. butter
3 qt. fruit

Bring 10 cups water and sugar to a boil. Mix 2 cup Therm Flo with 2 cups water until dissolved. Stir into hot sugar water. Remove from heat. Add Jell-O, vanilla and butter, then fruit. Use cherry Jell-O for cherry, orange for peach, raspberry for raspberry etc. For apple, omit Jell-O and add 4 teaspoons cinnamon. Use scant Therm Flo for apple. If this is too thick for your taste add more juice or hot water or use less thickener. Also add more or less fruit to your taste. This can be canned or frozen. If canning, process in boiling bath for 20 minutes. Leave ½" space at neck of jar.

Miss Miriam Miller

Freezing Strawberries

When freezing strawberries, add only a small part of the sugar so they freeze harder. When thawing, chop them up real well as soon as possible with a food chopper. This keeps them from getting watery, then add sugar to taste.

Mrs. Ernest Sara Schrock

Canning Beef Chunks

1 c. salt
2 tsp. soda
1 qt. water

1 tsp. salt petre
1 c. brown sugar

Mix all ingredients and bring to a boil. Let cool then add 1 gallon water. Pour over 16 pounds of meat chunks till covered. Put something on top to weight it down. Let stand in brine 5-7 days. Drain and cold pack. You don't need to add any liquid to can. Quart jars need to be pressure cooked at 10 pounds for 60 minutes. Pint jars at 10 pounds for 45 minutes.

Note: 40 pounds beef makes 50 pints.

Mrs. Howard Ellen Schrock

Jerky

1 lb. venison
½ c. Worcestershire sauce
⅓ c. soy sauce
2 Tbsp. liquid smoke

1 tsp. seasoned salt
¾ tsp. garlic powder
¾ tsp. onion salt
¼ tsp. black pepper

Cut in strips 1"x5" or whatever is easy to chew when done. Combine meat and all ingredients in a plastic bag. Refrigerate overnight, stir occasionally. Drain liquid and dry meat on paper towel. Bake 3 hours on an oven rack at 140°. Keep oven door cracked a bit.

Mrs. Monroe Elsie Miller

To Cure Ham

10 lb. ham
⅓ c. salt
1 tsp. salt petre

2 tsp. soda
⅓ c. brown sugar
1 Tbsp. liquid smoke

Bring to a boil, cool and add enough cold water to cover meat. Let stand for 3 weeks in refrigerator, then take out and wash off with cold water. Bake in roaster at 350° for 2-3 hours. Eat as is or use in casseroles that call for ham.

Mrs. Monroe Elsie Miller

Brine for Liver and Steaks

4 qt. water
1 c. sugar, scant
1 c. salt, scant

Heat enough water to dissolve sugar and salt. Slice liver and soak in water awhile so blood will drain out. Change water and soak again. Drain well. Then put 1 cup of brine in each quart jar and put meat slices in to fill the jar. Fill only to where the jar gets narrow. Close jars, and boil in hot water for 1 hour. When ready to use, drain water off and pour out. Dip liver in flour and fry in lard and butter, till browned. This is more tender than frozen liver and is good with tomato gravy and crackers so don't throw the liver out when you butcher.

Mrs. Ernest Sara Schrock

Curing Meats
turkey, ham, bacon, etc.

2 gal. water
2 c. salt
1 c. brown sugar
1 Tbsp. black pepper
½ c. soda
1 c. vinegar

Mix everything together and stir till dissolved. Pour over meat. Let soak 1 week for bacon and turkey breasts, and 4 weeks for regular ham. Set in a cold place. After soaking, smoke meat. This is also good to soak chicken. A good Tender Quick substitute.

Mrs. Wilbur Wilma Miller

Canning, Freezing

Smoked Turkey Thighs

1 c. Tender Quick
8-10 c. water
5 Tbsp. liquid smoke

15 lb. boneless, skinless
turkey thighs

Dissolve Tender Quick in water and add meat. Make sure meat is covered with water. Let stand 2 days in refrigerator. Pour off water and drain well. Sprinkle liquid smoke over drained meat. Let set 2 more days, stirring occasionally. Pack into jars and cold pack 3 hours. You can also pressure it at 10 pounds for 90 minutes. When filling jars leave good head space to prevent spoilage. Do not add liquid. It will produce it's own. Delicious! Tastes just like ham.

Note: You can take off fat if desired. You can also de-bone the drumstick and leave the fins in the meat. After canned pick out the fins.

Mrs. Ervin Ella Miller

Bacons

1 c. Tender Quick

7 c. water

Mix till Tender Quick is dissolved and pour over bacon. Make as many batches as necessary to completely cover the bacons. Soak 3 days, then smoke them. Have bacon cold and slightly frozen to slice. Is best if sliced thin.

Mrs. Wilbur Wilma Miller

Cheerfulness, joy and contentment
are preserves of youthful looks.

Bologna

30 lb. burger	1½ tsp. dry mustard
1 lb. Tender Quick	2 c. dry milk
2 c. brown sugar	1 Tbsp. garlic
2½ Tbsp. black pepper	1 Tbsp. Mace
4 Tbsp. Accent	2 qt. water
1 lb. oatmeal	¼-½ c. liquid smoke

Grind burger once. Mix all dry ingredients together, then add to burger. Grind again, then add water and liquid smoke. Grind another 2 times. Stuff into bags and let set for a few days. Wrap your rolls tightly in tin foil and bake at 200° for 4 hours or till 160°-170°. Smoke if desired. Slice and freeze. This takes quite a lot of time, but very handy once it is in the freezer.

Mrs. Leroy Barbara Weaver

Pork Bologna

25 lb. sausage	1½ tsp. garlic powder
¾ lb. Tender Quick	1 lb. powdered milk
2 c. brown sugar	1 qt. water
1½ Tbsp. black pepper	5 tsp. liquid smoke
1 tsp. salt petre	

Mix pork and Tender Quick, grind twice. Let set 24-48 hours, then add remaining ingredients and grind another 2 times. Stuff cloth bags. Wrap with heavy duty tin foil. Make sure your tin foil has no holes; handle carefully when putting in oven. Bake 6-7 hours at 170°. Meat is done when it tests 150° in center with meat thermometer. Cool immediately. Smoke.

Note: If you want to omit the Tender Quick, add 1.2 ounces vegetable powder and 1¼ cup salt instead of Tender Quick. Omit liquid smoke if you smoke your bologna.

Mrs. Wilbur Wilma Miller

Sausage Seasoning

1⅜ c. salt
¼ c. black pepper
¼ c. sage

1 Tbsp. red pepper
1 c. brown sugar

Mix together; sprinkle over meat and mix well before grinding. This is for 50 pounds pork. Can be frozen or canned. Cold Pack: Fry meat or put in oven to bake (stir several times.) Put sausage crumbs in jar and cold pack like other meat. Very good on pizza.

Mrs. Wilbur Wilma Miller

Sausage Seasoning

50 lb. ground meat
6 Tbsp. black pepper
3 Tbsp. dry mustard

3 Tbsp. garlic
1 c. salt
2 c. brown sugar

Mix all seasonings and brown sugar. Mix with meat and grind twice.

Mrs. Leroy Barbara Weaver

Sausage

40 lb. pork
1 c. salt

⅓ c. pepper
⅔ c. sage

Mix on table or in tub before grinding. Then freeze or cold pack. Meatballs can be baked on cookie sheets then cold packed.
Note: 40 pounds pork is 5 gallons.

Mrs. Ernest Mary Ellen Miller

Our Favorite Sausage

35-40 lb. pork
¾ c. Tender Quick
2 Tbsp. liquid smoke
2 Tbsp. black pepper, rounded
½ c. salt

Grind together 3 times and stuff in casings or make patties or balls. Cut casings in desired length. Prick with fork and roast. Divide juice in jars then fill with water. Pressure cook 30 minutes at 10 pounds pressue.

Mrs. Delbert Martha Schrock

Stuffed Sausage

25 lb. pork
½ recipe of sausage seasoning
2½ c. oatmeal
2½ c. water

Brine:
4 qt. water
½ c. salt
½ c. brown sugar
1 tsp. pepper

Sprinkle meat with seasoning, grind. Add oatmeal and water; grind another 2 times. Stuff casings, then smoke the sausages. If you don't smoke them you will need to bake them a little on cookie sheet or put in broiler. Cut to desired length and put in jars. Cover with brine. Cold pack like other meat. Yield: approximately 12-15 quarts.

Mrs. Wilbur Wilma Miller

When you help someone up a hill,
you are that much closer
to the top yourself.

Venison Bologna

30 lb. burger (venison)	4 Tbsp. Accent salt
1 lb. Tender Quick	½ c. liquid smoke
2 c. brown sugar	1 lb. oatmeal
1 Tbsp. black pepper, scant	1 tsp. dry mustard
1 Tbsp. garlic	2 c. dry milk
1 Tbsp. Mace	2 qt. water

Grind meat once and then mix in dry ingredients. Then add liquids and mix well. Grind again. When grinding the third time, put into bags or jars. Let set 48 hours to cure. When Cold Packing: Pressure it to 10 pounds for 45 minutes. To Bake Bologna: Wrap in heavy duty tin foil and bake in oven at 200°. Is done when temperature of bologna reaches 160°-170° with a meat thermometer. To Cook Bologna: Bring water to a boil, then put in bologna and time for about 40 minutes and then check to see if it reaches 160°-170°. When Baking or Cooking: Put in cold water 15 minutes as soon as done to make so bags come off easier. Very delicious!

Mrs. Clifford Rhoda Herschberger

Refried Beans

dry beans (pinto, red or black)	salt
garlic, several cloves per lb. of beans	water
several slices of bacon, opt.	½ tsp. cumin per lb. of beans, opt.

Sort the beans watching out for dirty beans or beans with spots on them. This will help with the taste! Soak the beans in water overnight. Next morning; wash the beans and put in kettle with plenty of fresh water. Your kettle should be only about half full of beans at this point as the beans will expand. Cover and bring to a boil. Let set 15 minutes. Drain off the water. Rinse beans well, add plenty of water, the bacon and garlic. Let simmer gently, adding water as needed. Once the beans are soft, maybe 4-6 hours, add salt to taste and mash with potato masher. Add water if needed to make them the consistency of mashed potatoes. Now they're ready to serve or cold pack. To Cold Pack: Fill clean jars, leaving about 1½" head space. Pressure cook 40 minutes at 10 pounds for quarts.

Mrs. Wilbur Wilma Miller

Canning, Freezing

Chili Sauce

½ bu. tomatoes
4 peppers
4 onions
4 celery stalks
1 pkg. Mrs. Wages chili seasoning
¼ c. salt
1½ c. Perma Flo
2 c. vinegar
2 c. brown sugar

Cook tomatoes and put through strainer. Grind peppers, onions and celery. Add rest of ingredients and thicken with Perma Flo, Pressure at 5 pounds for 3 minutes. Yield: approximately 15-20 quarts.

Mrs. Leroy Barbara Weaver

Sweet Baby Ray Barbecue Sauce

6 qt. chopped tomatoes
1 gal. juice
1 lg. onion
1 green pepper
1 clove garlic or
 ¾ tsp. garlic powder
½ c. water
2¾ c. brown sugar
⅓ c. Worcestershire sauce
4 tsp. dry mustard
4 tsp. chili powder
4 tsp. salt
½ c. vinegar
2 tsp. celery salt
2½ tsp. hickory smoke
2 c. honey
2 (16 oz.) bottles Sweet Baby
 Ray barbecue sauce
5 Tbsp. Perma Flo, heaping

Cook tomatoes, onions and peppers till tender. Put through victorio strainer, then add the rest of ingredients, except the Perma Flo mixed with juice to thicken. If you want it thicker add more Perma Flo. Hot water bath for 15 minutes. Yield: 8 quarts.

Mrs. Ervin Ella Miller

Barbecue Sauce

4 qt. ketchup
6 c. brown sugar
3 c. sugar
3 c. honey
3 c. molasses
½ c. mustard
6 Tbsp. Worcestershire sauce
1 Tbsp. salt
1 Tbsp. liquid smoke
1½ tsp. pepper

Make your favorite ketchup then add the rest of the ingredients. Bring to a boil and cold pack for 10 minutes. We use this on grilled meat like chicken and hamburgers, etc. Yield: approximately 8 quarts.

Mrs. Ervin Ella Miller

Barbecue Sauce

15 c. tomato juice
4 c. finely chopped onions
¾ c. ReaLemon
8 c. brown sugar
⅔ c. white sugar
3 c. vinegar
¾ c. mustard
⅔ c. liquid smoke
⅔ c. salt
2 c. Worcestershire sauce
⅓ c. paprika

Bring everything to a boil. Make a paste of 2 cups cornstarch and 3 cups water or tomato juice. Slowly add to hot mixture, stirring quickly with wire whip to blend. Bring to a full rolling boil. Fill jars and seal.

Mrs. Perry Delores Herschberger

Canning, Freezing

Smokey Honey Barbecue Sauce

4 qt. homemade ketchup
3 lb. brown sugar
3 c. honey
2 c. Worcestershire sauce
⅔ c. mustard
1 c. lemon juice
1 c. liquid smoke
3 Tbsp. salt
8 tsp. chili powder
1 c. vinegar
1 c. Perma Flo

Bring ketchup to boiling. Add rest of ingredients except vinegar and Perma Flo. Boil 15 minutes. Mix vinegar and Perma Flo then add to sauce and boil another 15 minutes. Pour into jars and seal. Yield: 12 pints.

IMPORTANT: Keep stirring all through cooking time to prevent scorching.

Mrs. Steven Katie Jantzi

Apple Barbecue Sauce

1 qt. homemade ketchup
1 qt. applesauce
2 lb. brown sugar
4 tsp. salt
3 Tbsp. mustard
1 Tbsp. chili powder
1 c. Worcestershire sauce
½ c. lemon juice
½ c. vinegar
½ c. Perma Flo

Bring ketchup and applesauce to boil. Add rest of ingredients except vinegar and Perma Flo. Boil 15 minutes. Mix vinegar and sugar then add to sauce and boil another 15 minutes. Pour into jars and seal. Yield: 6 pints.

IMPORTANT: Keep stirring all through cooking time to prevent scorching.

Mrs. Steven Katie Jantzi

Necessity drives where ambition can't cope.

Ketchup

2 gal. chopped tomatoes
3¼ c. sugar
⅓ c. salt
2 tsp. mustard
¾ c. vinegar
⅛ tsp. cloves
¾ tsp. pepper
1½ tsp. celery salt
½ tsp. cinnamon
¾ tsp. onion salt
40 oz. tomato paste

Cook tomatoes till soft. Drain off liquid and put pulp through victorio strainer. Should have approximately 1 gallon juice. Then return to stove and add all ingredients except tomato paste. When hot, add paste. You can also add some Perma Flo to thicken it. Put in jars and hot water bath for 10 minutes. This tastes similar to bought ketchup. Yield: 6 quarts.

Mrs. Ervin Ella Miller

Heinz Ketchup

½ bu. tomatoes
2 celery sticks
2 c. chopped onions
1 qt. vinegar
7 c. sugar
½ c. salt
1 tsp. cinnamon
1 tsp. cloves
1 tsp. nutmeg
½-1 tsp. red cayenne pepper
1 tsp. ginger

Chunk tomatoes, add celery and onions. Cook until soft then put through a victorio strainer. Take 8 quarts juice and add rest of ingredients, except spices. Make a small bag (3"x5") from thin material. Put spices in bag, tie shut and add to juice. Cook 15 minutes, then thicken with 3 cups mira clear or Therma Flo. Remove spices. Hot water bath 10-13 minutes. Yield: 10-11 quarts.

Mrs. Monroe Elsie Miller

Homemade Ketchup

20 qt. tomato juice, use paste tomatoes
3 sweet peppers
1 lg. onion
¼ bunch celery
3 qt. tomatoes
120 oz. tomato paste
1 gal. bought ketchup
2¾ c. vinegar
1 c. salt
10 c. sugar
¼ c. dry mustard
¼ c. paprika
1½ Tbsp. cloves
1½ Tbsp. cinnamon
1½ Tbsp. allspice
3 c. Perma Flo

Pour 20 quart juice into cloth bag and drain off about 5 qt. watery liquid. Reserve this. Cook other vegetables in tomatoes until soft. Put through victorio strainer, but do not drain this part. Bring all juice to a rolling boil. Cook 20-30 minutes. Add tomato paste, ketchup, vinegar, salt, sugar and spices. Mix spices with part of sugar to prevent lumping. Let boil 30 minutes or more. Mix Perma Flo with 3-4 cups reserved watery juice. Add to ketchup and boil another 15 minutes. Pour into jars and cold pack. Yield: 40 pints.

IMPORTANT: Keep stirring all through cooking time to prevent scorching.

Mrs. Steven Katie Jantzi

Chili Sauce

20 qt. kettle of tomato juice
4 c. chopped onions
4 c. chopped green peppers
1½ c. vinegar
2 lb. brown sugar
1 Tbsp. cinnamon
2 tsp. nutmeg
1 tsp. garlic powder
1½ tsp. celery salt
2 tsp. black pepper
5 Tbsp. salt
3 Tbsp. chili powder

Mix all ingredients together. Put into jars and process in boiling water bath 10 minutes. To make chili soup, fry meat of your choice: sausage, hamburger or venison. Add 1 quart chili sauce and 28 ounces Bush's baked beans. Thicken with a little Perma Flo if you prefer.

Mrs. Nelson Ruth Miller

Pizza Sauce

6 qt. tomato juice
¾ c. finely chopped onions
½ c. finely chopped green peppers
1 c. vegetable oil

2 Tbsp. salt
1½ tsp. oregano
1½ Tbsp. pizza seasoning
3 c. sugar

Mix all together in a large kettle. Bring to boil, then thicken with 2 qt. tomato juice and 2 cup Therm Flo. Bring to boil again. Put into jars and process in boiling water bath for 10 minutes.

Note: Two batches will fill a 20 quart kettle.

Mrs. Nelson Ruth Miller

Thick and Spicy Pizza Sauce

6 qt. tomato juice
8 celery sticks, chopped fine
9 onions, chopped fine
4 peppers, chopped fine
3 Tbsp. garlic powder or garlic buds
3 c. sugar
1 qt. ketchup
9 Tbsp. parsley

6 Tbsp. salt
2 Tbsp. pepper
6 Tbsp. paprika
3 Tbsp. chili powder
3 Tbsp. oregano
3 Tbsp. dry mustard
2¼ c. Parmesan cheese
1 gal. tomato paste

Cook tomato juice, celery, onions, peppers and garlic until tender. Mix in all the rest of the ingredients. If it tastes a little too rich, I add more tomato juice. Bring to a boil. Put in jars and cold pack 30 minutes or pressure cook 5 minutes at 10 pounds pressure.

Mrs. Samuel Dorothy Miller

Canning, Freezing

Pizza Hut Pizza Sauce

4½ gal. chopped tomatoes
4 green peppers
8-10 onions
2 c. olive oil
1 c. sugar
2 Tbsp. basil
2 Tbsp. oregano

6 bay leaves
½ tsp. red pepper
3 Tbsp. pizza seasoning
1 Tbsp. Italian seasoning
1 Tbsp. garlic powder
½ c. salt
1 gal. tomato paste, divided

Cook tomatoes, peppers and onions for 1 hour. Put through victorio strainer. Tomatoes should equal 2½ gallons juice. Add all ingredients except half of tomato paste. Cook 1 hour then add other ½ gallon tomato paste. If you don't have that much paste you can use mira clear or Perma Flo to thicken it. Put in jars and bake at 200° for 30 minutes. Yield: 25 pints.

Mrs. Ervin Ella Miller

Pizza Hut Pizza Sauce

2½ gal. tomato juice
8-10 onions, chopped
4 green peppers, chopped
2 Tbsp. basil
2 Tbsp. oregano
1 Tbsp. red pepper, scant
3 Tbsp. pizza seasoning

1 Tbsp. cumin
1 Tbsp. celery salt
2 c. sugar
½ c. salt
1 tsp. garlic powder
2 c. vegetable oil
1 gal. tomato paste

Mix all ingredients except half of the tomato paste. Cook together 1 hour, then add another ½ gallon tomato paste. Mix well. Put into jars. Process in hot water bath for 10 minutes. Yield: 25 pints.

Note: You can also thicken the sauce with Therm Flo instead of tomato paste.

Mrs. Kenneth Leanna Kauffman

Canning, Freezing

Pizza Sauce

3 gal. tomato juice
3 lb. onions
3 hot peppers
6 crumbled bay leaves
1 red pepper
1 green pepper
2 c. vegetable oil
2 c. vinegar
48 oz. tomato paste

1½ c. sugar
4 tsp. paprika
¼ c. basil
1 tsp. black pepper
½ c. salt
¼ c. oregano
1 tsp. minced garlic
1 tsp. red pepper
4-8 Tbsp. cornstarch, heaping

Stir everything together in a large kettle. Cook for 20-30 minutes. Stir often. Ladle into jars and seal. Yield: approximately 26 pints.

Mrs. Isaac Daisy Troyer

Canned Cheeseburger Soup

8 lb. hamburger, browned
2 c. chopped onions
3 c. butter
5 c. flour
7½ qt. chicken broth
7½ tsp. salt
2½ tsp. black pepper

½ lb. chicken base
4 tsp. parsley
4 tsp. basil
10 qt. shredded potatoes
4 c. cubed celery
7½ c. shredded carrots

Brown hamburger with onions. Brown butter; add flour to make a paste. Slowly add chicken broth. Add seasonings. Last add hamburger and raw vegetables. Put into jars. Pressure cook 1 hour at 10 pounds pressure. When opening, add 1 cup milk and some Velveeta cheese to 1 quart soup. Yield: 21 quarts.

Note: I needed to add more liquid so I added water.

Mrs. William Miriam Yoder

Canning, Freezing

Chunky Soup

2½ gal. water
¾ c. beef soup base
2 qt. beef broth
4 qt. tomato juice
1¾ c. sugar, opt.
¼ c. salt
4 qt. chopped carrots
2 qt. beans
3 qt. peas
4 qt. cubed potatoes
7 c. flour
8 lb. hamburger
2 lg. onions, chopped

Heat water, soup base, beef broth, tomato juice, sugar and salt. Cut vegetables into small cubes and cook separately in salt water, then add to mixture. Mix flour and add enough water to make a smooth paste. Use this to thicken soup. Season hamburger with salt, pepper and onions; fry. Add to soup, and stir well. Put in jars. Cold pack for 2 hours or in pressure cooker for 40 minutes at 10 pounds pressure. Delicious and nourishing. Yield: 30 quarts.

Miss Lovina Eicher

Chunky Chicken or Turkey Soup

2½ gal. water
4 qt. chicken broth
¾ c. chicken base
2 lg. onions
½ c. butter
4 qt. potatoes
3 qt. peas
2 qt. celery
2 qt. carrots
½ c. parsley
8 lb. chopped chicken
¼ c. salt
1 tsp. pepper
3½ c. flour

Bring water, broth and chicken base to a boil. Sauté onions in butter and add to the water. Add all the vegetables, chicken, salt and pepper. Mix flour with some water to make a paste. Add to the soup to thicken to desired consistency. Pressure cook 50 minutes at 10 pounds pressure. Yield: 23 quarts.

Note: When opening a jar for soup, we usually add some milk and cheese. Sometimes we add cooked noodles and eat it like a casserole.

Mrs. Ervin Ella Miller

Chili Soup

10 lb. hamburger
1½ c. chopped onions
2 Tbsp. salt
1 tsp. red pepper
2 Tbsp. chili powder, rounded
¾ c. chopped green peppers
10 qt. water
2 c. brown sugar
3 c. flour
4 qt. ketchup
1 gal. pork and beans

Fry the first 6 ingredients. Heat the water and brown sugar and thicken with flour. In a large container, mix everything well, then pack into quart jars, leaving an inch of space under the neck of the jar. Pressure cook for 1 hour at 10 pounds. Yield: 21-23 quarts.

Note: You can chop onions and peppers in season, freeze them in ice cube trays and toss them into the soup for additional flavor during cold winter days!

Mrs. Dennis Marilyn Hershberger

Chili Soup

20 lb. hamburger
2 c. flour
1 c. Worcestershire sauce
7 (15 oz.) cans hot chili beans
2½ c. brown sugar
60 oz. ketchup
10 qt. tomato juice
2 qt. water
4 qt. pizza sauce
4 med. onions, chopped
2 lb. spaghetti, broken and cooked
3 Tbsp. chili powder

Fry hamburger and onions, sprinkle salt and pepper on it to taste. Add the 2 cups flour to meat while warm. Cook spaghetti till almost soft. Mix all ingredients together in a tub. Taste to see if it has enough spices. Fill jars. Put in pressure cooker 45 minutes at 10 pounds pressure. Yield: 27 quarts.

Mrs. Ernie Freeda Yoder

Canning, Freezing

Chili Soup

20 qt. tomato juice
3 qt. water
12 lb. hamburger, fried
chopped onions
3 bunches celery, boiled soft
2 (28 oz.) cans crushed tomatoes

2 (28 oz.) cans Bush baked beans
3 (30 oz.) cans chili beans
7 (15 oz.) cans tomato sauce
5 lb. brown sugar
4 tsp. black pepper
⅔ c. salt
½ c. chili powder

Cold pack 3 hours. Yield: 40 quarts.

Mrs. Howard Ellen Schrock

Mom's Chili

1 bu. tomatoes
8 lg. onions
8 lg. peppers
diced garlic, opt.
4 c. brown sugar

½ c. salt
4 pkg. McCormick chili seasoning
1 lb. Perma Flo
2 c. vinegar

Juice the tomatoes. Dice the onions, peppers and garlic. Mix together. Add the sugar, salt and chili seasoning. Make a paste with Perma Flo and vinegar. Add to the soup to thicken. Bring to a boil again. Cold pack in hot water bath for 1 hour or 10 pounds pressure for 10 minutes. Yield: 35 quarts.

Note: I usually just can the sauce without the beans and hamburger, then when I open the sauce I add fresh hamburger and beans.

Mrs. Samuel Dorothy Miller

Jesus died for a reason — and you are it.

Miscellaneous

Miscellaneous

Butterscotch Topping 305	Horse Fly Spray.....................310
Coal Garden 310	Laundry Soap 310
Cottage Cheese 301	Magic Garden 311
Dish Cleaning Solution..............307	Melt Cheese (similar to Velveeta)........302
Drying Leaves 311	Oven Dried Roses 311
Eagle Brand Milk Substitute 305	Play Dough 308
Easy Play Dough 307	Play Dough 308
Egg Salad..........................304	Rehydration Drink 306
Egg Salad..........................304	Stainless Steel Cleaner 307
Farmer's Cheese....................301	Taco Seasoning Mix.................305
Finger Paint.......................309	Tomato Blight Recipe 312
Food for Feathered Friends 309	Velveeta Cheese 302
Gripe Water.......................306	Yogurt 303
Homemade Solution for Plants........309	Yogurt 303

Miscellaneous

Cottage Cheese

3 gal. skim milk
⅛ tsp. cheese culture

1 Tbsp. salt
cream and milk

Heat skim milk to 72°. Add culture and stir well. Place cover on stockpot and let stand approximately 12 hours. If you have any cream left on your milk, you can now skim this off and use it like store-bought sour cream. Cut in ½" cubes. Heat, stirring constantly, or you may use your hand trying to get the whey out of your curds. Heat to 115°. Let stand approximately 10 minutes. Pour in a cheesecloth lined colander. Drain several minutes, then run cold water over the curds while working with your hand, till curds are cold. Squeeze out all the water you can after draining several hours. Add salt, cream and/or milk till desired consistency.

Note: You may whip the cream before adding to curds.

Mrs. Wilbur Wilma Miller

Farmer's Cheese

4 gal. milk
¼ tsp. cheese culture
1 tsp. rennet

¼ c. cold water
3 Tbsp. salt

Very slowly heat milk to 92°, stirring occasionally. Add cheese culture, stir well, and let set for 1 hour. Add rennet dissolved in cold water. Stir well for 2-3 minutes then let set for 30-40 minutes. Cut curds into ½" cubes with a long-bladed knife. Stir while heating to 110-115°. Let set for 30 minutes. Drain off whey (15 minutes), then add salt and work in with your hands. Put curds in a press for 6-8 hours.

Note: You can soak the cheese in a salt brine for 3 days, turning it every day. Brine is 2 pounds salt diluted in 1 gallon of cold water. When cheese is sealed leave at room temperature or in cellar to age one month or more.

Miss Marietta W. Miller

Miscellaneous

Melt Cheese (similar to Velveeta)

1 gal. milk
2-4 tsp. citric acid
1 tsp. soda
¼ c. butter

2 tsp. salt or to suit taste
½ c. milk
3-6 Tbsp. cheddar cheese powder

Heat milk to 140°. Remove from heat and add citric acid. Stir gently until separated. Drain off whey. To curds add the rest of ingredients. Heat on low and stir briskly till lumps are dissolved. I then pour it into a greased glass bread pan and let set till cooled off a bit. Cover with plastic wrap and store in refrigerator. Melts well and tastes good.

Mrs. Ernest Ray Inez Miller

Velveeta Cheese

2½ gal. milk
2 tsp. soda
½ c. butter

½ c. cream
1 Tbsp. salt

Let milk sour till thick. Heat till scalded and pour into cheesecloth. Let hang until dry (12 hours) or overnight. Crumble curds to make fine crumbs, then mix soda into curds and let stand 2 hours. Place in double boiler and add butter. Melt butter with curds then add salt. Mix well. Add cream; if you want the cheese to be a spreading consistency, add 1½-2 cups cream. Stir until smooth. Pour into buttered container and cover. Let stand until completely cool, then slice.

Mrs. Jacob Elsie Mishler

God helps those who help others,
not themselves.

Miscellaneous

Yogurt

1 qt. milk
1 Tbsp. gelatin
2 Tbsp. water

¼ c. yogurt starter
½ c. maple syrup
dash of vanilla

Heat the milk to 180°. Dissolve gelatin in water, then stir into the hot milk. Let it cool to 110°, then stir in the yogurt starter. (Greek yogurt works well if you don't have your own.) Remove 4 tablespoons starter for the next batch, then stir in the maple syrup and vanilla. Set in a warm place for 4 hours, then refrigerate. This recipe works well with goat's milk.

Mrs. Dennis Marilyn Hershberger

Yogurt

1 gal. skim milk
2 Tbsp. plain gelatin
½ c. cold water

2 Tbsp. vanilla
4 Tbsp. plain yogurt
2 c. sugar

Heat milk in large kettle to 190°. While heating, soak gelatin in cold water. Add to milk once it reaches 190°, then cool to 130°. Add vanilla, yogurt and sugar. Beat until smooth. Pour through wire strainer into 5 quart ice cream pail. Cover and put in warm place for 7 hours, or till set. The oven with only pilot on works well. Chill. Add pie filling, preserves or peanut butter for variation. Thicken any fruit you add. Yield: 1 gallon.

Mrs. Monroe Elsie Miller

Miscellaneous

Egg Salad

4 lb. hot dogs or ham
14 dozen eggs
2 c. finely diced onions
3 c. finely diced celery
3 lb. shredded Colby cheese
2 qt. salad dressing

6 c. sugar
¼ c. liquid smoke
1 Tbsp. Worcestershire sauce
mustard to taste
salt to taste

Chop hot dogs or ham, eggs, onions and celery. Put in a 20 quart bowl; add cheese. Combine other ingredients and pour over egg mixture. You may need more salad dressing if it gets too dry. You can use a potato masher, grinder or salad master to shred eggs, ham, and cheese. This makes a large amount. Can freeze leftovers for several months. Thaw in refrigerator. Serves 100 people.

Miss Miriam Miller

Egg Salad

12 dozen eggs
3 c. chopped celery
1¾ c. chopped onions

4 lb. hot dogs
3 lb. shredded Colby
   cheese, opt.

Sauce:
2 qt. salad dressing
3 c. sugar
5 Tbsp. mustard

4 Tbsp. liquid smoke, scant
2 tsp. salt
1 Tbsp. Worcestershire sauce

Cook eggs around 10 minutes to hard-boil in a few 8-quart kettles. Cool and peel. Shred eggs and hot dogs, add chopped onions, celery and cheese. Mix sauce in a separate bowl, then add to egg mixture and mix well. Keep refrigerated till served. Serves 125 people.

Mrs. Ernie Freeda Yoder

 *Miscellaneous*

Butterscotch Topping

¾ c. brown sugar
2 Tbsp. corn syrup
¼ c. milk
3 Tbsp. butter

Combine all ingredients. Stir until boiling and simmer for 3 minutes. Serves 8 people.

Miss Rosanna Jantzi

Eagle Brand Milk Substitute

2 c. milk
1 c. sugar

Mix sugar and milk. Cook until 225°. Cool and use as Eagle Brand milk.

Miss Susie Eicher

Taco Seasoning Mix

2 tsp. chili powder
1 tsp. paprika
1½ tsp. cumin
2 tsp. parsley flakes
1 tsp. onion powder
½ tsp. garlic salt
½ tsp. oregano

Combine together and use whenever you'd use the boughten mix. Mix in larger amounts and store in a glass jar. ¼ cup mix equals to a 1¼ ounce package.

Miss Verna Kay Miller

A lot of kneeling will keep you in good standing.

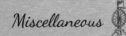

Miscellaneous

Gripe Water

6 oz. boiled sterile water
¼ tsp. soda

1 tsp. sugar
11 drops of flavoring, opt.

Dosage:
1 mo. = ½ tsp.
2-6 = 1 tsp.

over 6 mo. = 2 tsp.

This is similar to the Gripe Water sold in Canadian stores. The soda helps to bring up a baby's burps when he has a hard time doing so on his own. A dropper with teaspoon measurements on it comes in handy for this. Give as often as needed.

Mrs. Samuel Rachel Chupp

Rehydration Drink

1 liter boiled water
2 Tbsp. honey
¼ tsp. salt

¼ tsp. soda
½ c. frozen orange juice or
    a little mashed ripe banana

If your child has upset stomach and can't keep anything down, try this. Give the sick person a few sips every 5 minutes. This is a little sweet. If they can keep it down, try chicken broth, giving a tiny sip at a time.

Mrs. Leroy Barbara Weaver

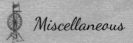

Miscellaneous

Dish Cleaning Solution

½ c. lye
1 c. liquid Tide
2 qt. bleach
15 qt. water

Heat until boiling. Dip (submerge) stainless steel using tongs to dip dishes. Let water cool off a little, then dip your Tupperware. You can also dip any glassware. Use rubber gloves to wash dishes, using regular dish detergent. Put vinegar in rinse water. Change dishwater frequently.

WARNING: Put lye in cool water; do not add lye to boiling water. Do not dip any aluminum or chrome. Enjoy your sparkling stainless pots and pans.

Note: remove any kind of knobs and handles.

Miss Miriam Miller

Stainless Steel Cleaner

½ canner water
½ c. lye
2 squirts dish detergent
¼ c. bleach

Be sure to put your ingredients in the water before it is too hot. Remove all knobs from your kettles and dip into hot water. Experiment on how long to leave it in the hot water. Take out of water and wash well, rinse in vinegar water. This also works well to clean any glass bakeware. It is fun to get out kettles that shine like new.

Mrs. Leroy Barbara Weaver

Easy Play Dough

1 c. salt
2 c. water
¼ c. vegetable oil
food coloring
4 tsp. cream of tartar
2 c. flour

Cook salt and water to almost boiling. Remove from heat. Add vegetable oil and food coloring, then dry ingredients. If this is too wet, knead in a bit more flour. If too dry, add a little water. Knead until smooth.

Miss Martha Miller

Miscellaneous

Play Dough

1 c. flour
1 c. salt
1 tsp. cream of tartar

1 tsp. oil
1 c. water
food coloring

Mix dry ingredients together. Add to water and food coloring, stirring constantly until mixture is consistency of dough. Remove from heat and let set until cool enough to handle. Keep in an airtight container and it will keep for weeks.

Mrs. Ervin Ella Miller

Play Dough

2½ c. flour
1 Tbsp. alum
2 c. water

1 c. salt
1 Tbsp. vegetable oil
food coloring

Place all ingredients in a saucepan. Stir constantly over low heat until mixture thickens into dough consistency. Remove from heat and let cool until it can be handled. Place on wax paper and knead until smooth. Store in airtight container.

Mrs. Joe Laura Hershberger

Miscellaneous

Finger Paint

½ c. cornstarch or clear jel
¾ c. cold water
1 Tbsp. unflavored gelatin
¼ c. cold water

2 c. hot water
½ c. powdered detergent
a few drops food coloring

In a saucepan mix cornstarch or clear jel with ¾ cup cold water. Set aside. Soak gelatin in ¼ cup cold water. Stir hot water into cornstarch mixture. Bring cornstarch mixture to a boil over medium heat and blend in gelatin mixture. Add powdered detergent and stir well. Then add food coloring. Store in airtight container in a cool place. Use the dull side of freezer paper or newspaper to paint on. Have fun. Yield: approximately 3 cups.

Miss Ruby Miller

Food for Feathered Friends

1 c. lard
⅓ c. sugar
2 c. cornmeal
1 c. bird seed

1 c. peanut butter
2 c. oatmeal
1 c. flour

Make lard warm or room temperature, then add rest of ingredients. Mix well and press in cookie sheet. Cool. Cut the size of your suet feeder. Yield: approximately 12 cakes.

Note: Old peanut butter or lard works well too, birds won't mind old tasting suet cakes.

Miss Verna Kay Miller

Homemade Solution for Plants

1 gal. warm water
1 tsp. Epsom salt
1 tsp. salt petre

1 tsp. baking powder
½ tsp. ammonia

Mix together and water plants. Use every 4-6 weeks. Makes the greens really grow! Be careful or you can kill the plants that bloom.

Mrs. Ervin Ella Miller

Miscellaneous

Horse Fly Spray

1 qt. Dawn
1 qt. white vinegar
1 qt. water

Mix all together and put in a sprayer bottle. Keep on buggy to spray the horses with.

Mrs. Ervin Ella Miller

Laundry Soap

1 bar Fels-Naptha soap
1½ c. Borax powder
1½ c. washing soda powder

Grate Fels-Naptha soap into bottom of 5 gallon bucket. Add 2 quarts boiling water. Stir till dissolved. Add 2 more quarts hot or boiling water and both powders. Stir again until dissolved. Fill bucket with cold water and stir well. Stir before each use, because it tends to clot. Use 1 cup per load. Adjust as necessary. Doesn't sud much.

Note: The price to make 5 gallons is about three dollars compared to ?? for commercial soap. I've thought that you could probably double the soaps and washing soda to make it stronger.

Mrs. Ernest Ray Inez Miller

Coal Garden

4-6 Tbsp. liquid bluing
4-6 Tbsp. water
4-6 Tbsp. salt
4-6 Tbsp. ammonia

Mix ingredients together and pour over broken pieces of coal or bricks, which are arranged in a bowl or pan. Set your little garden in a place where no one will bump into it. Watch it grow.

Miss Lori Miller

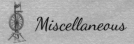 *Miscellaneous*

Magic Garden

1 Tbsp. ammonia
3 Tbsp. salt
¼ c. water
¼ c. bluing

Mix together then pour over charcoal that have been arranged in a glass bowl. Watch it grow, nice and colorful.

Mrs. LaVern Linda Miller

Drying Leaves

Gather a nice assortment of leaves. Place the leaves on the ironing board then cover with wax paper and iron each leaf individually with a hot iron. When wax seems to be ironed out of paper, get a new one. These leaves will then stay nice for a long time.

Note: You may want to cover your ironing board with a rag or towel as some color will come off leaves.

Miss Edna Mae Schrock

Oven Dried Roses

Remove all the oven racks except one, put rack on the highest notch in oven. Hang roses upside down using twist ties to fasten to the rack. Close oven door but make sure door is cracked (using spoon or pot holder) about 2" at the top so moisture can escape. Turn oven to scant 250° and bake for 1 hour. Cool completely before removing from rack. Make sure the stems are crisp again before putting in vases so the rose doesn't droop. This can also be used for other flowers. For smaller flowers, bake only 30 minutes. Use your own judgment.

Mrs. LaVern Linda Miller

Miscellaneous

Tomato Blight Recipe

1 gal. water
1 Tbsp. salt petre
1 Tbsp. Epsom salt
1 Tbsp. soda
1 tsp. ammonia

Mix well. Give each plant 1 pint every 2 weeks till plant has grown big and strong. Do not pour directly on plants and do not use in direct sunlight. I like to do it evenings or mornings. Often I add a little Monty's fertilizer, too. It just gives them a nice jump start.

Mrs. Samuel Dorothy Miller

Life is short. Pray hard.

Helpful Hints

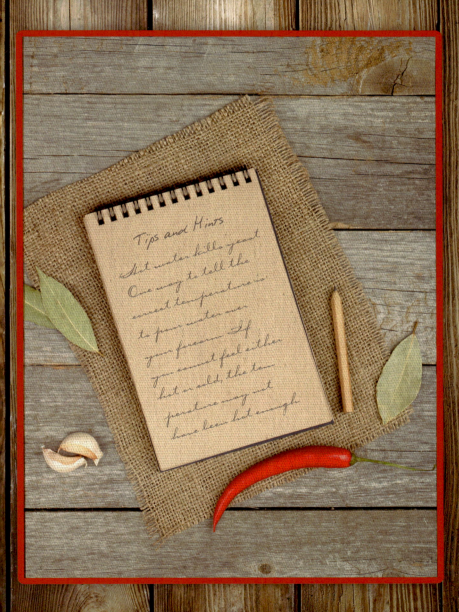

Helpful Hints

Abbreviations........................317
Food Equivalents....................318
Helpful Hints 315
Herbs for Vegetables 320
References 316
Substitutions for Emergencies..........321

Helpful Hints

🌾 When baking bread: A small dish of water in oven will help keep crust from hardening.

🌾 To prevent cheese from sticking to grater, spray the grater with cooking spray before beginning.

🌾 To cut down odors when cooking cabbage, cauliflower, etc. add a little vinegar to the water.

🌾 Perk up soggy lettuce leaves by soaking them in a mixture of lemon juice and cold water.

🌾 To keep hot oil from splattering, sprinkle a little salt in the pan before frying.

🌾 Hot water kills yeast. One way to tell the correct temperature is to pour water over your forearm. If you cannot feel either hot or cold, the temperature is right

🌾 Put honey in small plastic freezer container to prevent sugaring, it also thaws out in a short time.

🌾 You can lengthen the life of olive oil by adding a cube of sugar to the bottle.

🌾 Keep parsley fresh and crisp by storing in a wide-mouth jar with a tight lid. May be frozen.

🌾 Put ¼ cup vinegar in canner when cold packing meat. It keeps the jars from getting greasy.

🌾 Keep strawberries fresh for up to ten days by refrigerating them unwashed in an airtight container, between layers of paper towels.

🌾 Scaling fish is easier if vinegar is rubbed on the scales first.

🌾 To keep celery and lettuce fresh longer in refrigerator, store in paper bags instead of plastic.

🌾 Once an onion has been cut in half, rub the leftover side with butter and it will keep fresh longer.

🌾 Putting half of an apple in the cake pan will keep the cake moist.

🌾 Press wax paper on top of ice cream, that has been opened and used, to prevent wax-like film on top.

🌾 Store whole lemons in a tightly sealed jar of water in the refrigerator. They will yield more juice than when first purchased.

🌾 A rib of celery in your bread bag will keep the bread fresh for a longer time.

🌾 Store cottage cheese carton upside down an it will keep twice as long.

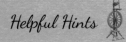

Helpful Hints

References

(For liquid and dry measurements use standard measuring spoons and cups. All measurements are level.)

dash	less than ⅛ tsp.
3 tsp.	1 Tbsp.
⅝ c.	½ c. + 2 Tbsp.
⅞ c.	¾ c. + 2 Tbsp.
1 jigger	1½ fl. oz. (3 Tbsp.)
4 Tbsp.	¼ c.
8 oz.	1 c.
1 c.	½ pt.
2 c.	1 pt.
2 pt. (4 c.)	1 qt.
4 qt. (liquid)	1 gal.
8 qt. (solid)	1 peck
4 pk.	1 bu.
16 oz.	1 lb.
32 oz.	1 qt.
8 oz. (liquid)	2 Tbsp.
1 Tbsp.	½ fl. oz.
1 c.	8 fl. oz.
1 Tbsp.	14.79 milliliters
1 c.	236.6 milliliters
1 liter	1.06 qt.
1 lb.	453.59 grams
1 oz.	28.35 grams
1 lb. butter	2 c.
1 lb. sugar	2 c.
1 lb. powdered sugar	3½ c.
1 lb. flour	4 c.
1 sq. chocolate	1 oz.
butter the size of an egg	¼ c.
8-10 egg whites	1 c.
12-14 egg yolks	1 c.
1 Tbsp. cornstarch	2 Tbsp. flour
1½ Tbsp. lemon juice plus sweet milk to make 1 c.	1 c. sour milk

Helpful Hints

If you want to measure part cups by the tablespoon, remember:

2 Tbsp.	⅛ c.
4 Tbsp.	¼ c.
5⅓ Tbsp.	⅓ c.
8 Tbsp.	½ c.
10⅔ Tbsp.	⅔ c.
12 Tbsp.	¾ c.
14 Tbsp.	⅞ c.
16 Tbsp.	1 c.

Can Sizes

Of the different sizes of cans used by commercial canners, the most common are:

8 oz.	1 cup
picnic	1¼ c.
No. 300	1¾ c.
No. 1 tall	2 c.
No. 303	2 c.
No. 2	2½ c.
No. 2½	3½ c.
No. 3	4 c.
No. 10	12-13 c.

Abbreviations

tsp.	teaspoon
Tbsp.	tablespoon
c.	cup
pt.	pint
qt.	quart
pk.	peck
bu.	bushel
oz.	ounce or ounces
lb.	pound or pounds
sq.	square
min.	minute or minutes
hr.	hour or hours
mod.	moderate or moderately
doz.	dozen

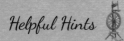
Helpful Hints

Food Equivalents

Almonds	3½ c.	1 lb.
Apple	1.	1 c.
Apples	1 lb.	3 med. (3 c. sliced)
Baking Powder	5½ oz.	1 c.
Bananas	1 lb.	3 med. (2½ c. sliced)
Banana, mashed	1 med.	⅓ c.
Bleu Cheese, crumbled	¼ lb.	1 c.
Bread Slices	4.	1 c. crumbs
Brown Sugar, packed	2¼ c.	1 lb.
Butter	1 lb.	2 c. or 4 sticks
Cake Flour	4½ c.	1 lb.
Cheese, American or Cheddar	1 lb.	4 c. grated
Chocolate, unsweetened	½ lb. pkg.	8-1-oz. sq.
Chocolate, unsweetened	1 oz.	1 sq.
Cocoa	4 c.	1 lb.
Coconut, shredded	1 lb.	5 c.
Coffee, ground	1 lb.	5 c.
Cornmeal	3 c.	1 lb.
Cornstarch	3 c.	1 lb.
Cottage Cheese	1 lb.	2 c.
Cream Cheese	8 oz. pkg.	16 Tbsp. (1 c.)
Cream, unwhipped	1 c.	2 c. whipped cream
Egg Whites	8-10	1 c.
Eggs, whole	4-5	1 c.
Egg Yolks	12-14	1 c.
Evaporated Milk	1 c.	3 c. whipped
Fat	2 c.	1 lb.
Flavored Jell-O	3¼ oz.	½ c.
Flour, sifted	4 c.	1 lb.
Flour, unsifted	3¾ c.	1 lb.
Graham Crackers	14 sq.	1 c. crumbs
Lemon	1.	3 Tbsp. juice
Lemon Juice	1 lb.	2-3 Tbsp.
Lemon Rind, lightly grated	1 lb.	1½-3 tsp.
Liquid	2 Tbsp.	1 oz.

Helpful Hints

Long-grain Rice, uncooked	1 c.	3-4 c. cooked
Macaroni, uncooked	4 oz. (1¼ c.)	2¼ c. cooked
Marshmallows	16	1 lb.
Noodles, uncooked	4 oz. (1½-2 c.)	2 c. cooked
Onion	1 med.	½ c.
Orange	1	⅓ c. juice
Orance Juice	1 lb.	⅓-½ c.
Orange Rind, lightly grated	1 lb.	1-2 Tbsp.
Powdered Sugar, unsifted	3½-4 c.	1 lb.
Raisins	1 lb.	3½ c.
Rice	2⅓ c.	1 lb.
Rye Flour	5 c.	1 lb.
Saltine Crackers	28	1 c. crumbs
Spaghetti	7 oz.	4 c. cooked
Sugar	2 c.	1 lb.
Unflavored Jell-O	¼ oz.	1 Tbsp.
Vanilla Wafers	22	1 c. crumbs
Walnuts, unshelled	1 lb.	1½-1¾ c. shelled
Whipping Cream	1 pt.	2 cups (4 c. whipped)
Whole Wheat Flour, unsifted	3½ c.	1 lb.
Zwieback, crumbled	4	1 c.

Nuts and Fruits most commonly used

	Nuts in shell	Shelled nuts
Almonds	1 lb.=1-1¾ c. nutmeats	1 lb.=3½ c. nutmeats
Pecans	1 lb.= 2¼ c. nutmeats	1 lb.=4 c. nutmeats
Peanuts	1 lb.=2¼ c. nutmeats	1 lb.=3 c. nutmeats
Walnuts	1 lb.=1⅔ c. nutmeats	1 lb.=4 c. nutmeats

	Whole	Pitted	Cut-up	Finely Cut
Dates	1 lb.=2¼ c.	2 c.	1¾ c.	1½ c.
Prunes	1 lb.=2⅓ c.	4 c.	3 c.	2⅞ c.
Figs	1 lb.=2¾ c.		2⅔ c.	2½ c.
Raisins	15 oz. pkg.=3 c.		2¾ c.	2½ c.
Candied Fruit	½ lb.		1½ c.	
Candied Peels	½ lb.		1½ c.	

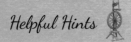

Helpful Hints

Herbs for Vegetables

The soul of a dish lies in its seasonings. Add the seasonings sparingly to bring out the natural flavor of the vegetables to enhance but not to destroy it.

Basil . . . . beets, eggplant, onions, squash, tomatoes
Bay Leaf (in water when cooking) . . . . carrots, potatoes, stewed tomatoes
Dill Weed . . . . asparagus, cucumbers, greens, green beans, potatoes
Marjoram . . . . green beans, mushrooms, peas, spinach, zucchini
Mint . . . . carrots, new potatoes, peas, spinach
Oregano . . . . broccoli, cabbage, lentils, tomatoes
Rosemary . . . . mushrooms, peas, spinach, squash
Sage . . . . eggplant, lima beans, onions, tomatoes
Savory Salsify . . . . beats, green beans, mushrooms, peas
Thyme . . . . beets, carrots, green beans, onions

Christians are only visiting this planet! Live that way.

Helpful Hints

Substitutions for Emergencies

It's best to use ingredients the recipe recommends:
but if you have to substitute, this list solution lends.

1 whole egg	2 egg yolks + 1 Tbsp. water
1 whole egg	2 egg yolks (in custards and such mixtures)
1 c. whole milk	½ c. evaporated milk and ½ c. water or 1 c. reconstituted nonfat dry milk and 1 Tbsp. butter
1 c. fresh sweet milk	½ c. evaporated milk + ½ c. water
1 c. fresh sweet milk	powdered milk + water (directions on pkg.)
1 c. fresh sweet milk	1 c. sour milk or buttermilk + ½ tsp. soda
1 c. sour milk	1 c. sweet milk + 1 Tbsp. vinegar or lemon juice
1 c. heavy sour cream	⅓ cup butter and ⅔ c. milk
1 c. sifted all-purpose flour	1 c. + 2 Tbsp. sifted cake flour
1 c. sifted cake flour	1 c. minus 2 Tbsp. sifted all-purpose flour
1 tsp. baking powder	1 tsp. baking soda + ½ tsp. cream of tartar
1 Tbsp. cornstarch (for thickening)	2 Tbsp. flour
1 c. powdered sugar	1 c. sugar + 1 tsp. cornstarch
½ c. brown sugar	2 Tbsp. molasses in ½ c. sugar
1 c. molasses	1 c. honey
1 c. honey	¾ c. sugar + ¼ c. liquid
1 sq. chocolate (1 oz.)	3-4 Tbsp. cocoa + ½ Tbsp. fat
1 sq. unsweetened chocolate (1 oz.)	1 Tbsp. cocoa + ½ tsp. shortening
1 c. canned tomatoes	about 1⅓ c. cut-up fresh tomatoes, simmered 10 min.
¾ c. cracker crumbs	1 c. bread crumbs
1 tsp. dried herbs	1 Tbsp. fresh herbs
2 oz. compressed yeast	3 (¼ oz.) pkg. of dry yeast
1 Tbsp. instant minced onion, dehydrated	1 sm. fresh onion
1 Tbsp. prepared mustard	1 tsp. dry mustard
⅛ tsp. garlic powder	1 sm. pressed clove of garlic
1 c. tomato juice	½ c. tomato sauce + ½ c. water
1 c. ketchup or chili sauce	1 c. tomato sauce + ½ c. sugar and 2 Tbsp. vinegar (for use in cooking)
1 lb. whole dates, pitted and cut	1½ c.
3 med. bananas	1 c. mashed
3 c. cornflakes	1 c. crushed
10 miniature marshmallows	1 lg. marshmallow
1 c. cake flour	¼ c. cornstarch + ¾ c. flour, sifted

Oh, mother, so wearied, discouraged,
Worn out with the cares of the day,
You often grow cross and impatient,
Complain of noise and the play.
For the days bring so many vexations,
So many things going amiss,
But, mother, whatever may vex you,
Send the children to bed with a kiss.

The dear little feet wander often,
Perhaps from the pathway of right;
The dear little hands find new mischief,
to try you from morning to night.
But think of the desolate mother,
Who'd give all the world for your bliss;
And as thanks for you infinite blessings,
Send the children to bed with a kiss.

For someday the noise will not vex you,
The silence will hurt you far more;
You will long for the sweet children's voices,
For a childish face at the door,
And to press a sweet form to your bosom,
You'd give all the world for just this,
For the comfort 'twill bring you in sorrow,
Send the children to bed with a kiss.

– Author Unknown

Canning Guide

Canning Guide

All information and measurements in this cookbook are accurate to the best of our knowledge. However, no guarantee is given. Responsibilities regarding accuracy and results evolve directly on those making use of these recipes.

Blanching and Freezing Vegetables 327
Boiling Bath 326
Pressure Canning....................325
Types of Syrup to Can Fruits..........327
Vegetable Equivalent Yields...........328

Canning Guide

Pressure Canning

Pressure Canning: Cover canner bottom with several inches of water, place jars in canner. Let steam vent for 5–10 minutes to expel all air from canner. Then close vent to build pressure. Start timing after the pressure reaches 10 pounds. Maintain pressure in the minutes listed:

Vegetables	*Pints*	*Quarts*
Beets	15 minutes	20 minutes
Carrots	15 minutes	20 minutes
Corn	15 minutes	20 minutes
Lima or Navy Beans	15 minutes	20 minutes
Pork and Beans	30 minutes	45 minutes
Potatoes	15 minutes	20 minutes
Pumpkin (cooked)	30 minutes	45 minutes
Snap Beans (green)	15 minutes	20 minutes
Soups or mixed vegetables without meats	15 minutes	20 minutes
Soups with meats or tomato juice	30 minutes	45 minutes

Tip: Adding 1 tablespoon lemon juice to each quart corn, lets you cut pressure time down to 10–15 minutes.

Meats (10 lb. Pressure)	*Pints*	*Quarts*
Raw	75 minutes	90 minutes
Cooked or Browned	30 minutes	45 minutes
Broths	30 minutes	45 minutes

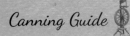

Canning Guide

Boiling Bath

For raw meat and anything with raw meat, boil for 3 hours. For other vegetables and broths, boil for 2 hours.

Raw Pack: Place jars in canner and fill with water to the neck of jars. Start timing when water reaches a rolling boil. Maintain at a boil for the minutes listed. Remove jars immediately.

Fruits and Vegetables — Pints & Quarts

Raw Pack

Apples, Applesauce	10 minutes
Apricots	10 minutes
Berries	10 minutes
Cherries	10 minutes
Peaches	10 minutes
Pickles	10 minutes
Pickled Beets	10 minutes
Pears	10 minutes
Plums	10 minutes
Rhubarb	10 minutes
Relish	10 minutes
Salsa	10 minutes
Tomatoes	10 minutes
Tomato Juice	10 minutes

Hot Pack

Pie Filling	20 minutes
Barbecue Sauce	10 minutes
Ketchup	10 minutes
Pizza Sauce	10 minutes

Tip: Store all canned goods in a cool dark place. It helps maintain the seal.

Canning Guide

Types of Syrup to Can Fruits

It takes about 1½ cups of syrup per quart to cover fruits.

	Water or Juice	Cups of Sugar	Yield
Very Light	1 qt.	½ c.	4 c.
Light	1 qt.	1 c.	4½ c.
Medium	1 qt.	2 c.	5 c.
Heavy	1 qt.	3 c.	5½ c.
Very Heavy	1 qt.	4 c.	6½ c.

Blanching and Freezing Vegetables

Heat water to a gentle boil and blanch for time listed. Drain well. Cool immediately in cold water or ice water. Drain and put in containers of your choice. Freeze.

	Blanching Time
Asparagus	2–3 minutes/diced 1 minute
Beans, snapped	3 minutes
Broccoli	2–3 minutes
Celery, diced	1–2 minutes
Corn, on the cob	5–7 minutes
Carrots, diced	2–3 minutes
Peas, in the pods	5–7 minutes
Peas, shelled	3 minutes
Peppers	need no blanching

Tips:
Beans: Cool on a towel, not in cold water. They don't become so rubbery.
Corn: Is not so messy if blanched on the cob, cooled, then cut off and put in containers.
Broccoli: Soak ½ hour in salted water (¼ cup salt per gallon water) to drive out insects. Rinse and blanch.

Canning Guide

Vegetable Equivalent Yields

Asparagus	1 lb. fresh		3 c. chopped
Beans	1 lb.		4 c. chopped
	1 bu.	30 lb.	15–22 qt.
Lima Beans	1 lb. shelled		4 c.
	1 bu., unshelled	32 lb.	6–8 qt.
Beets	1 lb. fresh		4 c. chopped
	1 bu. no greens	52 lb.	18–20 qt.
	1 bu. greens	12 lb.	4–6 qt.
Brussel Sprouts	1 lb.	4 c. quartered	1 pt.
Carrots	1 lb.		3 c. diced
	1 bu.	50 lb.	16–20 qt.
Cauliflower	1 lb.	1 med. head	4 c. florets
Celery	1 lb.		4 c. chopped
Corn	5–6 ears		3 c. kernels
	1 bu.	35 lb.	8–10 qt.
Cucumbers	1 lb.		4 c. sliced
	1 bu.	50–55 lb.	20 qt.
Lettuce	1 lb.		6 c. chopped
Onions	1 lb.		4 c. chopped
Peas	1 lb. unshelled		1¼ c. shelled
	1 bu.	30 lb.	6–8 qt.
Peppers	1 lb.	3½ c. diced	1½ pt.
Potatoes	1 lb. unpeeled		3 c. chopped
	1 bu.		50 lb.
Pumpkin	7 lb. whole		3½ lb. flesh
	1 lb. peeled		4 c. chopped
Rhubarb	1 lb. stalks		4 c. chopped
Spinach	1 lb. fresh		3 c. steamed
	1 bu.	12 lb.	4–6 qt.
Strawberries	1½ lb.	1 qt.	1 pt. mashed
Sweet Potatoes	1 lb. fresh		3 c. cubed
Tomatoes	1 lb.		2 c.
	1 bu.	50–55 lb.	18–20 qt.

You've not begun to live until you've prepared to die.